Data Protection Law in Ireland

Robert Clark

BA, LLM, PhD, BL

Statutory Lecturer in Law,
Faculty of Law, University College Dublin

WITH A FOREWORD BY

Donal C. Linehan

Data Protection Commissioner

THE ROUND HALL PRESS

This book was typeset by
Gilbert Gough Typesetting, Dublin
for the Round Hall Press Ltd,
Kill Lane, Blackrock, Co. Dublin

BRITISH LIBRARY CATALOGUING IN PUBLICATION DATA
Clark, Robert
Data protection law in Ireland.
1. Ireland (Republic). Computer systems Data protection
law.
I. Title
344.1702'858

ISBN 0-947686-59-2

Printed in Ireland
by Betaprint Ltd, Dublin

To Robert and Luke

Foreword

The Data Protection Act 1988 confers new rights on individuals. It entitles them to establish the existence of automated personal data, to have access to such data kept in relation to them, and to have inaccurate data rectified or erased. It also creates obligations for individuals or bodies who keep automated personal data. They have to comply with the data protection principles governing the collection, processing, use, disclosure and security of the data.

The Act enables the Council of Europe Data Protection Convention to be ratified by Ireland, thus ensuring the free flow of personal data between Ireland and other countries having similar laws.

Dr Clark's book *Data Protection Law in Ireland* provides a timely commentary on what is, in effect, a new branch of law. He examines in detail each of the Act's provisions and assesses their implications. Although, as he himself admits, it is unlikely that everybody will agree with all of his conclusions, his book provides a very thorough and stimulating survey of the new legislation. I am certain it will prove of great assistance not only to the individuals for whose benefit the new rights have been created but also to all those involved in the use and processing of personal data.

Donal C. Linehan
DATA PROTECTION COMMISSIONER

18 September 1989

Contents

Preface

At the risk of being charged with overestimating the importance of the subject, I wish to express the view that the 1988 data protection legislation is the most far-reaching legislative initiative of the decade. It is therefore somewhat paradoxical that the implementation of the 1988 Act, indeed its very existence, owes more to the work of the Council of Europe than to either the activities of the data processing industry or civil libertarians. This fact has at times led to the implicit charge that legislation has been foisted on Irish business interests when there is no apparent need for such legislation. Nothing could be further from the truth. Data protection law should be about the protection and validation of a right to privacy. Human persons need to be able to close out the rest of the world, at appropriate times, but the reconciliation of such a subjective and personal psychological requirement with other human or socio-economic interests is a profound and difficult task. The 1988 Act is open to the charge that the balance between rights of privacy for individual human persons and the rights of commercial organisations to distribute and disseminate personal data is too heavily weighted in favour of the latter interest. It is clear that the 1988 Act gives the data subject no real degree of control over the dissemination of personal data which is kept by data controllers and which the data controller may seek to provide to a third party. It may be that the provision of a veto, whereby any data, whether accurate or not, which is kept about a data subject, can be amended or deleted, at the insistence of the data subject, would be going too far, but the situation endorsed by the 1988 Act does not attempt to address the problem of data privacy in this wider context.

Although the Dáil and Seanad debates revolving around data protection cannot be said to have been extensive, it is evident that the 1988 Act is a complicated piece of legislation. However, it is in my view a significant improvement in several respects upon the UK Act of 1984. The draftsman has rejected many of the features of the UK Act in order to produce a more intelligible piece of legislation. Universal registration of data controllers has not been insisted upon. The codes of practice provisions in section 13 are a significant feature, signalling as they do the emphasis on self-regulation and the creation of elastic and practical standards within specific areas of business activity. An indication of how sensible some of these measures are can be gleaned from the fact that the UK Registrar has recently called upon Parliament to pass amending legislation which will, for example, produce a more selective and streamlined system of registration.

There are still many shortcomings in the 1988 Act. For example, the Act does not apply to manual or paper files; this will encourage avoidance and in particular the retention of some data on paper files. If privacy rights were to be effectively safeguarded the Act would apply to manual files also. The provisions regulating sensitive personal data suffer from the lack of definition that is a feature of the Council of Europe Convention and the fact that the special measures provided for in section 2(6) have not been drafted. The Commissioner should have been given powers to recommend or award financial compensation to data subjects. Most seriously of all, however, is the question of resources. Has the Commissioner been given the means of ensuring that the Act is capable of being fully implemented? The financial allocation for the first year of operation is the somewhat modest amount of £204,000 (see 391 *Dáil Debates* col. 327). Like all regulatory legislation, this Act is only going to be as good as the enforcement machinery allows it to be. In this context, it is likely that the ordinary law of contract and tort may be even more important to an individual who has some actual or perceived sense of grievance, to say nothing of the constitutional rights afforded by the *Norris* and *Kennedy and Arnold* litigation, discussed in Chapter 1.

I have attempted to produce a book that will be of interest and of some practical value to a wider audience than the practising lawyer or practising accountant. I hope that those involved in the information industry, the personnel management sector, indeed, any Irish business person who deals with computerised information, will find the book useful and informative. I have attempted to fit the Act into its wider legal context without making discussion about legal issues either too difficult or too simplistic. The speculative nature of this investigation into an important area of legal regulation inevitably means that there likely to be some errors of interpretation in this book. For these I apologise in advance.

I wish to thank Declan Madden, Joe Lynch, Raymonde Kelly and Peter Lennon. Each of them provided information and stimulating insights into how data protection law works, or should work. They are not responsible for any of the errors or uncertainties thrown up by this book, however. Patricia Garland is responsible for producing a typed manuscript with all her customary efficiency. The Publishers have been most helpful and have produced the finished product in what seems to have been an impossibly short period of time.

Disclaimer: Every effort has been made to ensure that the information and comment given in this book is accurate. Nevertheless I should be grateful to learn of any errors or omissions. However, no responsibility (legal or otherwise) is accepted by me or the publishers for any errors, omissions, or otherwise in that information or othewise.

Robert Clark
6 November 1989

Table of cases

1

The right to privacy

INTRODUCTION

While it is correct to assert the view that English law does not recognise that an inherent right of personal privacy exists in favour of individuals,[1] this is by no means a position that is reflected in Irish law. Ireland, through the Constitution, has adopted the common law[2] and common law rules, where these rules are not inconsistent with the Constitution. As such, cases like *Tolley v Fry & Sons Ltd*[3] appear at first sight to be good law in Ireland. Tolley, an amateur golfer, was caricatured by the defendants in the defendant's advertising material. Tolley's caddy was depicted as praising, in doggerel verse, a bar of chocolate, which he equated with the plaintiff's excellent drive from the tee. Tolley brought a civil action alleging defamation, alleging specifically that the use of his image, without his permission, was actionable as an infringement of privacy. While the plaintiff's action was successful it was decided on the narrow ground of innuendo. By using the plaintiff's image the defendants had implied that the plaintiff had been paid or remunerated in some way and had therefore compromised or prostituted his status of amateur golfer. In the Court of Appeal, however, Greer LJ bemoaned the absence of any remedy but for the defamatory innuendo. 'I have no hesitation in saying that in my judgment the defendants in publishing the advertisement in question, without first obtaining Mr Tolley's consent, acted in a manner inconsistent with the decencies of life and in so doing they were guilty of an act for which there ought to be a legal remedy.'[4]

There are other English cases which indicate that the unauthorised use of a person's image which is not itself defamatory is not actionable.[5] While isolated dicta in favour of some tortious action[6] for offensive intrusion of personal privacy can be found,[7] it is clear that the common law, as interpreted by the English courts, does not, in the absence of statutory provisions or some coincidental cause of action such as defamation, protect against the unauthorised interference with a person's seclusion of himself, his family, or his property, from others. Despite attempts in the UK Parliament to introduce Right to Privacy legislation[8] there seems little chance of establishing any general statutory right to privacy in the near future. Mr John Browne, in a private members bill, the Protection of Privacy Bill, 1989, has devised a statutory tort of invasion of privacy. Mr Browne's Bill attempted to establish that protection of privacy (which he believes is a fundamental human right along with freedom of speech, movement, and free association) should be recognised by British domestic law. While the Bill had been given a second reading and referred to Standing Committee, the Bill will proceed no further. On 21 April 1989 the British Government announced that a Home Office Committee would be established in order to review all aspects of the law relating to privacy. Further legislative action in this area will not, it seems, occur until the review has been completed. Mr Browne withdrew the Bill shortly after the Government announced the Home Office review.

PRIVACY PROTECTION BY INDIRECT MEANS: THE COMMON LAW

Before we consider the rights and remedies Irish Constitutional Law provides in respect of the unauthorised invasion of privacy, it is important to consider what coincidental causes of action are available to persons who have suffered some intrusion by others. These causes of action relate to rights that the law recognises and vindicates, such as property rights, contract rights, rights to a good name, as well as the possibility that one person may, in law, owe a duty of care not to cause physical or financial loss to others.

The law of confidence   The unauthorised use of, or disclosure of, information received on the understanding that the information is given in confidence, is actionable. While it is of course possible to provide expressly in a contract that information is to not be used or disclosed[9] and while the courts sometimes consider that the law of confidence may rest on an implied term[10] it is clear that, apart from any question of a contractual duty existing between the parties, there may still be a remedy, based on equitable principles, if three requirements are met. Megarry J, in *Coco v A.N. Clark (Engineers) Ltd*[11] summarised these requirements. 'First, the information itself . . . must have the necessary quality of confidence about it. Secondly, that information must have been imparted in circumstances imparting an obligation of confidence. Thirdly, there must be an unauthorised use of that information to the detriment of the party communicating it.'[12]

While the law of confidence is normally concerned with processes, formulae, marketable commercial or scientific ideas such plans, designs and working methods, personal data such as the names and addresses of persons, whether the address be a business address or private one, has clearly been within the concept of confidential information for a considerable time.[13] Despite the fact that infringement of the law of confidence has tended to take place within a commercial context — the defendant seeks to use confidential information which has a certain commercial value — it is now clear that the law of confidence is not restricted to providing a remedy for information provided within a commercial or business context. Professional persons such as doctors, lawyers and bankers, to give just three examples, are clearly bound by duties of confidentiality[14] for such persons are in a position to obtain personal information from clients that will be of considerable sensitivity. However, it is not essential that a professional relationship must exist between discloser and disclosee.

In the recent case of *Stevens v Avery and others*[15] Browne-Wilkinson VC ruled that there was no reason why the law of confidence should not be generally available to protect confidential information given by one person to another, especially when the information relates to the sexual activities of the person giving the information. Browne-Wilkinson VC rejected an argument addressed to the Court which sought to establish that, because the information was not commercial or industrial in nature, the law of confidence could not apply: Browne-Wilkinson VC to an extent turned this argument on its head by pointing out that, to most people, the details about their sex lives are high on the list of matters which they regard as confidential. *Stevens v Avery* therefore provides some support for the view that personal data, if abused by a data holder, may result in liability under the ordinary law of confidence.

The law of confidence does not create an absolute duty. A public interest defence may be asserted by disclosees who provide third parties with information given in confidence.[16]

The law of negligence The common law has provided some remedy through the law of negligence, e.g. a cause of action may arise when a negligent solicitor fails to obtain injunctive relief from a client who is being harassed by an estranged spouse.[17] This is only indirectly a vindication of privacy rights, as is the action under *Hedley Byrne & Co. v Heller & Partners*[18] where damages are available if economic loss results from failure to take reasonable care in compiling or holding information.

Trespass The possibility that a person may have a cause of action in respect of wilful or negligent interference with a person,[19] that person's goods[20] or that person's land[21] is well established, although the law is not very clear on several essential points. In relation to interference with the person, English law recognises that a willful act which causes physical harm — where a person falsely informs another that a close relative has been killed or injured for example, the person so informed suffering nervous shock, that person may have a remedy in tort.[22] Interference with goods is a possible cause of action but English and Irish case-law does not clearly identify the rationale for this cause of action. *McMahon and Binchy* point out that in the United States it is recognised that the tort is based on wrongful intrusion of privacy and, as such,

US law gives a right of action even if no damage can be shown *vis-à-vis* the good in question. Where the cause of action relates to interference with land there is a similar refusal to acknowledge that privacy forms an essential basis of the tort. In *Turner v Spooner*[23] a case in which the parties were litigating a dispute over the right to broaden windows in a building to let in more light, it was argued, unsuccessfully, that if windows were broadened this would increase the power to overlook others and thus constitute an actionable invasion of privacy.

Nuisance An actionable private nuisance may occur when a person finds that another has caused some physical interference with property by permitting water, noise, smoke, noxious fumes and the like to spread onto that persons land, thereby interfering with the right of enjoyment of the occupier. In *Lord Bernstein of Leigh v Skyview and General Ltd*[24] an aerial photograph, taken from an aeroplane which overflew the plaintiff's residence, did not result in liability in trespass or nuisance. Griffith J however pointed out that the basis for the decision was the absence of any persistent action on the part of the defendant. However, if there was constant harassment of the plaintiff, accompanied by the constant photographing of the plaintiff, Griffith J seemed to consider that, in such a case, a remedy would be available. It is interesting to contrast this decision with *Florida v Riley*, a decision of the US Supreme Court, handed down on 23 January 1989. The Supreme Court held that home-owners have no right to privacy in respect of low-flying aircraft at least 400 feet above ground. This kind of activity is undertaken by law enforcement officials so as to detect marijuana gardens.

Surveillance and intimidation The *Bernstein* case indicates that a cause of action in nuisance may be available if there is constant surveillance of an individual. It may be that a right of action for watching and besetting is also available. While this tort is generally considered as well established within the context of employment law and trade union law in particular, it is possible to argue that the concepts of watching and besetting, and the independent tort of intimidation, are available generally. In a recent Circuit Court case, noted in the *Irish Times* of 31 March 1988, damages of £2,000 were awarded against two men who had been repeatedly harassing the plaintiff. The plaintiff's business had run into financial difficulties and the two defendants had interfered with the plaintiffs business and social life. Judge Smith seems to have awarded damages for intimidation although it is generally thought that this relatively new tort operates soley within the context of labour law.[25]

Defamation This tortious cause of action is available where the reputation of a person is damaged by a statement made by another, that statement having the effect of disparaging the plaintiff or bringing him into ridicule or contempt amongst right minded persons.[26] As McDonald[27] points out, the Irish Constitution provides the basis for a significant development of the law governing defamation, by analogy with the impact that the US Constitution has had on common law rules relating to defamation.

Privilege Information given in confidence to professional legal advisers[28] and possibly to others such as priests[29] may be privileged against disclosure in the course of legal proceedings.

PRIVACY PROTECTION BY INDIRECT MEANS — STATUTE LAW

Copyright Under the provisions of the Copyright Acts, 1963 to 1986, the authors and other creators of copyright works are given a right to protect themselves against unauthorised copying, reproduction or adaptation of their works. The central element in deciding on the availability of copyright protection is whether the form in which information is held has been reproduced. The information itself is not an appropriate subject for copyright protection. This means that any unauthorised disclosure of personal details can only be protected if the form in which the information is held is reproduced (e.g. pages of a personnel file which are photocopied and published in newspapers may involve an abuse of copyright held by the author of the file but the person whose personal details are thus made public cannot have a remedy via the law of copyright).

Broadcasting The Broadcasting Authority Act, 1960, the legislation which establishes the national television and sound broadcasting service, RTE, and in particular the RTE Authority, contains the following provision:

> The Authority shall not, in its programmes and in the means employed to make such programmes, unreasonably encroach on the privacy of an individual.[30]

It is not clear whether an action for breach of statutory duty will lie against the Authority if this provision is not observed.

Confidential information Many statutes establishing public agencies contain legislative provisions requiring directors or employees not to disclose confidential information gleaned whilst performing duties, e.g. section 37 of the Postal and Telecommunications Services Act, 1983.

Miscellaneous In recent years two attempts have been made to provide greater protection for the individual citizen. The first attempt was made in 1985 by the introduction of the Postal Packets and Telecommunications (Regulations) Bill, 1985, a private members bill which attempted to provide a regulatory framework within which interference by the State with postal services and telecommunications could take place. As such, the Bill was a response to the Kennedy/Arnold telephone tapping case. The Bill lapsed and, it can be argued, the Constitutional protection afforded by Hamilton P's judgment in the subsequent 1987 litigation makes legislation less necessary than it was felt to be in 1985. Nevertheless, the Fianna Fáil/Progressive Democrat Government's *Programme for Government*, announced on 12 July 1989, includes a commitment to introduce legislation regulating telephone tapping.

The second attempt, also made by way of a Private Members Bill, in the form of the Public Offices (Privacy of Interviews) Bill, 1988, seeks to create a statutory right to have interviews which take place in public offices, e.g. ESB offices, the Department of Health, conducted in privacy. This right is to operate where business of a personal, private or confidential nature is transacted and the Bill seeks to give interviewees a right to insist that the conversation cannot be overheard or that the interview cannot be observed by other members of the public. The Bill, introduced by Deputy Jim Mitchell, was not enthusiastically endorsed by the Government although the Government accepted that the general principle of ensuring privacy for individuals being interviewed on matters of a personal nature at public offices was worthwhile. However, the Governments objection, principally based on cost factors, did not lead to the Government opposing the bill and it passed through its Second Stage in Dáil Éireann on 9 May 1989.

Codes of practice may also provide a degree of privacy protection. The Revenue Commissioners, in 1989, published a Charter of Rights for Taxpayers. This code of practice extends the following to taxpayers:

- courtesy and consideration
- a presumption of honesty
- information rights
- impartiality of treatment
- privacy and confidentiality
- right of independent review
- compliance costs to be given
- rights of consistent administration.

PRIVACY BY DIRECT MEANS — THE CONSTITUTION

The Irish Constitution does not in express terms provide any constitutional right to privacy but there is a line of authority which indicates that the citizen may invoke the personal rights provisions of the Constitution so as to require the State to protect and vindicate the citizen's implied right to constitutional privacy. It seems clear that the constitutional right to privacy has, as a parallel, basic principles of natural justice which may provide ancillary relief. Authority for this proposition may be found in the unreported judgment of Doyle J in *Murphy v PMPA Insurance*.[31] A statute required an Insurance company to issue insurance cover to acceptable applicants and keep records of cover so issued. The legislation also permitted members of the Garda Síochána access to premises where records were kept, as well as access to the records for inspection purposes; an officer was to be permitted to request information and be furnished with information relating to any policy. PMPA issued a policy to one Mellon, a member of the Gardaí. The complainant, an inspector in the force, requested access to all records kept by PMPA relating to Mellon, including proposal forms completed by Mellon. PMPA refused and were convicted of an offence in the District Court. PMPA appealed successfully against the conviction. Doyle J based part of his reasoning on the principle of *uberrima fides*, that is, the mutual duty[32] that applies as between insurance applicant and insurer. PMPA were bound under contract to keep this information confidential. On the other hand, the statute seemed to confer a right of access, thereby superceding the common law duty of confidence. Doyle J nevertheless resolved the issue by pointing out that, in this case, if a right of access were to exist it would encroach on the natural rights and natural liberty of a citizen. Mellon's career would be prejudiced if the employer could obtain all information held about him, e.g. information relating to health, personal habits and other information, and needed by the company as a legitimate aspect of its business.[33]

Recently, litigation has established a constitutional right to privacy which seems also to be predicated on elemental factors such as natural law and the dignity and individuality of the citizen. This principle has a somewhat tentative quality, but in future litigation the precise nature and limits of the principle will take shape. As the law presently stands it can be said that the right to privacy clearly operates in two contexts: firstly, in relation to consensual relationships between human beings and, secondly, in relation to the integrity and confidentiality of communications between persons.

Human relationships   Case-law seems to limit this aspect of the constitutional right to privacy to circumstances in which consenting adults seek to obtain redress against interference in sexual relationships but there is no reason to restrict the privacy right to this facet of human behaviour. The leading case is *McGee v Attorney General*.[34] The Supreme Court there struck down section 17(3) of the Criminal Law (Amendment) Act, 1935 which prohibited the importation into Ireland of contraceptives. A majority of the Supreme Court[35] relying on Article 40.3.1° of the Constitution, found an unenumerated right in the Constitution to privacy in respect of marital relations between the plaintiff and her husband, following *Griswold v Connecticut.*[36]

While subsequent academic comment centred inter alia on whether this question of constitutional privacy is dependent on the existence of a marital relationship between citizens,[37] subsequent case-law indicates that the right is not so dependent.

In *Norris v The Attorney General*[38] the plaintiff, a homosexual, sought a declaration in respect of criminal legislation dating from 1861 and 1885,[39] which statutes made acts or attempts to commit homosexual acts with other male persons criminal offences, as being acts of indecent assault and gross indecency respectively, and punishable as misdemeanors. The plaintiff asserted that these statutory provisions were incompatible with the provisions of the 1937 Constitution and, as such, had not continued to be in force after 1937, following the adoption of the Irish Constitution. Norris argued, firstly, that Article 40.1 of the Constitution, the equality provision, was incompatible with these criminal statutes and that in a case of conflict the statute must be declared unconstitutional. It followed, so the argument ran, that this legislation was an infringement of Article 40.3 of the Constitution. The second argument addressed to the High Court by Norris was that there existed a general right to privacy. In the High Court McWilliam J rejected both arguments. The relevant sections of the 1861 Act are gender free and could thus lead to a conviction of both men and women. As such there could not be an infringement of the Constitution. The relevant provision in the 1885 Act, whilst referring to males only, and while unsatisfactory in many respects, was not an infringement of Article 40.1 for this reason alone. A majority of the Supreme Court agreed with the High Court in concluding that the legislation did not infringe the equality provisions of Article 40.1. The Supreme Court, however, divided quite starkly on the second argument, the privacy argument, which was also addressed to the Supreme Court by the plaintiff.

Norris, in building on the privacy concept, also argued that by criminalising behaviour in private between consenting adults, the citizens constitutional right to privacy had been infringed. Even those members of the Supreme Court who held against Norris on this point conceded that a constitutional right to privacy can exist. O'Higgins CJ, with whom Finlay P and Griffin J concurred,[40] found that the right to privacy was not absolute and that certain acts, even though victimless crimes, can be condemned by the criminal law. O'Higgins CJ pointed out that the right 'to be let alone' cannot be absolute and the right of privacy in this case had been counterbalanced by the adverse consequences that would result for general moral well-being, the health of citizens and potential harm to the institution of marriage. In these circumstances any adverse affect the criminalisation of homosexual activities had on the plaintiffs health or freedom of association was justifiable as being necessitated by the exigencies of the common good.

McCarthy J and Henchy J, while dissenting on the substantive issue of the unconstitutionality of the legislation of 1861 and 1885, provided greater guidance on precisely what the right of privacy derives from and what it means. The general right to privacy, as an unenumerated personal right is, in Henchy J's view, based on 'the individual personality of the citizen.'[41] McCarthy J agreed in part with this formulation, but he preferred to consider the right of privacy as an inherent part of 'human personality' as distinct from being a right which is predicated on and reflective of 'the Christian and democratic nature of the State.' In these circumstances, Henchy J and McCarthy J seem to be saying, behaviour that is contrary to Christian moral teaching or, more controversially perhaps, is anti-democratic[42] could still be within the protective remit of privacy rights. Only if the State can adduce evidence to justify conduct by the State which *prima facie* infringes a citizen's right to privacy should this facet of human personality be regulated. In *Norris* Henchy J and McCarthy J held that the State had not offered any evidence to justify intrusion or interference with the general right to privacy.

While the Supreme Court's judgment in *Norris* has been overtaken by the 1988 ruling of the European Court of Human Rights, declaring that the 1861 and 1885 legislation constitutes an indefensible infringement of Article 8 of the European Convention of Human Rights,[43] it provides a firm basis for arguing that Irish constitutional law recognises a general right to privacy. Only future cases will develop the issue of how and in what circumstances the right to privacy is to be balanced and reconciled with other considerations such as the investigation of alleged criminal offences, public order, the effective running of penal institutions, and so on.

Communications Another obvious application of a general right to privacy relates to communications to or from a person. The knowledge that mail is being intercepted or read, or that telephones are being tapped, is a cause of great concern for most persons. In Ireland this has been recognised by successive governments. In relation to telephone interceptions by the organs of the State assurances have been given to Dáil Éireann that authorised interception only takes place in the most pressing circumstances and only upon the issue of a warrant signed by the Minister for Justice.[44] Any unauthorised interference could be the subject of a declaration that the interception is unlawful as an unconstitutional act, for which a remedy sounds in damages. There is no reason why the interception of mail or telecommunications by the organs of the State or private persons, e.g. by hacking into an electronic mailbox, should not be capable of redress under Irish constitutional law.

In *Kennedy, Arnold & Arnold v Ireland & the Attorney General*[45] it was stated

The dignity and freedom of an individual in a democratic society cannot be ensured if his communications of a private nature, be they written or telephonic, are deliberately, consciously and unjustifiably intruded upon and interfered with.

I emphasise the words 'deliberately, consciously and unjustifiably' because an individual must accept the risk of accidental interference with his communications and the fact that in certain circumstances the exigencies of the common good may require and justify such intrusion and interference. No such circumstances exist in this case.[46]

There is ample evidence to suggest that Irish law[47] provides a considerable amount of protection against intrusion. It should be noted that in *Kennedy, Arnold & Arnold* the personal right to privacy was available to the second plaintiff even though he was not a citizen of the State. Where an invasion of privacy is established damages for invasion of privacy can be awarded.[48] In *Kennedy, Arnold & Arnold*, warrants had been issued by the Minister for Justice authorising the Minister for Posts and Telegraphs to forward to the gardai information obtained by tapping the home telephone lines of the defendants, political journalists who had, through their newspaper columns made known Government decisions. These warrants were issued by the Minister for Justice and were directed at finding the sources of such information and ignored guidelines which indicated that warrants would only be issued where national security or the prevention or detection of serious crime was involved. The defendants conceded that while the tapping was improper, no interference with constitutional rights had occurred. Hamilton P rejected this submission. Upholding the plaintiffs submission that Article 40.3 of the Constitution included a personal right to privacy, the President of the High Court said

> The question to be determined in this case is whether the right to privacy includes the right to privacy in respect of telephonic conversations and the right to hold such conversations without deliberate, conscious and unjustified interference with and intrusion thereon by servants of the State, who listen to such conversations, recorded them, transcribed them and made the transcriptions thereof available to other persons.
> I have no doubt but that it does.

Basing his judgment on *Norris*, and in particular the speech of Henchy J, Hamilton P stated:

> The nature of the right to privacy must be such as to ensure the dignity and freedom of an individual in the type of society envisaged by the Constitution namely, a sovereign, independent and democratic society.

PRIVACY AND DATA PROTECTION IN THE UNITED KINGDOM

Despite the absence of any common law, statutory or constitutional right to privacy, a considerable amount of work has been undertaken in the United Kingdom on the question of whether legal recognition of a general right to privacy should be enshrined into the law. The Report of the Committee on Privacy, under the chairmanship of Kenneth Younger (hereafter Younger) is a landmark in terms of the identification and analysis of privacy generally. The Report, published in 1972,[49] provides a most convenient starting point for our discussion. For Younger, it was impossible to accept that a satisfactory definition of the right to privacy could be devised. The assertion that 'privacy is the right to be left alone' was said to go so far beyond any right which the individual living in an organised society could reasonably claim. Younger also argued that such an assertion would be useless as the basis upon which legal protection could be granted. A right of this kind would, Younger argued, be so open to qualification that it would be destructive of the general concept of privacy itself.[50] For this reason Younger, on balance, decided against recommending the enactment, into statute law, of a general right to privacy. Rather, Younger opted for specific proposals to be implemented which would directly address the problems raised by the Report.

Younger, as part of the process of identifying existing problem areas, regarded the law of privacy as having two main aspects. Firstly, there is the freedom 'from intrusion upon oneself, ones home, family and relationships. The second is privacy of information, that is, the right to determine for oneself how and to what extent information about oneself is communicated to others.'[51] Younger regarded these important human values as being closely linked but the Younger public attitudes survey revealed that public concern tended to focus on the latter value or definition: the treatment of personal information by others where there is an element of intrusion into areas of activity in which the information was hitherto private was identified as a unifying factor.[52] Particular attention was drawn by Younger to the following activities: 'intrusive gathering and dissemination of information by the publicity media, handling of credit information, unwarrantable intrusion into personal matters at work and in education and medicine, prying by neighbours and landlords, intrusive sales methods, investigations by private detectives and industrial espionage.'[53] Special attention was also paid to technological advances such as surveillance devices and computers.

Younger also identified the factors that make the issue of privacy such a controversial one in society. The public attitudes survey commissioned by Younger revealed that while the individuals need for privacy in personal affairs will vary from person to person, a generally held belief, that everyone needs privacy for their own personal and family affairs, was discovered. Medical evidence submitted to Younger indicated that privacy is of importance for physical and mental health. Younger concluded that privacy is a basic need for the maintenance, at a collective level, of a free and democratic society and, at an individual level, for the development and maintenance of a mature and stable individual personality.

The examination by Younger of technological advances and in particular the use of computers is instructive. Younger recommended that voluntary codes of practice should apply to computer users handling personal information.[54] Legislative measures were recommended for reviewing the growth of methods of gathering and handling personal information on computers[55] with powers to make recommendations. Steps towards identifying a responsible person for each organisation — the forerunner of the data controller — should be taken.[56] The Younger Commission however was not in a position to foresee the scale of the informatics and information technology revolution that began in the late 1960s.[57] It was not possible for Younger to really anticipate how new technology would make data processing a cheaper and more effective method of recording and effecting transactions.

By 1975 however, official concern about the potential for abuse that the new technology presented resulted in a White Paper, *Computers and Privacy*.[58] The speed and flexibility of computers for data storage, retrieval and processing had to be tested by reference to the dangers presented if information was inaccurate, or fell into the wrong hands, or was used in another context to that for which the information was initially kept.[59] Permanent supervisory machinery was recommended to oversee a set of objective standards covering the processing of personal information. These standards would include measures to ensure respect for privacy. This body, the Data Protection Authority, was to be a statutory agency and was to be capable of adopting and evolving so as to meet different circumstances, a clear reference to the potential within the data processing industry for rapid change and evolution. The White Paper led to the creation, in 1976, of the Data Protection Committee, chaired by Sir Norman Lindop, a body which was established to advise the Home Secretary on the permanent control machinery necessary to search existing and future computer systems, public and private, which hold personal information. Due regard for privacy was seen as an essential element in the creation of a set of rules and procedures governing the operation of computerised information systems. Lindop was required to identify the objectives that the relevant privacy legislation should aim to further. When the Lindop Report appeared in 1978[60] it continued the process begun by Younger by concentrating public debate on the use of information systems, to the detriment of the privacy of individuals. In particular, Lindop identified the data processing industry as requiring rules, which must evolve over time, or the rules would run the risk of becoming swiftly obsolescent. On the central question of whether a general privacy law was necessary Lindop took the view, after studying the relationship between privacy and data protection, that 'the function of a data protection law should be different from that of a law on privacy: rather than establishing rights, it should provide a framework for finding a balance between the interests of the individual, the data user and the community at large.'[61] Lindop recommended legislation to cover all automatic handling in the UK of personal data by any user or data processing bureaux. The legislation should declare a set of principles, to be observed by these persons and bodies. A Data Protection Authority was to be established and charged with the task of balancing competing interests. The data protection principles were to guide the Authority. Special consideration was to be given to privacy interests. The Authority was to be responsible for making codes of practice, which, if approved by Parliament, would acquire the force of law and breach of the code would constitute a criminal offence. A scheme of registration of all users in central and local government was recommended. The Authority was also to have powers to investigate complaints. Data subjects were to have a right to compensation by way of civil action, in the form of a statutory cause of action, in addition to any existing contract or tort remedy.

While Lindop proved influential in creating a climate within which data protection legislation came to be seen as essential it was really the British Government's signature of the Council of Europe Convention in May 1981, and the endorsement by Britain of the 1980 OECD Guidelines, that ushered in the 1984 Act. The 1982 White Paper *Data Protection: the Governments Proposals for Legislation*[62] stressed that legislation was needed for two reasons. Firstly, use of computers increased the danger to individuals that privacy would be infringed and, further, if the UK did not pass Data Protection legislation other Convention countries could decline to forward personal data to be processed or held in the UK.

Legislation eventually passed through the UK Parliament in 1984. The Data Protection Act, 1984 received the Royal Assent on 12 July 1984. The Act was implemented in three stages. The most important parts of the legislation, the subject access right and the power to refuse to accept applications for registration, became fully operative on 11 November 1987. Although the initial number of complaints to the Data Protection Registrar was small, the Registrar has experienced a fourfold increase in the number of complaints from members of the public. In the Fifth Report of the Data Protection Registrar, published in June 1989, there were 1,122 complaints made by members of the public during 1988, in contrast with 836 in the previous year. In this Report the Registrar has expressed the view that the registration process must be simplified and made selective and that amending legislation is necessary.

2

Data protection – the call for legislation

INTRODUCTION

In the previous Chapter we considered, amongst other matters, the extent to which Irish law provides a general constitutional right to privacy. It is likely that the intrusive collation of personal information, or the unauthorised dissemination of such information, may be protected in specific circumstances. The use of computerised data processing systems clearly accentuate the difficulties of balancing a variety of quite legitimate considerations. The right to be let alone is by no means absolute and it can be circumscribed by the public interest in freedom of information,[1] the investigation of criminal offences, or national security considerations, to name but just three obvious counterweights to the privacy right. In Ireland there has been no wideranging examination of data protection problems, much less an extensive debate on the need for legislative control of automatic data processing and data retention. The question, does Ireland need data protection legislation, has not really been addressed as an issue. The pressure for data protection legislation has, if anything, been largely but not exclusively external in origin.

THE NEED FOR DATA PROTECTION LEGISLATION

Despite the absence of any extensive Irish debate there is general acceptance, in Europe and elsewhere, that data protection legislation provides a potentially very effective method of advancing the concept of data privacy. Lindop[2] coined the phrase 'data privacy' to describe the individuals claim to control the circulation of data about himself. Lindop however noted that 'data privacy' becomes important, not because of the nature of the data itself, but because individuals have different privacy requirements. An individual, Lindop indicates, is less likely to insist on data being withheld if circulation of data will be to the advantage of the data subject, and *vice versa*. Nevertheless, this approach should not be dispositive of the issue of control of data. There is however a legitimate interest in data being freely available on certain matters

— Lindop instances personal credit details, and the balance between individual interests and collective interests is central to the debate. However, where personal data is held on an automated system, problems of control become acute. Automated data can be processed quickly. Such data can be accessed by many persons: often a greater degree of access is given on an automated system than is the case of data held on manual files, and access is often more difficult to regulate. Data held on an automated system may be easier to corrupt or gain access to, even if unauthorised by the data controller. Distribution of data on an automated system is extremely easy to effect. Data can be exported across national boundaries in seconds. In these circumstances a regulatory agency becomes important for, as Lindop points out, the balance between competing interests cannot be achieved simply by way of consensus reached as a result of agreement between data subject and data user.

> The means by which the balances are struck, and the conditions under which the agreements between data subjects and data users are reached, are of great importance. Where the agreement is voluntary, the result will not be fair unless each party fully understands the requirements of the other, and there is a clear understanding of what data are to be provided, and for what purposes they will be used. Fairness requires openness in such dealings and it also requires that no advantage should be taken of any disparities in bargaining power. But there are many cases where these conditions for fairness cannot exist. Data users cannot always be expected, or even be able, to appreciate fully the requirements of data subjects. Even less can data subjects be expected to appreciate fully the requirements of data users, let alone the relevant technicalities of information handling. In many cases, especially where the relationship is between the government and the governed, there can be no question of equal bargaining power; in yet others it may turn out that agreement simply cannot be reached. In all such cases, only an independent third party can fairly weigh all the interests involved — those of the data subject, the data user and society at large — and determine the best point of balance.[3]

Lindop notes that essentially it is the speed and ease with which a computer, as part of an information system, can effect the processing, selection, transformation and distribution of personal data, that makes regulation necessary. This argument is clearly accepted in Ireland. In introducing the Data Protection Bill, 1987 at Second Stage, the Minister for Justice Mr Collins had this to say about the rationale behind data protection legislation in Europe:

> In the early seventies large information systems had become computerised to such an extent that fears began to be expressed on an increasing scale

about the threat to privacy that they could pose. The fears were not based primarily on the amount of the information stored in the systems. The real basis for the concern was the ease and speed with which computerised information could be collected, rearranged, transferred and retrieved, and the fact that this information could include sensitive personal information and could be used for all kinds of purposes without the knowledge of the individuals to whom it related. Moreover, the ability to link computerised information systems gave rise to apprehension that the state would be in a position to have virtually instant access to all the information it held separately on each individual and, through file matching, to build up a comprehensive profile on every member of society. There were fears, too, that computerised personal information could more easily be stolen or copied or otherwise obtained improperly by those to whom it should not be disclosed.[4]

As the Minister himself later acknowledged in the same speech, the pressure for legislation has come from a variety of sources, both in Ireland and elsewhere.

INTERNATIONAL DEVELOPMENTS

Although the European Convention for the Protection of Human Rights has not been directly called into play in the field of data protection, Article 8 is still significant. The recent European Court of Human Rights ruling[5] in the *Norris* case suggests that Article 8, while not part of Irish domestic law,[6] will prove influential. Article 8 declares

1. Everyone has the right to respect for his private and family life, his home and his correspondence.

2. There shall be no interference by a public authority with the exercise of this right except such as in accordance with the law and is necessary in a democratic society in the interest of national security, public safety or the economic well being of the country, for the prevention of disorder or crime, for the protection of health or morals, or for the protection of the rights and freedoms of others.[7]

Many countries have strengthened domestic law so as to provide specific measures to counteract abuse of privacy rights. For example, Sweden has had data protection laws in operation since 1973. Austria followed in 1978, as did France. The Federal Republic of Germany implemented its 1977 data protection legislation in 1979, as did Luxembourg. Norway implemented its 1978 Data Protection law in 1980. Iceland's 1981 law came into force in 1982. Israel passed privacy laws in 1981, implementing these laws in the same year. The UK Act was passed in 1984 and became fully operational in 1987. The Netherlands enacted a Data Protection Act in December 1988 and it is expected that this Act will become operational in late 1989. Action on the legislative front is not confined to Europe. Canada, as part of its vast programme of constitutional rights following the constitutional changes ushered in at the beginning of this decade, has passed limited measures which cover the federal government and federal agencies. This reflects the US position which seems to demonstrate that concern exists about public sector activities and freedom of information issues rather than data privacy. Australia too has passed freedom of information legislation but no data protection legislation exists as such, although Australian case law indicates that privacy implications are involved in freedom of information issues.[8]

As the various national legislatures began to respond to the perceived dangers to privacy presented by data processing by automatic means, it became clear that there was a danger that national laws would be divergent and incapable of responding effectively to the threat posed by the exportability of personal data. Further, the fear that some unscrupulous regime may refuse to pass or implement data protection laws raised the spectre of the 'data haven', i.e. that sensitive personal data could be kept in one country and used in any manner without any effective control or sanction being available. Action at international level was forthcoming, at two levels in particular. The OECD (Organisation for Economic Cooperation and Development) of which Ireland is a member, undertook work in the 1960s and 1970s on automatic data processing and transborder data flow. The fears expressed in OECD and elsewhere on dangers to privacy were a primary cause of OECD action but, perhaps just as importantly, it was the view of experts involved that disparities in legislation would interrupt the free flow of personal data across frontiers. Restrictions would possibly result from such disparities, and, as such, would seriously affect important sectors of the economy such as banking and insurance. Indeed, it can be said that at an international level, pressure for legislation has been industry or commerce led rather than the result of any political or civil libertarian lobby. The OECD, through Council Recommendation of 23 September 1980, and the accompanying *Guidelines on the Protection of Privacy and Transborder Flows of Personal Data*, recommended that OECD states take into account in their domestic legislation the guidelines, undertake to remove or avoid creating barriers to transborder data flow, and cooperate so as to implement the Guidelines. The OECD Guidelines set out basic principles which national governments are to strive to observe. They presage the data protection principles set out in the Data Protection Act, 1988. Ireland was involved in OECD activities in this field and the principles were endorsed in Paris on 18 December 1986 by the Irish Ambassador to France.

The second level at which the problem of data privacy was addressed in an international context has, if anything, been even more influential in Ireland. The Council of Europe *Convention for the Protection of Individuals with Regard to Automatic Processing of Data*, of 28 January 1981, was signed by Ireland on 18 December 1986. This Convention is similar in many respects to the OECD Guidelines but its emphasis is much more on rights of privacy for individuals than facilitating the transfer of data across international boundaries. The Convention provides a set of data protection principles which the controller of data files must observe. Personal data must be collected fairly and lawfully and be accurate and kept up to date, when necessary. Safeguards in terms of security measures must be in place, particularly in relation to sensitive data, that is, data relating to racial origin, political opinions, religious and other beliefs, health or sexual life and criminal convictions. The Convention also gives data subjects the right to establish the existence of personal data, to receive a statement on what the data records about the subject, and to rectify or erase incorrect personal data. While the Convention does not require the signatory state to establish a supervisory agency, the Convention does establish a Consultative Committee.[9] Each party to the Convention is to nominate a representative and deputy representative. The functions of the Committee are set by the Convention. These functions are:

(a) to make proposals with a view to facilitating or improving the application of the Convention
(b) make proposals with a view to amending the Convention
(c) give opinions on proposals to amend the Convention
(d) express an opinion, on request by a Party, on any question concerning the application of the Convention.[10]

While the Convention is limited to natural persons in terms of 'persons' who may rely on the data protection principles, and while the Convention is limited to the 'automated data file', the Convention is permissive in that Parties may, when ratifying the Convention declare (a) that the Convention will also apply to data relating to non human 'bodies', whether or not such bodies possess legal personality, and (b) that the Convention will also apply to manual personal data files.[11] Article 12 of the Convention regulates the extent to which Parties may limit or prohibit the export of personal data. The protection of privacy *per se* is not a legitimate basis for the prohibition of transborder data flows.

Because the Council of Europe Convention is binding and signatories have the obligation to implement the Convention by adopting its central provisions into domestic legislation, the Convention is probably the most influential factor in explaining why and how the Irish Act was implemented in its present form.

Before leaving the work of the Council of Europe mention should be made of the Council of Europe's recommendations on data protection. The Council of Europe has followed up the Convention with a series of projects, undertaken by committees of experts, to produce specific recommendations which are designed to apply and expand upon the data protection principles *vis-à-vis* certain spheres of activity. The first recommendation provides for the regulation of automated medical databanks. The recommendation is confidentiality focused: information given in respect of individuals which is kept on automated databases by medical practitioners, hospital nursing and health authorities should, as far as law and practice allows, be accessible only by essential medical and health care personnel.[12]

The second recommendation[13] is directed at protecting the interests of users of computerised legal information services. A computerised database relating to legislation, judicial decisions and legal literature is of obvious utility, especially when laws and legal information become ever complex, and the recommendation seeks to promote greater use of such services and to prohibit discriminatory rules which seek to close off access to persons, even though they may have the ability to meet the costs of using the service.

The third recommendation,[14] relating to the protection of personal data used for scientific research and statistics, is directed at ensuring that parties adopt procedures which allow persons who give information for research and statistical purposes to know and consent to user for that purpose. The recommendation also prohibits data obtained for research or statistical purposes from being used for any other purpose.

Of particular significance in Ireland is the direct marketing recommendation.[15] Where goods or services are offered, or where messages are posted, telephoned or transmitted by direct means, in order to solicit a response, the recommendation is likely to be applicable. The recommendation is particularly concerned to regulate the method of compiling mailing lists. Information gleaned from publicly available sources or as a result of informed consent can legitimately be held and used for direct marketing purposes. However, if the data subject objects to user, or transmission to third parties, then the recommendation permits erasure from the list, on request. Section 2(6) of the Irish Act implements the direct marketing recommendation into Irish law.

The recommendation[16] relating to the protection of personal data used for social security purposes is of great practical importance. Given that greater mobility of labour within Europe means that many workers will have social security records in more than one state, and that eligibility for benefits may depend on establishing a worker's affinity with various social security systems, computers provide a very speedy and efficient method of processing and transmitting data. However, much of this data will be particularly sensitive. The recommendation seeks to prohibit the processing of data concerning racial origin, political opinions, religious or other beliefs unless absolutely necessary for the administration of a particular benefit. Most importantly, the recommendation seeks to limit disclosure outside the social security network to essential situations and requires either the consent of data subjects to such disclosure or the existence of national laws to provide guarantees against invasion of data privacy.

It is understood that work on a recommendation in respect of the protection of personal data relating to employees is at an advanced stage in the Council of Europe and that a committee of experts has been convened to address the implications that data protection legislation has for newspapers and publishers, with particular reference to the balancing of privacy rights with the competing interest of freedom of information.

THE EUROPEAN COMMUNITY

By the middle of 1989 seven EC Member States have data protection legislation in place. The five States who have not yet implemented general data protection legislation, that is, Greece, Portugal, Italy, Spain and Belgium, do provide some protection *via* sectoral initiatives or constitutional law but the enactment of general legislation is a priority within each of these States. Developments and initiatives in the Council of Europe and OECD have to some extent overshadowed the work within the European Community in respect of data protection. The European Parliament has passed several resolutions which have directed community institutions to the problems of protecting individual rights, urging in particular the Commission in 1979 to prepare a proposal for a directive relating to harmonisation of national legislation on data protection. Commission recommendation 81/679/EEC, of 29 July 1981 welcomed the Council of Europe Convention and advanced the view that the Convention is appropriate for the purpose of creating a uniform level of data protection in Europe. However, the Commission reserved the right to propose to the Council the adoption, by the Council, of an Instrument under the EEC Treaty if Member States did not, within a reasonable time, sign and ratify the Convention. The Commission accordingly recommended that Member States that have not already done so should sign the Treaty during the course of 1981, and ratify the Treaty by the end of 1982. This deadline was not of course met by all Member States but, as yet, the Commission have not pressed the Council to adopt a directive or other instrument. Rather, the Commission, principally DG XIII, Telecommunications, Information Industries and Innovation, has sponsored research into sectoral initiatives and in particular initiatives which do not deal with general principles but which seek to define provisions which are suitable for specific sectors of activity. These areas include banking, transport, insurance, electronic information systems and Public Sector activities. Work on assessing the effect of data protection legislation, both in the seven EEC countires that have legislation in place and the five who have not, is to take place under the IMPACT programme. If legislation is thought to have an effect on competition conditions in such a way as to distort competition it may be that measures at effecting harmonisation will emerge, probably in 1991.

DOMESTIC CONSIDERATIONS

A decision to accept the Council of Europe Convention was made at Government level at a relatively early stage following the opening for signature of the Convention. On 15 July 1982, the then Minister for Justice Mr Doherty announced that legislation allowing Ireland to give effect to the Convention was in the course of preparation.[17] In 1985 the Joint Oireachtas Committee on Legislation was established to investigate and hear submissions on the need for data protection and freedom of information legislation. This coincided with the publication of Senator Brendan Ryan's first Freedom of Information Bill.[18] That Bill attempted to provide persons with rights of access to official documents (Part II) and also give rights of personal privacy (Part III) in respect of private individuals, where public bodies, companies and financial institutions maintained records of personal information. The Bill also contained restrictions on the right of such bodies to disclose personal records to third parties, save in certain circumstances. Access rights were to be generally available and the personal record could be amended, upon request by the person concerned. The Bill contained no obvious link with the Convention e.g. the data protection principles included in the convention were not referred to or included in the Bill.[19] The Bill also relied on litigation in the District Court for its enforcement mechanism: no provision for a Privacy Commission or Data Protection Commissioner was made in the Bill. The Bill was referred to the Oireachtas Committee but the Bill lapsed when that session of the Oireachtas ended. While a second Freedom of Information Bill was presented to the Seanad by Senator Ryan in 1988 it failed to enlist Government support. The Bill, like its predecessor, included provisions on personal privacy but it was the freedom of information aspect of the Bill that proved unacceptable to the Government.[20]

Some members of the business community are prepared to see data protection legislation as a boon to efficient and responsible data processing and data handling activities. Recent studies[21] on data processing security reveal that many organisations have inadequate security measures in place. Unauthorised physical access to sensitive data processing areas, failure to provide disaster and backup plans and procedures, easy access to data via portable terminals without supervision, are seen as common failures. When it is realised that the provision of incorrect data may lead to contractual[22] or tortious[23] liability when the employer has not exercised reasonable care, it will be appreciated that considerable advantages can follow from adherence to the data protection principles. In 1986 the Institute of Chartered Accountants in Ireland, in its publication, *Security and Confidentiality of Data*,[24] stressed how important it is for a data security programme to be in place if a business is to protect itself against legal liability. The statement emphasises that it is essential that the integrity and confidentiality of stored data be maintained. 'Data is a valuable resource, and organisations which fail to secure it can and do suffer financial loss. At worst, they may go out of business'.[25] Indeed, it can be argued that adherence to data protection legislation, once the initial task of establishing a data audit and data security measures are completed, allows a business to manage data more effectively. Efficent data management can be compared, in this respect, to good stock control or good personnel relations within a company. A recent survey completed on behalf of the European Economic Community indicates that most of the European business organisations surveyed took the view that data protection legislation currently in force reflect sensible security provisions.[26]

The primary explanation for the need for data protection legislation given by the Minister for Justice Mr Collins when introducing the Bill at Second Stage to Dáil Éireann was as follows.

> The Bill is designed to provide adequate safeguards to individuals against any abuse of their privacy arising from the automatic processing of personal data concerning them. It does this without imposing any undue burdens on industry or the taxpayer and without unnecessarily restricting transborder flows of data, including flows of data to this country for processing from countries which have ratified the convention.
>
> There are other positive benefits. The Bill will encourage Government Departments and agencies and private sector companies to adopt better practices in the handling of personal data, such as keeping data up to data and not keeping data for longer than necessary. That should lead to greater efficiency in the use of information technology in both the public and private sectors.[27]

It must be added that a failure to adopt data protection legislation could, in theory at least, have serious implications. A state that does not adhere to the Council of Europe Convention could acquire the stigma of being a 'data haven', and, as such, Convention States could legitimately inhibit the export of data to that state on the ground that infringement of privacy could result.

THE TIMETABLE

The Data Protection Bill, 1987 was presented to Dáil Éireann on 19 October 1987. The Second Stage took place on 17 November 1987. Committee and all subsequent stages in the Dáil took place on 28 June 1988. The Bill passed all stages in the Seanad on 6 July 1988. The Bill was signed by the President on 13 July 1988. It must be said that while this is a complicated piece of legislation, debate in the Oireachtas was not extensive. The Committee Stage in Dáil Éireann was shortened by guillotine and discussion on specific sections ceased on section 6. The Committee Stage in the Seanad was shorter still.

The registration process[28] began on 9 January 1989. The rest of the Act, save for sections 6(2)(b) and 10(7)(b), came into effect on 19 April 1989.[29] Ratification of the Council of Europe Convention was expected in the middle of 1989, but the dissolution of the 25th Dáil and the loss of Dáil time, within which the formal process of ratification could commence, means that ratification will not take place until the autumn of 1989, at the earliest.

3

Definitions

INTRODUCTION

It is standard procedure for a piece of legislation to include a definition section which will provide a method of identifying what a term, phrase or word means within the context of the Act or, indeed, within the context of a Part or section of the Act in question. Where the term, phrase or word is not defined in the legislation the courts may have recourse to the Interpretation Act, 1937 in order to discover whether that Act provides a definition. In the absence of a definition in either Act it is an accepted, if not universal,[1] practice for the courts to strive to give the word or words under review their plain and ordinary meaning. The search for the plain and ordinary meaning of the statute is at times an impossible task, given the extraordinary range of meanings that an individual word may evoke, but in this regard the courts are aided by a range of basic rules and presumptions — the so called canons and maxims of construction[2] — some of which will be pertinent to our analysis of the Data Protection Act, 1988.

Section 1(1) of the 1988 Act declares that, in this Act, certain words and phrases have a meaning fixed by the Act 'unless the context otherwise requires'. This is somewhat more flexible than the definition section found in the 1984 UK legislation. Section 1 of that Act purports[3] to set out an exhaustive definition of several terms, save for the definition of 'processing' which is only to include certain activities, leaving the possibility that unspecified activities may be included in the term 'processing'. The question of whether a word in a statute can be given different meanings was considered in the House of Lords in the recent case of *Payne (Inspector of Taxes) v Barrett Developments (Luton) Ltd*.[4] Lord Keith of Kinkel, giving judgment for a unanimous House of Lords said:

> The rule that the same word occurring more than once in an enactment should be given the same meaning whenever it occurs is a guide which must yield to indications of contrary intention.

It is submitted that section 1(1) of the Data Protection Act, 1988 contains just such an indication and it is possible that the definitions that follow in this Chapter may possess, according to context, nuances that will only emerge in the course of interpretation by the Commissioner and the courts.

We shall now consider the definitions of some of the most important words and phrases, as set out in section 1(1) of the 1988 Act. These extremely technical definitions produce layers of meaning, many of the words intersecting with, or being part of, composite definitions which attempt to restrict the scope of the legislation. This is achieved without the draftsman having resorted to words and phrases that have a physical or technological meaning[5] and which therefore would have the potential for making the legislation obsolete when future scientific advances displace existing technology. The statutory definitions are discussed, not in the order in which they appear in section 1(1), but by reference to their relationship with other defined words or phrases.

DATA

Section 1(1) defines data as 'information in a form in which it can be processed'. This definition is a somewhat different one to that which was initially put forward when the Bill was introduced into Dáil Éireann. The original definition — 'information undergoing automatic processing' — was clearly defective in that, firstly, it would only apply to data that was being processed *vis-à-vis* data that could, or was about to be processed or reprocessed. Secondly, the original definition was, in several respects, both too wide and too narrow. By including the phrase 'automatic processing' the definition would have been narrow insofar as it would clearly exclude data recorded on manual files; but the definition, as initially presented to Dáil Éireann, would have also been too wide because information recorded on magnetic tape or on a gramophone record would, arguably, be within the original definition of data: it would be undergoing automatic processing. The idea that the original definition would have brought dictation tapes and gramophone records into the definition of data caused obvious concern, and several definitions were altered in an attempt to avert such a possibility. Of particular significance is the amendment of the word 'processing' so as to exclude all acts of recording and storage. Therefore, the words 'processing' and 'processed' no longer envisage that personal information recorded on a cassette or gramophone, or on any other medium, is *ipso facto* data. This problem of definition illustrates just how difficult it is to limit the scope of the legislation for data simply means raw information: the existing legislation purports to narrow down the definition to information kept 'in a form in which it can be processed'. The amendment to the definition of data does not include a reference to automatic processing at all. The long title to the Act itself makes it clear that the Act is not directed at all information relating to individuals: the long title refers to 'certain information relating to individuals that is processed automatically'. Both the long title[6] and the definition of 'processing' serve to restrict the otherwise open-ended definition of data. In a recent article[7] Piragoff illustrates the distinction between data and information. Information, he points out, is not a thing but a process or relationship that occurs between a person's mind and some sort of stimulus. Data, on the other hand, is merely a representation of information or of some concept. Piragoff illustrates this by giving the example of drawings or markings placed on the walls of caves by early cave dwellers: do they represent cave decorations or represent information or concepts? Only when the intellect is directed at deciphering this material — or indeed any code or language — can a meaning be extracted. For this reason the Canadian Criminal Code provides a useful alternative definition of data: subsection 301, 2(2) is part of the Canadian law which provides for new criminal offences in relation to computer crime, but only in relation to data, which is there defined as 'representations of information or concepts'.

The Commissioner, in his *Guide to the Data Protection Act, 1988* gives some examples of what is or is not covered by the Act. Information inputed onto the main memory of a computer or stored on a diskette is data because it is capable of being processed automatically. On the other hand, a typed document is not data because it cannot be processed automatically. Even if an optical character recognition device can read the document the document *per se* is only capable of being processed automatically when the document is inputted. On the other hand, audio cassette tapes, information transmitted by fax, telex or stored or recorded on an answering machine is not data because it cannot be processed automatically: computer printout, as a manifestation in physical form of a processing operation performed on a computer is not data: nor is information displayed on a screen. The information which produces this, e.g. information stored on a mainframe memory or floppy disc is data because *in that form* it is capable of being automatically processed. The Commissioner also states that microfiche or microfilm, as a 'photographically produced document' is not data unless it can be automatically processed. If this can be done, e.g. by bar-coding or other means which involve an automated information retrieval system, then this document will be data. If the microfilm is produced directly from information recorded on a computer as COM (computer output microfilm), the Commissioner views this as being in the same position as a computer printout.

PROCESSING

Like the word data, the statutory definition of processing was amended radically at Committee Stage in Dáil Éireann. Processing is defined in the Act as

> performing automatically logical or arithmetical operations on data and includes —

(a) extracting any information constituting the data, and

(b) in relation to a data processor, the use by a data controller of data equipment in the possession of the data processor and any other services provided by him for a data controller,

but does not include an operation performed solely for the purpose of preparing the text of documents.

The key phrase in this definition is 'performing automatically logical or arithmetical operations on data'. The essential element in this definition is the power of a machine to sort, list, arrange, manipulate, select, amend and add to, a given amount of data. If the machine does not automatically do any of these things then there is not processing of data within the statutory definition. Because of the extremely vague definition of data in the Act it is essential that the definition of processing be clearly stated. The definition of processing initially incorporated into the Data Protection Bill, 1987 was much less satis-factory. Firstly, the initial definition included recording and storage of data. Any dictation tape or gramophone recording on which data was stored was therefore within the statutory definition, even though recordings of this kind are not capable of being further processed, by reference to a given set of commands, by a machine. The dictation tape or gramophone recording can be played automatically. The dictation tape can be altered — by re-recording for example — but the combination of human voice and tape recorder do not process data automatically because no logical or arithmetical operations are carried out on the data. Dictation tapes and other means of making sound recordings, which are in turn used only to create the text of documents e.g. letters, memoranda, are in any event outside the definition of processing because of the proviso. It follows that if a system is created merely to store data without in any sense being capable of changing the order or composition of the data then there is no processing. A machine used to record telephone messages in no sense processes the data recorded thereon even though the machine can be automatically played back. The use of fast forward on a recording machine does not change the order in which the data is recorded so there is not processing. However, once data is capable of being manipulated in some further way there will be processing, if done automatically. If material is stored on microfiche then the mere act of storage is not an act of processing. Once the material is highlighted by a microfiche reader there *may* be processing, e.g. if the margin of each fiche is bar-coded so as to allow the machine, upon command, to select automatically a particular fiche and display the relevant part of the document.[8] Library activities of this kind may therefore involve data processing.

To return to the question of storage of data for a moment, where information exists in a form in which it can be processed, this means that the information in question is data. Whether that data is processed simply by transferring it from one medium to another is no longer answered by the definition of processing: recall that initially the Bill's definition of processing expressly included recording and storage. If the transfer of the recording takes place by a method which then makes it possible to, in some way, manipulate, rearrange or add to the data, then recording of this kind would appear to come within the definition of processing. There would have to be some logical or arithmetical process for these events to occur and, where this is possible, processing can be established. The sorting and arranging of documents by using a logical or arithmetical process e.g. information in machine code which is recorded magnetically and sorted by computer will be processing. Documents with machine readable codes printed on them and processed by computer are similarly within the definition. Information in microform seems also to be within the notion of data processing. Microform data is not of itself capable of being read into a computer but a computer, by reference to machine readable codes on the microform, may select and extract information held on the microform.

This leads onto the problem of printed matter which, by definition is not processed but which is capable of being automatically processed by means of an optical character recognition device (OCR) or text character recognition device (TCR). In dealing with this issue in Dáil Éireann the Minister for Justice Mr Collins drew a distinction between data, as distinct from information recorded in typescript or in printed form.[9] The printed form of the information is not data because, in that form, it is not capable of being processed. Once the printed or typed document is processed into a form in which it can then be processed automatically, e.g. inputted into a mainframe computer or onto a hard or floppy disc, it will then be processed data. Similarly, a book is not within the Act simply because an OCR or TCR machine can potentially load the contents into a computer. Once the book is recorded than data processing takes place. The definition specifically includes, but is in no way limited to, extracting information found in the data. It was obviously necessary to expressly stipulate this because the statute is otherwise silent on whether automated information retrieval by accessing a database is processing.

The Irish definition of processing is extremely broad. There is no requirement that the information relate to individual data subjects. The information could relate to a manufacturing process, fishing or farming conditions or the meteorological situation. Even if a data subject does not appear anywhere in the data, the automatic processing of information held in a form in which it can be processed brings the activity within the words 'data' and 'processing'. Other words and phrases in the legislation serve to narrow down the sphere of activity regulated by the Act, particularly the phrase, personal data.

The Irish definition of processing differs radically from the definition in the UK legislation in a further respect. The UK definition of processing refers to personal data and provides that processing of personal data means amending, augmenting, deleting or rearranging the data or extracting the information constituting the data by reference to the data subject.[10] This definition of processing personal data has produced a fairly subtle distinction. The UK Registrar's Guidelines indicate that 'processing by reference to the data subject' will occur whenever the data user intends to locate and process information *because* it relates to an individual whatever the technical means by which this object is achieved'.[11] The Guidelines go on to illustrate this point. If data held on computer can provide the text of articles relating to manufacturing methods but the articles also hold personal data, e.g. on the authors of those articles, the fact that the articles contain personal data on data subjects does not bring the data user within the Act. If the data user intends to process the data with a view to extracting information about individuals then there would be processing within the UK Act. The Irish Bill initially drew this narrow distinction between processing generally and processing personal data specifically, but the distinction was deleted at Committee Stage in Dáil Éireann. The Minister for Justice Mr Collins said of the definition of processing as set out in the Bill, as introduced,

> The present text confines it to 'processing by reference to individual data subjects or categories of data subjects.' This means that unless an individual can be searched for automatically by name or other identifying particulars the data about him or her would not come within the scope of the Bill. On further consideration it appears to me that this restriction is not justified and that the safeguards of the Bill should apply to personal data. Otherwise the test as to whether data is covered by the Bill would often depend on the degree of sophistication of the equipment and the software. The revised definition, therefore, deletes the reference to processing by reference to individual data subjects so that the safeguards in the Bill will apply.[12]

Therefore, if a database can be operated automatically there can be processing within the Act, even if the operator is prevented from searching for data by reference to a key word or key name facility.

If a data processor lends equipment to a data controller, the data processor is not to be held to be processing that body of data unless the equipment remains in the data processor's possession. This is the impact of the words that follow (b), set out above. It is possible to foresee that this will produce difficulties for someone who owns or possesses data equipment and who allows someone to access the equipment for their own purposes. Take the example of an employer who allows an employee or a friend to have access to a personal computer in order to establish and maintain a file. While the equipment will remain in the possession of the employer, the employer will not be a data controller for the person who opens the file — the employee or friend — will control the contents and use of the file and, as such, that person will be the data controller. Even if the file in question has no conceivable link with the employer, for example, it may be opened in order to keep a record of donations made by workers to a charity, it is probable that the employer becomes a data processor in respect of that file and the employer becomes registrable even if no other processing activity takes place and even if the employer is not registrable as a data controller or data processor in respect of normal business activities. Nor does the fact that, in our example, the employer takes no commercial benefit from the activity, assist the employer. While the activity does not take place wholly or partly for business purposes the Commissioner still views this employer as caught by the obligation to register. The view that is taken of the question of whether there can be such a person as a non-registrable data processor is narrow: only if the processing is a one-off or intermittent activity will the person possessing the equipment be outside the Act in the sense that that registration as a data processor will not be necessary.

PROCESSING AND MANUAL FILES

The most controversial aspect of the Irish Act relates to the automatic processing requirement. Because a manual file is not covered by the legislation until such time as the file is actually inputted to a machine or is set out in a form in which the file can be automatically processed, many commentators and Parliamentarians have been critical of the Council of Europe Convention and have questioned whether it is an appropriate model for legislative action. While the Convention is flexible on this point in the sense that Article 3.2.c. allows states to extend the Convention to personal data files which are not processed automatically, the Irish Act follows the UK legislation in excluding manual files. The arguments in favour of extending the legislation to all files are formidable. The most overwhelming argument is one of effectiveness. It is possible to evade the legislation by keeping data on a combination of manual file and automatic system. If the data subject is only allowed access to information on the automated system it may be coded or incomplete. If the legislation is intended to reassure individuals that data holders and data processors meet minimum standards of practice which are designed to protect the privacy of individuals, the distinction between manual and automatically processed files provides a convenient opportunity for the unscrupulous. An ancillary argument is often used to undermine the exclusion of manual files. Because the data protection principles and the other elements in the legislation, e.g. registration, only apply to automated information systems the law actually creates an incentive for business organisations and individuals to retain manual filing methods rather than adapt to newer and more efficient automated systems. The law therefore fosters antiquated and less effective work and business practices.

Both these arguments surfaced during the debates in Dáil Éireann on the Data Protection Bill, 1987.[13] It is evident from the Minister for Justice's response that the decision to exclude manual files was taken on pragmatic grounds. While it is correct to point out, as the Minister for Justice did at Second Stage, that the initial demand within the Council of Europe for a Convention was precipitated by fear that automatic processing of data produced particular difficulties because of the greater speed and efficiency of new processing and information systems, this seems to be a quantitative rather than a qualitative point: serious infringement of privacy may result from a breach of confidence no matter how the information is recorded. The central argument used to resist attempts to include all personal data files is the cost that business would incur in responding to the requirements of the Act. The Minister for Justice however buttressed this argument by implying that it is the norm for data protection legislation elsewhere to exclude manual files.[14] In fact the data protection legislation in force in other European Community Countries often includes manual files: the Danish, French, Luxembourg and Federal Republic of Germany have laws in force which are not confined to data which is capable of undergoing automatic processing. It is likely that some Countries which intend to implement the Convention will not include manual files: this is certainly true of draft legislation in Belgium and Portugal (and possibly the Spanish bill when it emerges) but Dutch legislation and Greek draft legislation cover manual files as well. The Minister for Justice did not rule out the possibility that the law, would, at some future date, be amended to include personal data held on manual files.[15]

PROCESSING — TEXT OF DOCUMENTS

The possibility that 'processing' by automated methods would include the use of micro-processors which are used exclusively for the preparation of letters, memoranda, and other documents, led to a specific provision which excludes any operation performed solely for the purpose of preparing the text of documents. This follows a similar exclusion in section 1(8) of the UK Act. It is not the intention of the legislature to exclude all work tasks that can be discharged by a word processor: the essential question is whether the operator uses the word processor soley to prepare the text of a document. So, if the word processor is used to discover whether a particular document was sent out to an individual this would not be an exempt function. The Registrar's Guidelines in the United Kingdom explain that the exemption is designed to exclude a text which is entered into a computer, whether it is a dedicated word processor or not, so as to enable a person to more easily edit and print a document by using the machine. Even if the text is simply retained on the machine the exemption does not apply. In Ireland too the text of document exemption will of necessity be narrowly construed. The kind of situation that will come within the exemption would include a case where a professional typist undertakes to prepare a report or thesis on a word processor. When the document is completed, to the satisfaction of the person who has commissioned preparation of the document, the file on the word processor should be wiped. If this takes place then the exemption will operate. Retention of the file would take the typist outside the exemption even if no further processing is envisaged for the test is whether the information or data is capable of being automatically processed, not whether this is envisaged.

The fact that data is loaded onto a computer with the view to creating a document at some future date will not always bring the activity within the exemption. It is clear that if an operator opens a file in order to create a document from the information contained therein, the activity is not exempt. If the file is added or amended, or if the file is accessed for information purposes, it is likely that the operation is being undertaken for a multiplicity of purposes. Even if the text is loaded onto a computer and edited in the manner set out in the UK Guidelines, it is possible that related activities will bring the situation within the definition of processing. If a standard letter is set up and retained but the word processor is directed to search in order to find out if a copy of the letter has been sent to a particular individual, or if the word processor is required to decide which of two separate standard letter is to go to a particular individual (e.g. by reference to the sex or place of residence of the individual) then processing takes place.

Difficulties may arise in the future on the meaning of document. The word is not defined in either the Irish or the UK legislation. There are examples of statutes which provide a definition of the words 'document' or 'documents'[16] for the purpose of specific pieces of legislation but these meanings are not generally reliable. It is often necessary for the courts to rule on the question of whether an item is a document within the context of pre-trial motions relating to discovery and service of documents. Within this somewhat limited context plans,[17] and account books[18] have been held to be documents. A tape recording was held to be a document in *Grant v Southwestern and County Properties*[19] and x-ray plates[20] as well as films[21] have been held to be documents for the purpose of discovery proceedings. The general question, what does a document consist of, was addressed by Humphreys J in *Hill v R*.[22] The learned judge stressed that the meaning to be attributed must be such as would be agreeable to the ordinary educated business person. The underlying principle is that it must be something which teaches, something which gives information, something which makes evident that which would not otherwise be evident. The Data Protection Act, 1988 uses the phrase, text of documents rather than the word, document. It follows that the meaning is narrower than that attributable to document. Making a transcript of a tape-recording, or the speech on a videotape or film would be clearly exempt, as would the use of a computer to produce captions to accompany photographs.

DATA CONTROLLER

Data controllers, are, in effect, the persons who are most likely to be subject to responsibilities and obligations under the Act. Deciding whether a person is a data controller will involve a close analysis of work practices within an organisation and may also require the organisation, or indeed an individual who processes personal data, or in some way assists in this regard, to look closely at the terms of any contract which purports to govern how and in what circumstances data is to be processed. The distinction between a data controller and data processor is in most cases quite obvious but there will be borderline cases in which data will be processed in different ways, for different purposes, and it is conceivable that while the parties may believe that all these activities have the same legal quality, the Act will compel us to reach a different conclusion.

The definition of data controller is found in section 1(1): 'a person who, either alone or with others, controls the contents and use of personal data'. In opting for this definition the draftsman has selected the concept of the 'controller of the file', as found in Article 2(d) of the Council of Europe Convention, as distinct from the 'data user', which is the corresponding term in section 1(5) of the UK Act. This is a wise choice. The UK term, data user, is a complex and complicated way of trying to get across a relatively simple idea. The UK expression also contains a concept within a concept. A person is only a 'data user' if that person 'holds' data. A person holds data if three requirements are met. In the UK firstly the data — note it need not be personal data while the Irish definition of data controller specifies personal data only — must form part of a collection of data processed or to be processed automatically. The collection of data requirement is absent from Irish law so any personal data kept is, under the Irish definition, consistent with the controller being controller of that data. The second requirement to meet the 'holds' requirement under the UK Act, approximates to the substance of the Irish definition. That person must (either alone or jointly or in common with other persons) control the contents and use of the data within the collection. The word jointly is designed to cope with situations where the UK data user is not the person with sole control over contents and use; i.e. control over the data is exercised jointly with others such as fellow employees or other compilers of a database. Control in common will arise where each data user shares a source of information but each user can use, change or amend this information without reference to the others. The third element to be satisfied before a UK data user holds data is that the data must be in a processed or processable form, or if already so processed, in a form intended to be further processed.[23]

In contrast with this cumbersome piece of drafting the Irish Act simply requires that a person control the contents and use of personal data. A person who contributes to these two functions will be a data controller, so, in relation to a given set of data, there exists the possibility that there will be several data controllers. If a person has the power to decide what information about a data subject is to be recorded or amended by automatic means, or if that person has the power to decide what use is to be made of the data, then that person will be a data controller. The problem of how we are to discriminate between persons who have some degree of access to data (who do not thereby become data controllers) and persons who exercise control over contents and use is not addressed by the Act. In reality this problem arises in its most acute form in relation to 'disclosure' of personal data. The Act does however deal with the problem of joint access to control over contents and use. Rather than use the terms 'alone', 'jointly' or 'in common', the Irish Act uses an omnibus phrase — 'either alone or with others'. This covers the case of joint or common control.

The word 'person' is not defined in the Act but the Council of Europe Convention makes it clear that a person means a natural or legal person: Article 1(d). A corporate body that employs individuals to do work which involves the processing of personal data will of course be a data controller. Individuals concerned in this activity may also be within the definition, data controller. Employees in the personnel department of a corporation, journalists, trade union officials who compile profiles of individuals, may be separate and distinct data controllers. Yet it cannot have been intended that each employee register separately. It is suggested that an appropriate way of limiting the sphere of activity and responsibility can be effected by an appropriately worded phrase set out in the conditions of employment of individual workers, i.e. 'Personal data to which the employee has access in the course of the employee's employment is not data which the employee may control, either as to its contents or its use.' However, the Commissioner would be perfectly entitled to look at the facts of the case and decide that a particular employee is engaged in activities that make the employee a separate data controller (e.g. a personnel manager who maintains a separate database at home). Similar difficulties can arise in relation to voluntary activities. Unless the activity is an exempt activity, e.g. social, recreational or domestic, the compiler of a database on behalf of a school, church, sports association, or youth club or similar body may be a data controller even if the activity is undertaken on behalf of that body or association. Of course even if a person is caught by the definition of data controller he is unlikely to be registrable unless the data is sensitive personal data within section 16(1)(c).

A contractual allocation of data controller status is also likely where data is not processed exclusively by one organisation or individual: e.g. an information provider relies on others to service it with data, the data being automatically processed by the data service. The information provider will no doubt be a data controller but will the service provider, who after all, is hardly likely to control the use of the information? Rather than leave the difficult factual problem of control unresolved, it would be sensible for the contract to decide that, in the light of a realistic appraisal of what the service provider does, the contract should deem one (or indeed, both) of them to be data controller for the purpose of the Act. This can also be achieved implicitly: the contract could make it clear that a service provider is not to have control over the contents and use of personal data. In cases where access to data is shared between organisations or individuals a contractual allocation of data controller will have to meet the reality of the situation. Because information contained in the data or part of the data may be of great commercial value to an organisation, it may be unwise to allow another person — a processing service provider, for example — to have access and control simply to effectively allocate data controller status elsewhere. Conversely, if the service provider is intimately involved with the day to day management and control of an aspect of an organisation's business it may be prudent to rationalise the relationship in such a way as to make it clear that the service provider is data controller. Take for example a case of a management consultancy firm that undertakes to cut down office overheads, e.g. by introducing flexitime and telephone logging of calls where these activities involve the automatic processing of personal data. A decision which designates the consultancy firm to be a data controller in respect of that personal data would probably be appropriate.

DATA CONTROLLER — *EQUIPMENT SUPPLIERS*

The Bill, as initially presented to Dáil Éireann, created a measure of uncertainty for business organisations that manufacture, sell or otherwise make available data processing equipment. It was possible that the Bill could, unwittingly, bring suppliers of equipment within the definition of data controller if the supplier retained a right of access to, or a right to repossess, the equipment. Clauses giving such rights to the supplier are of course common in leasing contracts and this has caused some concern in the business community. It is submitted that a business equipment firm could not be held to be a data controller even if the leasing contract gives the equipment firm a right to repossess the equipment. That contractual term would not give the equipment firm a right to control the contents of use of personal data although it would clearly interfere with the ability of others to control the contents and use of personal data stored or processed on the equipment, as the case may be. Nevertheless, a standard contract for the leasing of equipment should provide that the lessee *vis-à-vis* the equipment provider should be sole data controller of personal data kept or processed on that equipment.

DATA CONTROLLER — *PROCESSING AND TRUSTS*

The UK Guidelines make the point that where a contractual arrangement is made between trustees and a service provider (e.g. the trustees of a pension scheme contract with a bank, an insurance company or a pensions administrator with a computerised system) 'it would be appropriate to consider the application of trust law'[24] and seek legal advice before designating which of them is to be data user (or in Ireland data controller). The possibility of a breach of trust, by delegation of trust powers, is a possibility although if delegation is necessary and if the delegate is carefully selected, and generally supervised, this is not a very likely eventuality. Legal advice should be taken however on each individual situation.

DATA CONTROLLER — *PARTNERSHIPS*

Specific attention was drawn in Dáil Éireann to the difficulties that are presented by this legislation when a business is run, not as a corporate body, but by way of partnership. The creation of a partnership does not involve the creation of a new and distinction legal entity. A partnership deed and the Partnership Act, 1890 create contractual and fiduciary relationships and duties for each partner.[25] Liability of each partner for the debts contracted by individual partners in the course of trading is joint and several, i.e. partner A may be personally liable on contracts concluded by partner X with third parties. The absence of a distinct legal entity when a partnership is created may be a source of annoyance under the Data Protection Act, 1988. If a partnership — a medical or accountancy partnership or a firm of solicitors for example — maintains automated personal data on clients or others, the Act does not allow the partners to designate one of them to be data controller on behalf of 'the firm'. If a single partner has control over personal data , that partner may have to register as the sole data controller. An amendment at Committee Stage[26] was moved by one opposition deputy to allow for designation of a single data controller within a firm but the amendment was not acceptable. The Minister for Justice[27] indicated that section 20 regulations would, via the procedural rules governing registration, make it easier for partners to register than would otherwise appear be the case. The obligation to register will nevertheless extend to every partner in every partnership firm, where a partnership activity comes within section 16. The registration form requires the name and address of each partner to be provided to the Commissioner.

THE DESIGNATED DATA CONTROLLER

Many of the difficulties that arise from the scope of the definition of data controller, and its inherent vagueness when the file or data can be accessed and in some way changed by a multitude of persons, are avoided in respect of the activities of the Civil Service. Section 1(3)(a) provides that an appropriate authority, within the meaning of the Civil Service Regulation Acts, 1956 and 1958,[28] being a data controller or data processor, may designate a civil servant, in relation to whom that body is the appropriate body, to be a data controller or data processor in respect of all or some of the personal data kept by that authority. The effect of such a designation is to make that person a data controller or data processor, thereby making the Act apply to that person. The Act however is not to apply to the appropriate authority once the designation has taken place. This provision is intended to allow a Minister, for example, to delegate responsibility for compliance with the Act to a person within the Department who is responsible for keeping personal data on an automatic system. This specifically means that when a delegation has taken place an action for non compliance with the Act, and in particular a tort action for breach of the section 7 duty of care, will not lie against the Minister who heads the Department within which the designated data controller or data processor is employed. However, during Committee Stage in Dáil Éireann amendments to the designated data controller provisions were moved by two opposition deputies to firstly, introduce a notification of designation procedure and, secondly, to make it clear that any civil servant who breached the Act while acting in his or her capacity as a designated data controller, would not be personally liable in damages.[29] These amendments were not accepted by the Government. On the second of these amendments Mr Collins indicated that there was no intention to transfer liability to compensate onto the shoulders of the designated civil servant: Mr Collins said, 'if anybody is wronged the State will be responsible in the normal way'.[30]

Section 1(3)(b) also provides for a similar delegation of function and responsibility in regard to the keeping of personal data by the Defence Forces. The Minister for Defence is authorised by the section to designate a commissioned officer of the Permanent Defence Forces to be a data controller or data processor. While the designation is in force the data controller or data processor is deemed to be such for the purpose of the Act and, in respect of the Act, it shall not apply to the Minister for Defence, as respects the data concerned.

Section 1(3)(c)(i) makes two consequential amendments whereby a civil servant who is employed in a Department where no designation has taken place is deemed to be the employee of the appropriate authority. If a designation has taken place the civil servant is deemed an employee of the designated data controller or data processor. Section 1(3)(c)(ii) similarly directs that if no designation in respect of the Permanent Defence Forces has taken place, a member of the Defence Forces is deemed to be an employee of the Minister for Defence. If a designation has taken place then that Defence Forces member is deemed an employee of the designated officer. Section 1(3)(c)(iii) directs that a member of the Garda Síochána (other than the Commissioner of the Garda Síochána) shall be deemed to be an employee of the Commissioner.

DATA CONTROLLER — *CONCLUSIONS*

The simplicity of the data controller concept is more apparent than real. There will be considerable difficulties for companies and partnerships on the basic issue of who has to appear on the register as a data controller. It is perhaps unfortunate that the designated data controller procedure, used in the civil service, could not be extended into all sectors. The reason given for exempting Ministers from the provisions of the Act, namely, that day to day data processing activities are not within a Minister's remit, may hold true for a great number of private sector employers who, nevertheless, alone or with others, control the contents and use of personal data. We shall return to this question when we examine the registration process in Chapter 7. It must however be pointed out that the registration process envisages that data controllers, presumably companies and other registerable organisations, are to name the person to who inquiries in respect of the Act are to be made. While this person is not the data controller — the company or organisation whose name appears on the register remains data controller — this can avoid some of the difficulties that arise from the troublesome definition of data controller.

DATA SUBJECT

Data subject is defined as 'an individual who is the subject of personal data'. In contrast with the terms 'data controller' and 'data processor', a data subject will always be a living human person. The Council of Europe Convention is permissive in the sense that states are free to apply the Convention to 'groups of persons, associations, foundations, companies, corporations and any other bodies consisting directly or indirectly of individuals, whether or not such bodies possess legal personality'.[31] The refusal of most countries with data protection legislation in place to extend the protection to all legal persons — in the European Community only Luxembourg and Denmark have done so — is largely the result of a feeling that data protection laws involve fundamental issues of privacy as a human right.[32] While corporations have trade secrets that it may legitimately seek to protect, there already exist a variety of criminal and civil law remedies which can effectively prevent or inhibit others from unlawfully obtaining or using sensitive or valuable technical or commercial data. The law of contract, the law of confidence, intellectual property law, aspects of criminal law, such as the property offences under the Larceny Act, 1916[33] are all directed at protecting such data. Whether the automatic exclusion of data relating to deceased persons is justifiable may be questioned. While the deceased will no longer be capable of being hurt by any invasion of privacy that results, friends and members of a family may be grievously affected by breach of the data protection principles.[34]

Despite the fact that some European States allow organisations to use subject access rights and other parts of data protection law — Austria, Norway, Iceland, Luxembourg and Denmark for example — the International Chamber of Commerce, in an influential study[35] concluded that the International Business Community had not demonstrated any desire to have corporate organisations brought within the scope of persons entitled to exercise rights under data protection laws. Indeed, hostility to the expense, the bureaucratic interference and possible loss of information that would result, were far more common reactions within the business world. The ICC supported the view that data protection legislation is essentially about privacy rights and human persons.

It is nevertheless recognised that the exclusion of all commercial organisations and all non human entities may be inappropriate. In a recent survey Walden and Savage[36] acknowledge that it may at times be impossible to distinguish between the entity and the person or persons who direct and control the entity. Information about a company and its solvency or reputation are closely linked with the persons who run the company, particularly when the entity is a one-person business in effect. Groups having ethnic, religious, cultural physical homogeneity for example may need to be protected but if information held on a group is incorrect, rights of rectification cannot be exercised by representatives of the group. Individual action must be taken by persons comprising the group. Walden and Savage conclude that while the automatic extension of data protection privacy laws to all legal persons would be unwarranted, they support the ICC's view that where problems exist in relation to data held on 'small legal persons', that data should be classfied as a kind of sensitive personal data. This balance seems a sensible one but difficulties of definition and regulation are formidable.

DATA PROCESSOR

At least one Dáil deputy felt that the phrase, data processor is a potential cause of confusion because it will normally be used in relation to a machine rather than a person or organisation.[37] The Act defines data processor as 'a person who processes personal data on behalf of a data controller' but the definition does not extend to 'an employee of a data controller who processes such data in the course of his employment'. The data processor in Irish law approximates to the computer bureaux which is defined in section 1(6) of the UK Act. The idea that a data controller will obtain processing services, typically on-line or batch processing of data, is straightforward enough. Where however the data controller obtains the use of data equipment which is still in the possession of the data processor, and any other service provided by the data processor for the data controller, there is still processing by the data processor. Only if the data processor parts with possession of the equipment to the data controller will there be a transfer of sole responsibility to the data controller.[38] An employee of the data controller who processes data 'in the course of employment' will not be a data processor and will not, for example, have to register under section 16. It will therefore be of critical importance to consider when an employee acts 'in the course of employment'. The phrase appears in English and Irish law as part of a composite phrase, 'arising out of and in the course of employment'. The phrase is found in workmen's compensation and occupational injury legislation[39] and it has provided the test by which eligibility for industrial accident compensation is, in a causal sense, established. It is generally accepted that the words 'in the course of employment' require the employee to show 'he is doing what a man so employed may reasonably do within a time during which he is employed, and at a place where he may reasonably be during that time to do that thing.'[40] The fact that an employee does something which is ultimately of benefit to the employer does not always bring the activity within 'the course of employment'.[41] By analogy with the workmen's compensation cases, processing of data at home by an office worker, particularly when this takes place outside normal office hours, would probably be outside the course of employment.[42] The same principles will apply should processing take place on the way into the workplace[43] (e.g. using a laptop computer while on a train) or possibly during working hours but for purposes unrelated to the employment.[44] The person who falls outside the course of employment test would, in relation to that activity, be obliged to comply with the Act, on an individual basis, and perhaps even to register, unless the activity is an exempt activity.

If a company or a person, on a voluntary basis, keeps automated records or processes data automatically, on behalf of others, that company or person may be a data processor. Many employers are data processors and therefore registrable even though the work undertaken is of no practical or economic value to the employer. An employer who runs a social club or savings scheme or the like on behalf of employees may be registrable, even if this is the only automated activity undertaken and the file is maintained by an employee, on a voluntary basis, on the employer's equipment.

THE DESIGNATED DATA PROCESSOR

Problems of this kind are largely side-stepped in respect of data processing within the Civil Service and the Defence Forces. Section 1(3) permits the relevant Minister or the Minister for Defence to appoint a civil servant or commissioned officer, respectively, to be a data processor. The effect of any such designation is to make that designated civil servant or designated officer the data processor. A designation has the effect of rendering the Act inapplicable to the relevant Minister in respect of personal data covered by the designation for as long as the designation is operative. A similar procedure has been more extensively discussed above in regard to data controllers.

PERSONAL DATA

The definition of personal data found in the Irish Act is considerably broader and less technical than that found in the definition of personal data in section 1(3) of the UK Act. In Ireland, personal data means 'data relating to a living individual who can be identified either from the data or from the data in conjunction with other information in the possession of the data controller.' The requirement that the data relate to a living individual prevents information about corporations, unincorporated associations or statutory bodies from being personal data, except insofar as the data relates to human persons who participate in the affairs of such entities. The Irish Act does not draw a distinction between 'data as data' and 'data consisting of information', as the UK Act does, but it covers the disclosing of data as data, i.e. raw data in a undigested state. It is not clear whether there is any significance in the UK distinction between data as data and data as information.

The identification of the living individual either from the data itself or from information already held by the data controller is a significant counter-evasion provision. In most cases if the data contains a person's name then data about that individual will lead to that person being identifiable. However, if the name is a common name the data controller and processor may encode the data to avoid confusion. If the name and code accompany the data then personal data will exist. A further possibility is that the individual's name will not accompany the data at all. Where a large volume of work is to be carried out a coded prefix may be used for individuals. The code could be devised specifically for processing purposes or it may be some existing number e.g. a PRSI number, a VAT registration number or, in the case of an employee, a works number. If the data controller holds a key to the code and can therefore identify the individual then the key to the code will constitute 'other information' in the data controller's possession.

The Irish Act does not follow the UK Act in drawing the problematical distinction between statements of intention (which are not personal data) and statements of opinion (which are personal data). In Ireland therefore all personal data, regardless of whether the data relates to issues of intention or opinion, come within the data protection principles. However, the distinction between statements of fact and statements of opinion remains important in one particular context. Because of the definition of 'inaccurate', that is, something which is incorrect or misleading as to any matter of fact, a statement of opinion is not inaccurate as long as that opinion is actually held, even if it is, in the data subject's opinion, incorrect. The data subject cannot insist on deletion or amendment of that statement. However, the other data protection principles are relevant to statements of opinion, e.g. the data subject should be allowed access to the statement; the statement should not be held for longer than is necessary.

DISCLOSURE

The word disclosure is not exhaustively defined in the Act. As a word it retains the ordinary meaning to be attributed to it. In the Data Protection Act, 1988 it is reasonably clear that the word is intended to convey little more than displaying, stating, telling or imparting the actual data or information contained therein, yet the use of the word disclosure is problematical in one context. Suppose data or information is released but the person to whom it is released already knows about the data or information? Despite the probability that the data protection principles may not have been observed there is Australian authority to support the view that it is not possible to disclose a fact to a person about which that person is already aware: there is a difference, so the argument goes, between 'disclosing' a fact and stating a fact.[45] The Act however makes it clear that disclosing generally includes 'the disclosure of information extracted from such data and the transfer of such data . . . and, where the identification of a data subject depends partly on the data and partly on other information in the possession of the data controller, the data shall not be regarded as disclosed unless the other information is also disclosed.' It is clear from this that disclosure covers disclosure of the data in a raw form and disclosure of information which is taken or extracted from the data. It is the view of the UK Registrar that disclosure will occur when the data, or information, is made available in written form but also if the data or information is displayed on a screen and shown to another person.[46] If information is provided by extracting it from the data, or if the data, as a whole, is provided to another person, there will only be a disclosure if that individual can be identified therefrom. However, if the information or data is released with other information which will enable identification to take place — by cross referring the data or information with that other information — there will be a disclosure. It is noteworthy that the Minister for Justice was advised that the release of personal data, or information extracted therefrom, with identifying information is caught by the definition of disclosure regardless of whether the identifying information is disclosed, before, after, or simultaneously with, the personal data or information[47] which has been automatically processed.

The definition of disclosure excludes a disclosure made, directly or indirectly by a data controller or data processor to an employee or agent of his for the purpose of allowing the employee or agent to carry out his duties. Disclosure to a data processing manager, the manager then informing employees that personal data must be amended, is not a disclosure within the Act for the data processing manager is the conduit by which the data controller or data processor indirectly informs employees of matters that are essential for the performance of contractual duties. If a data controller informs an employee of a data processor there would be a disclosure unless that employee meets the description of agent: the informant must inform an employee or agent of his if the exemption is to apply.

4

The section 2 data protection principles

INTRODUCTION

It must be emphasised at the outset that the data protection principles are not, strictly speaking, legal obligations in the traditional sense of the term. So, if data controller does not observe the principles, a sanction, in the form of a fine or an award of damages, will not be automatically imposed on the data controller. The data protection principles provide guidance for the Commissioner, data controllers and data processors and in particular any body which is representative of data controllers, as well as trade associations and the professions, on the technical and ethical standards that should be achieved if minimum standards of data privacy are to be afforded to individuals. The data protection principles serve a variety of functions.

Educative role for data controllers and others   These principles will provide those actively engaged in data processing with a somewhat bald statement on data gathering and data processing activities which are acceptable. This in itself is an important development, particularly in relation to computer security and the unauthorised disclosure of personal data. Data controllers will need to revise standard procedures to meet the requirements of the data protection principles.

Jurisdictional role for the Commissioner   The Act does not make it an offence or a tort to fail to meet the standards set by the data protection principles but it does provide the Commissioner with a proper legislative basis for intervention if an individual complains that the data protection principles have not been observed. Indeed, the Commissioner has the jurisdiction to initiate investigations on whether, *inter alia*, the data protection principles have been contravened, even without a complaint having been received.[1] Section 10(3) of the Act emphasises the importance of the data protection principles by affording the Commissioner additional powers if an enforcement notice relates to non-compliance with the data protection principles by a data controller. It is however likely that the Commissioner will seek to mediate and persuade data controllers to meet the relevant legislative standards before resorting to enforcement notices as a coercive method of attempting to obtain compliance.

Legislative role The Irish Act allows data controllers and representative bodies an initial power to decide what the data protection principles require of them. This emphasis on self regulation is a significant feature of the Irish data protection scheme. The Commissioner has a statutory duty[2] to encourage trade associations and other representative bodies to prepare codes of practice, to be complied with by persons involved in these activities. These codes of practice may, in turn, be approved by the Commissioner[3] and, following the laying of each code before each House of the Oireachtas by the Minister for Justice and, following the approval of each House, by resolution, the code shall have the force of law.[4] Although the Act does not directly address this point it is difficult to see how an individual can complain about an alleged departure from the data protection principles if a data controller meets the standards set in a code approved in this manner. This procedure contrasts sharply with the UK Act. Under the UK Act the codes of practice, even if representative of trade practice, do not have the force of law and are merely a guide to standard and accepted procedures within the sphere of activity concerned. It would still be possible for the Registrar to hold that the UK Act requires higher standards to be achieved and the Registrar could ultimately resort to use of enforcement powers to set such higher standards.

The data protection principles are found in Chapter II of the Council of Europe Convention. These principles are based on the recommendations of the Lindop Committee and are predicated on the Preamble to the Convention which assumes the existence of an individual's right of privacy. The Convention sets out principles relating to the quality of data (Article 5), sensitive personal data (Article 6), data security (Article 7), and also access rights and remedies for infringement (Article 8). These principles are set out in the body of the Data Protection Act, 1988, specifically sections 2, 3 and 4.

THE 'FAIRLY' OBTAINING AND PROCESSING PRINCIPLE

The first principle set out in section 2(1)(a) of the Act corresponds with the principle found in Article 5.a. of the Convention. Section 2(1)(a) requires the data controller to ensure that as regards personal data

> the data or, as the case may be, the information constituting the data shall have been obtained, and the data shall be processed, fairly.

It is clear that if the data is not personal data the principle does not apply. For example, the compilation or use of technical data that does not contain data about individual persons — scientific data, specifications, trade secrets and the like — is not compromised by this principle. It is possible that some technical data, if recorded automatically and in a way which includes references to the designers and researchers responsible for the project, or persons involved in testing or validating of the project, could provide a somewhat indirect method of counteracting certain kinds of industrial espionage. If the technical data, indispersed with personal data, is not obtained fairly it is possible to hold that the personal data has not been obtained fairly. The Act does not distinguish between attempts to obtain personal data as the sole or primary objective, as against a case where the data obtained is of an economic or scientific nature but happens to include personal data.

This first principle is directed at data controllers and it should impose an obligation in relation to data and information gathering, regardless of whether the data or information is obtained or provided orally, in writing or in a form in which it can be automatically processed. However, the use of the word data may, as a matter of bad drafting, frustrate this for it is arguable that only when the data or information is recorded by the data controller in a form in which it can be automatically processed (i.e. inputted) does it become data within the terms of the Act. So, if information is obtained about an individual, for example from a tape recording, but the data controller decides not to process that information into data, the fact that the information exists on tape does not breach the first principle because the information, in that form, is not data within the terms of the Act. The use of the word 'information' adds nothing in this context for the information, until in processable form, is not part of the data. If however the word data is, in this context, given a broader interpretation then unfair compilation in any form would breach the first principle.[5] Section 2(5)(b) imposes an immediate limitation on this principle by providing that use for a purpose which was not disclosed at the time data was obtained does not of itself lead to breach of this principle. The Irish Act is otherwise silent on this principle but there are some useful pointers set out in the UK Act[6] and in the Registrar's Guidelines.[7] The Act requires that, in relation to the question whether information was obtained fairly, regard shall be had to the method by which it was obtained, in particular whether the person from whom the information was obtained was deceived or misled as to the purpose or purposes for which it is to be held, used or disclosed. This is fleshed out by the Guidelines. Was the informant[8] given an explanation about why the information was needed and when it might be used or disclosed? If so, was the explanation complete and accurate? If the informant asked about use of the information, what reply was made? Could the informant, without explanation, be expected to understand why the information was needed and to what purposes it would put? If not, why was an explanation not provided to the informant? Was the informant under the impression that the information would be kept confidential, once disclosed by the informant? Was this belief justifiable? Was it intended that this confidence would be preserved? Were inducements, threats or improper pressure, brought to bear on the informant? Was the informant led to believe that failure to provide the information would be personally disadvantageous?

The UK Guidelines envisage that the informant will be advised as to why the data is required unless this is obvious from the context in which the question is asked. Even if this is the case, if some further use of this data is possible or contemplated, the informant should be told of these other uses. A form of constructive knowledge is also envisaged by the UK Guidelines. The informant could be told the information is needed for the purposes set out on the data controller's entry on the Register (if applicable). This would put the onus on the informant to check the Register. For this reason the UK Registrar considers this to be 'less satisfactory'[9] than to require the data controller to provide a brief explanation of the intended uses and disclosures.

Although the first principle is applicable to data controllers there is an obligation to process the data fairly. This is because it is for the data controller to determine the contents and use to which the data is put. If the data controller decides to process data for purposes that are seen as socially harmful, insensitive or offensive, there may unfair processing. The compilation of a database of persons listed in *Stubbs Gazette* with a view to the automatic processing of these names so as to make offers of loans, at high rates of interest, may be unfair processing. The processing of names of recently deceased persons so as to produce a list of surviving spouses, the processed data to be used to sell to surviving relatives graveyard memorials to the deceased is insensitive in the extreme and may therefore constitute unfair processing. A local authority that processes data held on local rates defaulters in order to decide whether discretionary educational grants should be paid to children of the taxpayer may also process data unfairly.[10]

The most significant feature of the first principle however relates to the failure of the draftsman to include any reference to lawfully obtaining and processing. Both the Convention and the UK Act refer to obtaining and processing 'fairly and lawfully' and it is clear that a distinction can be drawn between 'fairly' and 'lawfully'. Fairness involves an examination of moral and ethical standards and values that members of Society, as a whole, would agree upon. 'Lawful', in contrast, can refer to a value-free and completely objective issue: in obtaining or processing this data has any legal rule been infringed? Obviously a given activity may satisfy both criteria — murder or theft of documents in order to obtain data for example — but there will be many borderline situations, in a heavily regulated society such as ours, where a technical infringement of the law will occur in circumstances where no obvious moral or ethical value is at issue, and *vice versa*. The inherently subjective nature of 'fairness', even if we individually believe that reasonable fellow citizens would agree with our assessment, makes it a difficult standard to apply. In Dáil Éireann the failure of the Bill to refer to 'fairly and lawfully' produced a lively debate at Committee

Stage. An opposition amendment to include this phrase was met by the argument that the amendment was unnecessary because 'fairly' included 'lawfully'.[11] This response did not persuade the opposition, particularly when it was pointed out that section 2(1)(c)(i) refers to 'specified and lawful purposes'. Nevertheless, the Act refers simply to an obligation to obtain and process 'fairly'.[12] It must be assumed that there is no intention to derogate from the Convention and that the draftsman is correct in the view that 'fairly' will, *a fortiori*, include 'lawfully'. The case-law relating to the admissibility of unfairly and unconstitutionally obtained evidence[13] provides some guidance or whether data or information is obtained lawfully. Data or information may be obtained unlawfully in a variety of ways, e.g. by trespass, or the use of listening devices, by criminal fraud or by infringement of a citizens personal rights under the Constitution. It appears however that once data is unfairly or unlawfully used or disclosed, the citizens only recourse is for compensation under the Act. The data is not invalid for evidentiary purposes in the same way that illegally or unconstitutionally obtained evidence may be under the 'fruits' doctrine.[14]

The exclusions If information or data is kept for, or intended for, use in the following activities then the fairly obtaining and processing principle is not applicable if the activity in question would be likely to be prejudiced.[15] The listed actives are

(i) preventing, detecting or investigating offences:
(ii) apprehending or prosecuting offenders:
(iii) assessing or collecting any tax, duty or other monies owed or payable to the State, a local authority or health board.

The exclusion of the first principle is permitted by the Convention if, to use the words of the Convention, derogation is necessary in a democratic society to protect the monetary interests of the State or assist in the suppression of criminal offences.[16] This section does not exempt the activities of the Garda Síochána, law enforcement agencies such as the Office of the Director of Public Prosecutions, the Chief State Solicitor, the Revenue Commissioners, and other agencies, from this principle. Data kept for unrelated activities by these bodies — information recorded by a local authority to assist in deciding whether individuals are 'suitable' for grants for example — would still have to be obtained and processed fairly.

The statutory power to provide additional safeguards Article 6 of the Council of Europe Convention requires Parties to the Convention to provided appropriate safeguards in respect of particularly sensitive data, that is, personal data revealing racial origin, political opinions or religious or other beliefs, and personal data concerning health or sexual life as well as criminal convictions. The Convention directs that if domestic law does not provide appropriate safeguards then this data may not be processed automatically. The Data Protection Bill, 1987 was amended in the Dáil at Committee Stage to make it possible for the Minister, by statutory instrument, to amend the data protection principles so as to provide additional safeguards in respect of such sensitive personal data.[17] The Minister for Justice explained[18] that this amendment would be a prudent measure for the Oireachtas to approve for the introduction of some degree of flexibility would reduce the possibility that another Party State would prohibit the export of sensitive personal data — health data for example — on the ground that Irish domestic law did not provide specific guarantees in respect of particularly sensitive personal data.

No regulations have been laid before the Oireachtas.

THE ACCURACY PRINCIPLE

The second principle, set out in section 2(1)(b) of the Act, corresponds with the principle found in article 5.d. of the Convention. Section 2(1)(b) requires the data controller to ensure that 'the data shall be accurate and, where necessary, kept up to date'. The Act gives guidance on the meaning of accurate by providing that data will be inaccurate if 'incorrect or misleading as to any matter of fact': section 1(2). This means that if a statement found in the data is a statement of opinion there can be no challenge to this opinion on the ground that it is inaccurate once it can be shown that the opinion was held. It does not however follow that a statement of opinion cannot at the same time involve a statement of fact. It may be that there are difficulties of proof which have to be overcome but, nevertheless, it is possible to show that a given opinion was not actually held. If X gives an opinion that Z is a reliable person, or 'a most desirable tenant'[19] when other facts known to X at the time the statement was made make it clear that Z is not reliable, or a desirable tenant, as the case may be, there may still be a misrepresentation of fact. The statement may be held to contain an implied assertion that there are no facts known which would justify a contrary opinion. Similarly, if a commercial landlord represents to a prospective tenant that the property to be let to the tenant is capable of producing a stated income for the tenant, if put to a certain use, the landlord may give, as an implied statement of fact, an implied assertion that due care and diligence has been taken in estimating the productive capacity of the business activity involved.[20] Similar considerations will apply to statements which look rather like statements of intention rather than statements of fact. If collateral evidence reveals that a statement of intention was not genuinely held, i.e. the person making the statement clearly intended to do something quite different, then there will be an inaccurate statement within the Data Protection Act, 1988.[21] Thus, the form in which the promise was made will not defeat the substance of the complaint.

Statements that cannot be statements of fact include statements of opinion which are not predicated on any factual basis at all. If it is clear that the person professing to hold that opinion has no experience or expertise in the area in question, there is little prospect of a court being able to hold there is a incorrect or misleading statement as to any matter of fact. The leading case is *Bisset v Wilkinson.*[22] The vendor of land situated in New Zealand was asked about the capacity of the land to carry sheep. The vendor gave a view which fell short of the actual capacity of the land. The parties knew that the land had never been used to farm sheep and that the vendor, unlike the purchasers, had never been engaged in this business. It was held that there was not a misrepresentation of fact. There was, in the circumstances of the case, a mere statement of opinion by the vendor. If fraud is shown or if the representor, the person making the statement, fails to show that a reasonable man, with the knowledge of the representor, could have come to this conclusion, the fact that the statement is described as an opinion does not necessarily protect him.[23] A statement about the intention or opinion held by a third party may be a misrepresentation if, as matter of fact, that intention or opinion was not held. In *Smelter Corporation of Ireland v O'Driscoll*[24] the defendant agreed to sell land to the plaintiff after being told by the plaintiff that if the sale were not voluntarily negotiated, then the local authority would compulsorily acquire the land from her. This statement, although it was believed by the person making it, had no foundation in fact. The sale was held not to be specifically enforceable because the statements made produced a fundamental unfairness in the transaction.

If the statement is a laudatory statement that occurs in advertisements or in publicity material — 'Zipo washes whiter' — the courts are sometimes prepared to hold the statement to be a 'mere puff'. The extravagance or imprecise nature of the statement may indicate that no reasonable person would rely on this statement.[25] Although consumer protection legislation had provided greater protection against these statements it is still possible that this concept will inhibit a court in holding a statement to be a misleading statement of fact.

Back-up data   The obligation to keep all personal data capable of undergoing automatic processing accurate is not absolute. The obligation only applies 'where necessary'. Back-up data,[26] that is, data stored to provide material which can be used in the event of accidental data loss, or theft, for example, will not always be up to date or accurate. If the data is needed then the data controller will have to update or revise the data, not only because it would be necessary under the Act but because the data, if used in an unrevised form would be unreliable and likely to cause financial or commercial difficulties for the end user. However, back-up data itself is not necessarily going to be used at all in that state and it follows that it is not necessary to keep back-up data accurate until such time as it will be used. The Act makes this absolutely clear in section 2(4) by expressly providing that the accuracy principle does not apply to back up data.

Updating The accuracy principle requires the data controller to keep the personal data up-to-date. The Commissioner's *Guide to the Act* indicates that if, for example, an organisation keeps a list of undischarged bankrupts, it will be in breach of this obligation if it makes no effort to keep itself informed of persons whose bankruptcy have been annulled or discharged.

THE PURPOSE PRINCIPLE

Section 2(1)(c)(i) provides that the data 'shall be kept only for one or more specified and lawful purposes'. Given that 'specified' is not defined in the Act it is at first sight difficult to determine what this means. The Council of Europe Convention sets out a similar principle in Article 5.b.: personal data undergoing automatic processing shall be 'stored for specified and legitimate purposes and not used in a way incompatible with those purposes.' The only conceivable ways in which the purpose may be specified is if it is either specified to the source of the personal data or to some authority charged with supervision of the Act. As such, the word specified most obviously seems to mean the purpose expressly or impliedly set out in the register which the Commissioner is obliged to establish and maintain under section 16(2) of the Act. However, not every data controller is required to register and, in the case of data controllers who fall outside the categories of registrable data controllers, it is at first sight difficult to see how this principle is fully applicable and how it can be breached. If the data controller is registered then the entry on the register will be conclusive. As long as these purposes are adhered to and are adequately described in the register, the data controller will not infringe this principle. However, this point underlines just how important it is for a data controller to compile a thorough census of personal data held or controlled. There must also be a periodic review of the kind of personal data held and the use to which it is put so as to ensure that the activities of the data controller do not diverge from those originally compiled for the sake of initial registration. If new purposes arise the entry on the register can be revised. If a registered data controller knowingly keeps personal data of any description which is not on the register, or keeps or uses personal data for a purpose other than a purpose described in the register, the data controller commits an offence.[27] However, there are two incidental or fringe meanings of 'specified' that could be upheld. Firstly, by section 3 of the Act, a data subject may ask a person who is suspected of keeping personal data on an automated system the purposes for which data is kept. That person must respond by stating a description of the data kept by them and the purposes for which it is kept. Should the data be kept for other purposes not described then it is possible that the principle is breached. Secondly, the Commissioner, by section 12, is given a power to seek such information as is specified in the Commissioner's written notice, from any person as long as the information is such as is necessary or expedient for the Commissioner to have in order to perform his functions. Should the response be inaccurate it is arguable that section 2(1)(c)(i) is not complied with. There would in any event in such a case be the likelihood of a separate criminal offence having been committed under section 12(5).

The purpose must be 'lawful'. Again the Act does not define lawful. It may be that a data controller, at the time of registration, may stipulate a purpose which the Data Protection Commissioner believes to be unlawful. The Commissioner may, under section 17(2)(b), decline to accept the application for registration. This again begs the question of what is unlawful. If a criminal offence is likely to occur e.g. the personal data is to be used to make threats amounting to blackmail, then there will be no difficulty. If personal data is kept in order to write libelous articles about the data subject or to intimidate the data subject, or infringe constitutional rights of privacy, then the purpose is not lawful. Personal data kept in order to interfere with the business activities of another (e.g. an employee keeps commercially sensitive information on a former employer's customers) may be within this notion of unlawful purpose. However, if no statute is breached or criminal offence committed, or civil wrong is perpetrated, it is not possible to hold that an unspecified use of personal data can be affected by this part of the principle, even if the Commissioner is of the view that the information is inappropriate. Thus, trade association, trade union or employer blacklists of persons are not *ipso facto* covered by this principle unless some unlawful activity is envisaged:[28] the list itself may not be unlawful even as an actionable civil conspiracy.[29]

In practical terms this principle may be difficult to monitor. The registration process is intended to be as straightforward and as easy as it can be made to be. The purposes for which data is kept will be described in fairly bland terms. Data held by a data controller in circumstances where the Commissioner may fear or apprehend unlawful use of data can be investigated by the Commissioner via enforcement notices and information notices, as well as by the Commissioner responding to registration applications by holding that the applicant has not provided sufficient information to allow registration to take place.[30]

THE USE AND DISCLOSURE PRINCIPLE

Section 2(1)(c)(ii) provides that the data 'shall not be used or disclosed in any manner incompatible with that purpose or those purposes'. This principle is based on the latter part of Article 5.b. of the Convention which directs that personal data undergoing automatic processing is not to be used in a way which is incompatible with the specified and legitimate purposes for which the data is stored. So, in order to determine whether the principle has been breached it is necessary to look to the entry on the register to discover what specified and lawful purposes are recorded in respect of the data controller. It should be noted that section 2(1)(c)(ii) refers to use and disclosure while the Convention talks, more imprecisely, about use in a way which is incompatible with those purposes, and, as such, the Act clearly stresses that disclosure to third parties, whether accidental or not, will breach the data protection principles if the register does not record that use or disclosure. It is essential to note that the use and disclosure principle is directed at providing protection against an invasion of privacy but it does not do this by conferring upon the data subject a right to veto or prevent any further use or disclosure of the data. The entry on the register rather than the wishes of the data subject determine how use and disclosure is to be policed by the Commissioner. If, for example, the data subject is mislead by the data compiler (e.g. by a false or misleading account of how the data will be used) then there may be a breach of the fairly obtaining principle in section 2(1)(a) but not the section 2(1)(c)(ii) principle.

If the data subject discovers and objects to use and disclosure in a particular way the most important step to be taken is to find out if the use or disclosure is included in the entry on the register made by the data controller. The keeping or use of personal data for a purpose not mentioned on the register,[31] or the disclosure of personal data to a person not described in the entry, other than a section 8 disclosure,[32] are criminal offences if committed knowingly.[33]

Section 21(1) of the Act provides further protection for the data subject by providing that a data processor, his employees and agents, shall not disclose personal data unless so authorised by the data controller. To do so knowingly constitutes an offence under section 21(2). The Commissioner does not have jurisdiction to control such breaches of the Act by way of the enforcement notice procedure because data processors are not bound to observe all the data protection principles and, because section 21 creates a criminal offence, section 10(2) excludes the enforcement notice procedure in such cases.

THE SUFFICIENCY PRINCIPLE

In the Council of Europe Convention, Article 5.c. attempts to prevent personal data from being stockpiled when there is no obvious or immediate need for the data at that time. Accordingly, section 2(1)(c)(iii) requires the data controller to ensure that personal data 'shall be adequate, relevant and not excessive in relation to that purpose or those purposes', i.e. the specified and lawful purposes for which data is kept. This requirement embraces a variety of issues. Firstly, the data must be adequate. This seems to impose an obligation to gather sufficent information in such a way as to provide a satisfactory basis upon which to make decisions which will touch and concern the data subject. As such, this seems to overlap with the accuracy principle. However, it is arguable that if data held is accurate but incomplete, the accuracy principle may not be breached but the adequacy requirement may be. Suppose data records that a judgment has been given against a data subject in respect of a debt but it fails to record that immediately afterwards the data subject settled the debt by a cash payment, the data subject being unaware, through no fault of his own, that court proceedings were pending. In a marginal case of this kind the adequacy requirement may be called into operation by the Commissioner. The requirement that the data be relevant is a little more difficult to analyse. If data held by a data controller is in no way material then the principle is breached but whether data is relevant will require some difficult decisions to be made. We may take as an analogy the law relating to pre-contractual disclosure of information to an insurance company by a person seeking some kind of insurance. Is it relevant to a motor insurance policy that the applicant has previously been turned down for fire insurance?[34] Is it relevant to an application for a policy protecting against loss of property by theft that the applicant was born in Rumania[35] or that the applicant has many years before been convicted of certain criminal offences[36] or that a close relative[37] has been convicted of (or even accused of committing)[38] criminal offences. These illustrations point up the fact that many personal details may be legitimately held by a data controller even though a reasonable lay person would not consider these matters to be material or relevant. In disputed cases it will be for the Commissioner to decide whether data held is relevant or otherwise. Issues of this kind illustrate the importance of codes of practice and specialist industries and organisations should avail of the opportunity to release authorised codes of practice under section 13, thereby ensuring some degree of self-regulation, and perhaps uniformity of approach, throughout a given sphere of activity. The value of such self-regulatory practices has been recently demonstrated in the United Kingdom. Many local authorities have been found to be acting contrary to the Data Protection Principles *vis-à-vis* the questions asked in relation to the Poll-Tax. The lack of any uniformity of approach is perhaps an unfortunate side-effect of the much more centralised nature of the UK Act.

The requirement that data kept must not be excessive is designed to inhibit data controllers who load personal data that is in no way material to the specified or lawful purpose for which the data may be kept. The loading of personal data because there is a slight chance that the data may be useful at some time in the future infringes this aspect of the principle. There are obvious overlaps with the accuracy principle as well as the time principle, discussed below.

THE TIME PRINCIPLE

The sufficiency principle is designed to prevent the initial compilation of personal data on an automated system because it is not relevant *at that time* to the activities of the data controller. The time principle is directed at a different problem. Personal data may, at the time of processing, have been relevant but it may at some time in the future have outlived its usefulness *vis-à-vis* the activity for which the personal data was initially required. Section 2(1)(c)(iv) provides that personal data 'shall not be kept for longer than is necessary for that purpose or those purposes'. It is obvious that the principle is directed towards preventing the accidental or unauthorised disclosure of personal data, or the unauthorised acquisition of personal data — by hackers, for example — by requiring the deletion of personal data which is, strictly speaking, not required any longer. Data controllers must therefore operate an effective system for reviewing personal data held and, whenever possible, delete personal data which is no longer required. The principle cannot be evaded by arguing that the data is needed for historical, statistical or research purposes for it is within the remit of the Commissioner to examine the circumstances and hold that the exception given by section 2(5)(a) is not applicable in a given case: a mere assertion that the data is required for any of these three purposes will not suffice. In some respects this principle is of greater practical importance than the other data protection principles because the indiscriminate retention of personal data on a system is likely to lead to the data controller being found to be negligent and therefore liable to a data subject under section 7, assuming of course that the word 'collection' in section 7 extends to retention of data.

It is however not safe to operate on the basis that personal data must be deleted if the relationship which necessitated the initial compilation of the data is at an end. It would not be wise to delete an employee's personal file once the employment is terminated without reviewing all the circumstances. If, for example, an employee is dismissed for poor timekeeping or absenteeism it would be acceptable to retain the relevant details, if recorded on an automated system, until such time as it becomes clear that the employee is not going to bring a complaint about alleged unfair or wrongful dismissal.

The exemption given in section 2(5) in respect of personal data kept for historical, statistical or research purposes is not as broad as may first appear. Clearly the Commissioner has the jurisdiction to rule on whether the exemption is applicable in a given situation. Further, the exemption is not applicable if the data is used in a way in which damage or distress will or is likely to be caused, to any data subject. It is not clear whether the personal data held indefinitely must relate to the data subject who suffers, or is likely to suffer, damage or distress. Personal data held indefinitely about X could be kept on an automated system even after X's death. Could Y, a relative of X, complain that the data should be deleted, even though necessary for statistical reasons, on the ground that, if disclosed, it is likely to cause damage or distress to other members of the family of X and Y?

Presumably this principle can be sidestepped by keeping hard copy of the personal data, while deleting the data from the automatic system.

THE SECURITY PRINCIPLE

This principle differs somewhat from the data protection principles considered above because it applies to both data controllers and data processors: section 2(2). In the Council of Europe Convention Article 7 requires appropriate data security measures to be taken and, to this end, section 2(1)(d) directs that 'appropriate security measures shall be taken against unauthorised access to, or alteration, disclosure or destruction of, the data and against their accidental loss or destruction'.

This requirement cannot be examined in insolation from the nature of the material controlled, or processed, as the case may be. If the data material is material that is generally available to the public — matters recorded on the electoral register or marriage records held by local authorities and available for inspection for example — then it hardly seems to be worthwhile to expect security measures of any real substance to be imposed at all. On the other hand, data of an extremely sensitive kind, such as health records and sexual history of a data subject, will require substantial security measures to be in place. It will also be necessary to consider whether the data in question is data which, if it is accessed by unauthorised persons, is likely to result in financial loss, personal distress and embarrassment, and cause a considerable loss of self-esteem to the data subject. Accordingly, there will be a direct correlation between the nature of the material and the security measures to be adopted. The more sensitive the material, the greater the onus will be to adopt rigorous security measures, hence the use of the word 'appropriate' in section 2(2). The security measures that are to be adopted are directed at unauthorised access, alteration or disclosure. This may of course occur in relation to intruders who seek to obtain data, e.g. by hacking or theft, but is may just as easily apply to unauthorised access or use of data within an organisation. If it is common practice for passwords to be divulged to persons who are not, strictly speaking, authorised to use that or any password, there will be unauthorised access[39] even if the individual gaining access is an employee of the data controller. The security principle is intended to discourage improper practices for, where security and accountability within an organisation is not adequate, the possibility of a data subject being compromised will be so much greater. It should be remembered that the definition of disclosure is extremely wide. If a data file can be accessed or displayed in a part of the office where all employees (and indeed the public generally) may habitually be, then security measures will have to be reviewed. Security measures against criminal acts — by burglary or arson for example — may also be required. Because the security principle also extends to guarding against accidental[40] loss or destruction it will be appropriate to consider if after office hours security — are cabinets and rooms locked — and precautions against fire or flood and the like are adequate. Staff recruitment and training should also be directed at ensuring that the employees discharge their responsibilities in a satisfactory manner.

Back up copies of material should be made but of course security measures will be needed in relation to back up data also! The exemption in section 2(4) *vis-à-vis* back up data is only an exemption for the purpose of the accuracy principle.

5

Subject access rights

INTRODUCTION

The subject access provisions are probably the most publicised aspect of data protection legislation but this in turn leads to a fundamental misunderstanding of the whole thrust of data protection law. The data subject may have a statutory right to establish what personal data relating to himself/herself is held on an automated system, but data protection legislation does not represent a substantial movement towards freedom of information when the subject of the inquiry is not the individual making the request. Indeed, there are statutory restrictions which permit the data controller or processor to refuse to disclose personal data about other persons when a subject access request has been made. Freedom of Information legislation is often directed at opening up the Public Sector to make it responsive to inquiries about matters of government policy, public administration and maladministration but, it is arguable, data protection legislation cannot do this very effectively because of the very sweeping exemptions that are recognised by the Council of Europe Convention. The subject access rights provide a useful and somewhat straightforward method of amending errors on an automated file, once the file is located, but, as we shall see, the Irish Act is seriously defective insofar as the Commissioner has no power to award, or even recommend the award of, compensation to data subjects who have suffered loss, following from the contravention of the data protection principles set out in section 2(1) of the Act.

THE RIGHT TO ESTABLISH THE EXISTENCE OF PERSONAL DATA

Section 3(1) provides that an individual who believes that a person keeps personal data may request that person, in writing, to

>(a) inform the individual whether that person keeps personal data, and
>(b) if this be the case, to give a description of the data and the purposes for which the data is kept.

This general right is exercisable regardless of whether registration takes place or not. Of course, if a person keeping the data is registered but responds to a section 3 request by stating that data is kept for purposes which are not set out on the entry in the register, an offence may be committed under section 19(2)(b) so it will be necessary to correlate section 3 responses and the entry on the register, if any. Despite the opening words of section 3, it is not necessary for the individual making the request to 'believe' that personal data is kept. A request based on mere suspicion or even a speculative request could not be rebuffed by stating that there is no basis for the individual's belief that personal data is kept. Note also that the request under section 3 can be made, even if personal data is not kept relating to the individual making the request.

Section 3 was strengthened by a Government amendment which was moved at Committee Stage in Dáil Éireann. As initially introduced, section 3(1)(b) only required the keeper of the data to disclose the existence and purpose for which data is kept. The amendment moved also requires that there be supplied to the inquirer a description of the data. The Minister for Justice opined that this will not be a burden on data controllers but it will be of considerable help to individuals who use section 3 as a preliminary step in exercising subject access rights.[1] Given that not all data controllers are required to register under the Irish Act this section 3 request — for which no fee may be charged — will prove an important method of establishing whether personal data is held but, of course, the request under section 3 cannot legitimately include a request to know if personal data is held about a named individual.

THE RIGHT OF ACCESS TO PERSONAL DATA

The right of access stipulated in Article 8 of the Council of Europe Convention finds expression in section 4 of the Act. Subject to some quite substantial limitations set out in the Act, an individual who so requests a data controller, in writing, shall be informed whether the data kept by the data controller includes personal data relating to that individual and, further, the applicant shall be supplied with a copy of the information constituting the data: section 4(1)(a). The subsection goes on to stipulate that the request must be complied with, as soon as may be, but not later than 40 days after the applicant has satisfied the procedural requirements laid down in section 4. Although section 4 is said by the explanatory memorandum accompanying the Act to be complimentary to section 3, it is not a condition precedent to an application under section 4 to show a section 3 application has been made: the register will of course indicate whether personal data is kept by a registered data controller and in such a case a section 3 request would seem to be wasteful. Simply by consulting the register an individual can see whether a data controller is registered, thereby avoiding a possible delay of 40 days before a section 3 request is answered. When the information is provided following a right of access request the Act requires that, if the information is provided in a form which is not intelligible to the average person, without explanation, the information should be accompanied by an explanation of those terms. This would be extremely useful to data subjects who access technical or medical records, for example. Although section 4(1)(a) distinguishes between a request to know if personal data is held on the applicant and a request for information constituting the data, section 4(1)(b) stipulates that unless the application states otherwise, a request for information on whether personal data is held on the applicant is to be regarded also as a request for a copy of the information also. Despite the language used in the section, a 'request' does not really take place for the data controller 'shall' provide the information sought. If the data controller fails to comply with a subject access request no criminal offence or civil wrong is committed. The enforcement notice procedure found in section 10(2) is applicable and a subsequent failure to comply with an enforcement notice will possibly result in prosecution and conviction. However, the absence of any general statutory right to compensation for data subjects and the failure of the section 7 duty of care to address section 4 at all — the section 7 duty of care only applies to a refusal to comply with the data protection principles set out in section 2(1) — means that there is no independent course of action open to a data subject who finds that a data controller refuses to comply with a subject access request. This reflects the view that emotional distress or tangible economic loss is not likely to occur simply because a data controller declines to comply with a subject access request when compared, for example, with the very real prospect of such harm being a direct result of inaccurate data being kept or the security principle being breached. There remains the possibility that a refusal to comply with a subject access request may significantly impede or delay the process by which the data subject can verify that the other data protection principles are being observed, or breached, as the case may be.

Procedural reasons to justify non-compliance with the request

Non-payment of the fee   The Act provides in section 4(1)(c)(i) that a fee may[2] be payable to the data controller when a subject access request is made. The fee is not to exceed either the amount prescribed by regulation — a figure of £5 is set by the Regulations[3] — or an amount regarded by the Commissioner as reasonable, having regard to the estimated cost of compilation. It is possible that individual data controllers may attempt to regulate the volume and timing of subject access requests by providing that if subject access requests are made in a particular week or in a particular month, no fee, or a much reduced fee, will be charged for requests made at that time. This will allow a data controller to organise work activities in such a way as to minimise any disruption that can result from responding to subject access requests. Although the Act is silent on this point, if the fee chargeable is not paid then the data controller would presumably be entitled to refuse to respond to a subject access request until such time as the fee is paid. It is clear that only on compliance with the requirements of section 4 does the 40 day period begin to run: see section 4(1).

Where separate entries are lodged in the register in respect of data kept for separate purposes, section 4(2) provides that a separate request must be made by the data subject and a separate fee may be payable for each entry.

Inadequate information supplied by data subject Section 4(3) obliges the data subject to provide the data controller with such information as the data controller may reasonably require so as to satisfy the data controller on the identity of the individual, and assist the data controller in locating any relevant personal data or information. What is a reasonable requirement will be a question of fact and should the data controller impose requirements the applicant feels to be unreasonable, a complaint to the Commissioner would be possible. It should be remembered that if the data controller responds to a subject access request by providing personal data which relates to a person other than the applicant, e.g. a relative residing at the same address, because inadequate information was provided, this may itself be a breach of the disclosure principle in section 2(1)(c)(ii) of the Act. The reasonableness requirement may fluctuate by reference to the material kept by the data controller. Data that is not particularly sensitive could be released when the applicant provides a relatively modest amount of identification such as a signature or home telephone number. Where the data is particularly sensitive — on racial origin, religious or other beliefs, health and sexual history for example — the data controller would be justified in seeking more substantial proof of identity such as a passport, PRSI number, even a letter from a person of standing such as an employer, TD, or parish priest. The Commissioner has expressed concern about organisations that give out personal information held on computer in response to telephone requests. Because of the difficulties of establishing the identity of the caller in such a case it would be prudent for such organisations — local authorities, public utilities and the like — to decline to give information over the phone (e.g. data on the state of an account) but instead send hard copy to the address on the file.

The identification requirement is included in the Act not simply to provide a safeguard against personation or information being improperly disclosed. There is also some concern to keep the cost of satisfying subject access requests down to an acceptable level. The fee chargeable may not provide adequate compensation to the data controller if a particular search is going to take some time to complete. In such a case it may be reasonable for the data controller to request further information: the data controller could, if it will reduce the time and cost of compliance significantly, seek information on the names of persons with whom the data subject has been in contact or the location of the branch office where the data subject has had previous dealings.

The personal data relates to another individual   The general duty to disclose personal data relating to a data subject following an access request is constrained by section 4(4) which states that a data controller is not obliged to disclose personal data if it relates to another individual, unless that other individual has consented to the disclosure. This provision therefore provides the data controller with a power to refuse to give out personal data relating to a third party but it does not prevent the data controller from releasing personal data about a third party if the data controller wishes to do so. Only if the personal data is used or disclosed for a purpose not mentioned on the register, can a data subject make a valid objection, and this is the result of a contravention of section 2(1)(c) rather than section 4(4).

The data controller's privilege to withhold data relating to an individual other than the applicant is limited by the proviso to section 4(4) which requires the data controller to make the disclosure, if it is reasonable in all the circumstances to delete references to the identity of the third party so as to prevent that person's identity from becoming known. The data controller, when responding to a subject access request, is not entitled to refuse to respond on the ground that dislosure is likely to lead to data relating to a colleague, relative or associate of the data subject, being disclosed. The data controller must edit the data, whenever it is reasonable to do so, so as to conceal the identity of the third party but the data controller should not edit out all references to the third party. It is not clear in such a case whether the data controller is obliged to approach the third party in order to secure consent to a disclosure request: in the opinion of the UK Registrar there is no obligation on the data controller (data user in the UK) to take active steps to secure the third parties consent to disclosure.

Particular difficulties are going to arise where the subject access request will relate to an assessment or evaluation of the data subject. Because the Act does not exclude statements of opinion from the remit of the subject access provision, delicate situations are likely to arise when a data subject may come into possession of an assessment of his or her abilities and performance (e.g. at or in the workplace) which is not particularly favourable. Even if the assessment is unsigned or the name of the author or assessor is not disclosed, it will be obvious to the data subject who the author or assessor is (e.g. the personnel manager or a college professor). In order to ensure that such assessments can be made with candour the Act envisages that the assessment in such a case would be withheld under section 4(4).

The time factor   When a subject access request is made in a manner which satisfies the procedural requirements laid down in section 4, the 40-day time period begins to run from the date of application. However, the question that arises for the data controller is whether the data controller is to release the data in the state in which it existed at the date of receipt of the subject access request or whether the data controller can give access to personal data which has been revised or amended subsequent to the subject access request being received. Personal data may be amended or updated or added to at any time of course, but if the data controller was able to amend the data as a result of an subject access request being made, this could lead to wholesale evasion of the subject access principle. The Act provides that the data controller may release personal data about a data subject so as to take account of any amendment made to that personal data, as long as the amendment would have been made irrespective of the fact that a subject access request has been made. No other amendment is possible, a provision which is designed to prevent the editing or deletion of personal data. Failure to observe the provisions of section 4(5), i.e. the release of personal data in an edited or amended form, is not specifically a criminal offence but the provisions of section 4(5) are subject to the Commissioner's power to issue an enforcement notice under section 10.

Examination results The Irish Act follows the UK legislation in making specific provisions in respect of examination results but there are some problems and difficulties following on from the way in which the Irish Act is drafted. First of all, the Irish Act refers specifically to 'the results of an examination'. Section 35 of the UK Act employs the much broader phrase 'personal data consisting of marks or other information' to be used in determining the results of an examination. The UK legislation would therefore include continuous assessment notations, personal data such as medical history, and other personal details that may conceivably be used by a board of examiners in deciding whether a student should be awarded a particular mark or a particular degree or diploma. The Irish phrase seems directed exclusively at examination performance.

Section 4(1) allows a data subject to make an application to a university, college or other educational establishment to obtain all personal data kept in relation to that individual. Obviously the section 4(1) procedure would allow a student to obtain all personal data processed automatically, including examination marks, as long as the data is processed automatically. The 40-day limit may prove very uncomfortable for some institutions and examining bodies that take some months to complete the process of examining and the final assessment of candidates, so section 4(6)(a) gives an extension of time in respect of access requests made by examination candidates: a request in relation to the results of an examination is deemed to have been made on the date the examination results are first published or the date the request is made, whichever is the later date. Once the date of the application is fixed the data controller has 60 days in which to respond to the request for examination results. Section 4(6)(b) defines examination as 'any process for determining the knowledge, intelligence, skill or ability of a person by reference to his performance in any test, work or other activity.' This definition seems to exclude the possibility that material other than that used to test the student must necessarily be disclosed to the candidate as part of the 'results of an examination.' If a student is awarded a low mark because an examiner is of the view that the paper or essay has been plagiarized, or the student has been found guilty of cheating, any examiners report would not necessarily be disclosable as part of the results of the examination. The student would nevertheless seem to be entitled to obtain all automated personal data held by the institution under the provisions of section 4(1), within the 40-day period, so the narrowness of section 4(6) will allow students to obtain some personal data held on an automated system within the 40-day period set by section 4(1). If that personal data is used to determine the level of degree or diploma awarded but it is not, strictly speaking, evaluative, e.g. notes on medical or family problems, attendance records and the like, a subject access request to that information will be governed by section 4(1), not section 4(6).

The Irish Act differs significantly from the UK Act in another respect. There seems to be no obligation under the Irish Act to release all the changes and alterations made to the marks, e.g. by internal and external examiners when reviewing the mark originally awarded, for these changes, when made, irrespective of the receipt of the request, are governed by section 4(5). If the mark which has been ultimately awarded is released, this will satisfy the requirements imposed under Irish law.

Apart from the question of obtaining examination marks which are the result of an educational course or programme, there are other applications to which this provision can be put. All assessments made in order to assess competence or performance seem to be within the remit of section 4(6). A test prepared by or on behalf of a prospective employer or an agency in order to test the suitability of a person for employment would also be covered. An agency seeking to test the competence of a person seeking work as a freelance translator, the grades being kept on computer, would be obliged to disclose. The Commissioner's *Guide* gives another example: 'A firm holding a typing test to recruit secretaries, for example, would come under this provision'.

REFUSALS TO RELEASE PERSONAL DATA

Subject access requests which are made in accordance with these statutory requirements should be complied with although no criminal offence is committed by a data controller who declines to provide personal data. The Act obliges the data controller to provide notification of a refusal to the applicant.[4] The notice, in writing, must include a statement of the reasons why the personal data is not being made available. The statement must also indicate that the applicant may complain to the Commissioner about the refusal. If no written notice is given, or the notice is deficient, the data controller does not, it seems, commit a criminal offence but if the individual complains to the Commissioner the enforcement notice procedure under section 10 could be used to compel compliance with this obligation by the data controller.

Modification of subject access rights by the Minister The Act generally presupposes that it is in the best interests of the data subject that personal data held by others is readily available to that individual. The subject access right provided by Article 8 of the Convention is however not unqualified. The Convention itself, in Article 9, allows contracting parties (i.e. states) to restrict subject access where this is necessary to protect the data subject. In other words, the Convention recognises that, in certain circumstances, it may be as well for the data subject not to discover certain details about himself or herself. Section 4(8) permits the Minister, by regulation, to modify the subject access rights generally conferred by section 4. Section 4(8) specifies that modification may take place in respect of personal data relating to physical or mental health or personal data kept for, or obtained in the course of, or while carrying out, social work.

Physical or mental health The most obvious modification may relate to subject access requests, which, if complied with under the general subject access provisions in section 4, may be positively harmful to the individual concerned. The drafting of the Irish statutory instrument which brings about this modification was clearly influenced by the Council of Europe Recommendation on automated medical data banks.[5] The recommendation provides detailed regulations which member states are 'recommended' to adopt as a measure towards ensuring the confidentiality, security and ethical use of personal data contained in medical health records. On the sensitive question of subject access the detailed principles set out in the annex to the recommendation require measures be taken to ensure that every person is to know of the existence and content of the information held about that person in a medical data bank.[6] Access should be provided, if national law provides, via an intermediary in the shape of that person's physician. One of the exceptions that national law may provide for relates to information, the knowledge of which may cause serious harm to the data subject. The explanatory memorandum gives as an example the case of a patient who may be detrimentally affected by learning that he or she is recorded on a cancer registry. Again, some patients may conceivably be relieved to learn of the worst and it is by no means clear whether the physician of the data subject will be required to decide whether *this patient* should be given a full or an incomplete account of the physical or mental condition, and prognosis, recorded on the data bank. Speaking at Committee Stage in Dáil Éireann, the Minister for Justice Mr Collins promised that regulations would be narrowly drawn: the section did not allow for modifications in the interest of administrative convenience and a Minister who sought to make such regulations would probably find the regulations subject to judicial review. A somewhat less obvious subject access restriction, necessary in order to protect the data subject's right to privacy, is foreseeable even if the applicant seeks personal data in order to satisfy a third party about the individual's medical history. Situations could arise whereby an employer, an insurance company, a bank or other lending institution, to give just a few examples, may insist that the individual provide a summary of that person's medical history, from an automated data bank, as a precondition of getting a job, insurance cover, or a loan, as the case may be. Because section 4(8) uses the term modification rather than restriction, it would be possible for regulations to require the data subject to keep his personal details confidential and not allow third parties to acquire this information. Section 4(8), in such a hypothetical case, overlaps considerably with section 2(6) and additional safeguards under both sections could, conceivably, allow the data controller to decline to release personal data if the data controller has reasonable grounds for believing that the sensitive medical data is to be made available by the data subject, to a third party, and that such disclosure would not be in the best interests of the data subject.

Before we look at the regulations in detail, it should be recalled that a data controller who wishes to avoid the obligations imposed by the Data Protection Act, 1988 need only keep the data in question on paper file to deny a data subject any right to access the information held about the data subject. Even if the data controller keeps personal data on an automated system the data subject may be deprived of any section 4 right of access under the health exemption, as set out in section 4(8) of the Act. The provisions of section 4(8) enable the Minister for Justice, whenever he considers it desirable to do so, by regulation, to modify the application of the subject access rights in certain circumstances. Section 4(8)(a)(i) directs that the operation of the subject access rights found in section 4 can be so modified when the personal data relates to the physical or mental health of the data subject. The regulations which effect the modification, the Data Protection (Access Modification) (Health) Regulations, 1989[7] came into effect on 19 April 1989.

These regulations were made after consultation with the Minister for Health, the Minister for Finance, the Minister for Education, the Minister for Social Welfare, the Minister for Defence and the Minister for Labour. The regulations follow a basic principle found in Article 4(1) of the regulations:

Information constituting health data shall not be supplied by or on behalf of a data controller to the data subject concerned in response to a request under section 4(1)(a) of the Act if it would be likely to cause serious harm to the physical or mental health of the data subject.

'Health data' is defined as 'personal data relating to physical or mental health'. While this is clear enough, it is not however apparent that data about personal habits may have a direct effect on health, e.g. a person's consumption of tobacco, alcohol or use of other stimulants, may be health data. This kind of information is collected by insurance companies and employers for example. The problem in this context however is not a real one because the data subject is bound to know his or her personal habits. However, diagnosis on the effects of such consumption is going to be 'health data'.

The regulation draws a fundamental distinction between health data held by or on behalf of a health professional and health data held by others.

1. In the first instance a health professional is defined as

(a) a person who is a medical practitioner, dentist, optician, pharmaceutical chemist, nurse or midwife and who is registered under the enactments governing his profession, and

(b) a chiropodist, dietician, occupational therapist, orthoptist, physiotherapist, psychologist, child psychotherapist or speech therapist.

Where health data is held by or on behalf of such a data controller the data controller may made up his or her mind about whether the personal data can be released. In the usual course of things a medical practitioner who provides data about patients to a hospital authority, the data maintained on files put up on a computerised system, would not always be a data controller. If the medical practitioner is employed under a contract of service the employing authority or health board would be the data controller rather than the medical practitioner. A subject access request to the authority or health board would have to be made. Conversely, if the health practitioner is self-employed — a consultant who has a private practice, for example — data about patients which is put up on an automated system in such circumstances, at the direction of that health practitioner, would make that health professional the data controller. Even if the information is put up on a system owned by a health board the issue of control would be crucial: in such a case the health board would be a data processor acting at the direction of the health practitioner who would in all likelihood be the data controller. Where it is resolved that the health professional is the data controller the health data can be provided to the data subject without reference to another health professional, as long as the general principle is observed, that is, the data is not likely to cause serious harm to the physical or mental health of the data subject. The fact that the Statute authorises disclosure in these circumstances is not however the end of the matter. If the health professional has not been intimately or recently involved with the data subject it is submitted that the provision of health data without taking steps to either verify the accuracy of the data, or seeking information from others who have been recently or intimately involved in providing care to the data subject, would be foolhardy. The health professional would expose himself or herself to a claim in negligence if health data were released, the disclosure causing harm to the data subject, in circumstances where a reasonable and prudent practitioner would have, for example, sought information from other practitioners. A dietician or speech therapist may, for example, be given sensitive personal data about a person in clinically acceptable conditions, and, while the Act authorises disclosure, it would be prudent to discuss this data with, for example, the information source before making disclosure.

2. Where the data controller is not a health professional then the disclosure of health data to the data subject, or a decision to withhold health data, cannot be taken without reference to 'the appropriate health professional'. The regulation states that the 'appropriate health professional' means either

(a) the registered medical practitioner, or registered dentist, currently or most recently responsible for the clinical care of the data subject in connection with the matters to which the information, the subject of the request, relates,

(b) where more than one such person, the person most suitable to advise on those matters,

(c) where no one in (a) or (b) is available, a health professional who has the necessary experience and qualifications to advise on those matters.

In this second situation, the data controller will be an insurance company, a solicitor, a State body such as the Department of Justice or the Department of Social Welfare. Before the health data can be disclosed consultation must take place. However, the fact that an assessment has been made by a health professional does not mean that the data controller can immediately release that data to the data subject: suppose, for instance, an insurance company sends a potential insured for a medical examination to a doctor employed by the insurance company. If a report is sent to the insurance company, the company, as data controller, must not immediately disclose the report even though the report is the result of a medical practitioner's assessment. Consultation with the appropriate health professional must take place. It could be that the doctor examining the data subject is not 'the appropriate health professional.' If the data subject's own GP, for example, has recently treated and examined the data subject, the issue may be tested in such a way as to lead to the conclusion that the GP is either the most recent health practitioner to provide care for the data subject or, alternatively, that, while both are currently and recently responsible, the GP is the person most suitable to advise. Note that 'care' is defined so as to include investigation and examination.

Even if the data controller forms the view that the release of personal data would be likely to cause serious harm to the physical or mental health of the data subject, the data controller is obliged to edit the data in such a way as to release that part of the data that would not cause harm. On the question of editing and in particular section 4(4), the regulation provides that the exemption in section 4(4), which generally allows the data controller to withhold personal data because it contains personal data about someone else (e.g. an assessment of the data subject by a third party) is not to apply where the third party is a health professional who has been involved in the care of the data subject and the data relates to him in his capacity as such. For example if the data controller is a health board it cannot refuse to provide personal data on the ground that to do so would reveal a nurse's, or a doctor's, assessment of, or opinion about, the data subject.

The social work exemption The relevant regulations,[8] also made under section 4(8), came into force on 19 April 1989 and were made after consultation with the Minister for Health, the Minister for Social Welfare, the Minister for Education, the Minister for the Environment and the Minister for Labour. The basic principle set out in the regulation is that social work data is not to be supplied to a data subject if it would be likely to cause serious harm to the physical or mental health of the data subject or the emotional condition of the data subject. The regulations only apply to social work data, as defined in the Act. The legislation reflects a preoccupation with social work data held by a public or a publicly funded social work organisation and this, it is submitted, is a very serious shortcoming. Wholly private or entirely voluntary organisations are outside the regulation.[9] 'Social work data' is defined as

> personal data kept for, or obtained in the course of, carrying out social work by a Minister of the Government, a local authority, a health board, or a voluntary organisation or other body which carries out social work and is in receipt of moneys provided by such a Minister, authority or board, but excludes any health data within the meaning of the Data Protection (Access Modification)(Health) Regulations, 1989 (SI No. 82 of 1989), and 'social work' shall be construed accordingly.

A distinction must be drawn between social work data which is provided to the data controller by persons who are not employees or agents of the data controller and those who are. In the first instance one can think of instances

Data protection law

where a health board would come across personal data about a person, the information being supplied by a member of that person's family, the gardai, or an employer. Before that personal data can be passed onto the data subject the regulations require consultation with the data source but, it seems, consultation in good faith will suffice. The data source does not have to give permission before disclosure is made. This could be problematical when, for example, the data is such that the data subject will be able to glean from the data itself that it could only have been provided by one other person, as for example occurred on the facts of *Stephens v Avery* (see Chapter 1). Where however the source of the data is an employee or agent of the data controller, no process of consultation is necessary.

The regulations require that even where the data is likely to cause any of the three harmful consequences stated — physical harm, mental harm, emotional distress — it must be released in edited form if in edited form the harmful consequences can be avoided. The editing of data by reference to section 4(4) is not permitted if the person identified is an individual engaged in carrying out social work and the data relate to him in that capacity. The regulations are also stated to be without prejudice to the power of a court to withhold from a data subject social work data kept by it and constituting information provided in a report supplied to it in any proceedings.

RESTRICTION OF SUBJECT ACCESS RIGHTS: SECTION 5(1)

The subject access provisions contained in section 4, which have been discussed above, do not apply to certain categories of personal data. The Act does not exclude the holders of the data in question from the registration requirements, when applicable, but, rather, the provisions of section 5 enable a data controller to respond to a subject access request by writing that the data controller does not keep personal data which the law requires be revealed to the applicant. The Act includes in section 5 a list of circumstances in which a subject access request may be so declined. As we shall see, some of these do not confer a blanket power to turn down a subject access request: the data controller can be required to explain to the Commissioner why, in the particular circumstances of a given case, it was necessary to rely on the exemption in question. For this reason each individual subject access request should be examined and processed on its own merits by a senior member of the data controller's staff: if the applicant feels that the request made should have been complied with a complaint to the Commissioner may follow.

(a) **The crime and revenue exemption** The Act, in section 5(1)(a), follows the Convention by stipulating that, where personal data is kept for any of the following purposes, the subject access provisions are inapplicable where their application would be likely to be prejudicial. These purposes are

    (i) preventing, detecting or investigating offences,
    (ii) apprehending or prosecuting offenders,
    (iii) assessing or collecting any tax, duty or other moneys owed or payable to the State, a local authority or health board.

This exemption does not operate in a blanket manner. The data controller can withhold personal data only in a case where the application of subject access rights would be prejudicial to these purposes.[10]

(b) **The collateral investigation exemption** If personal data is held for any of the purposes stated in (a) above, it is foreseeable that the holder may pass this data or information on to others who may require it for some statutory purpose. The example given by the Commissioner brings this out clearly. If the gardai hold personal data for the purpose of investigating an offence alleged to have been committed, either by a gardai or another person, the Garda Complaints Board would have a legitimate right, indeed a statutory duty, to investigate a complaint relating to the alleged offence if that complaint was made within the context of the Garda Complaints Act, 1986. As such, the Board should be entitled to see relevant data to carry out the investigation. This collateral investigation, based on a statutory obligation, does not come within (a) above, but section 5(1)(b) makes specific provision for a subject access exemption.

(c) **The prisons exemption** Subject access rights cannot be exercised where it would be likely to prejudice the security of, or maintenance of good order and discipline in, specified penal institutions. These institutions are

    (i) *a prison* The word prison is not defined by the Act. However, section 3 of the Prisons Act, 1972 provides that the Minister for Justice may from time to time specify a place or places to be used as a prison. Each place so specified shall be a prison to which the Prisons Acts, 1826 to 1970 shall apply.
    (ii) *a place of detention provided under section 2 of the Prison Act, 1970* Section 2 of the 1970 Act empowers the Minister for Justice to provide places of detention which are to promote the rehabilitation of offenders who have been sentenced to penal servitude or imprisonment or detention in St Patrick's Institution.

(iii) *a military prison or detention barracks within the meaning of the Defence Act, 1954* Section 232 of the 1954 Act empowers the Minister for Defence to set aside a building or part of a building and declare it to be a military prison or defence barrack, as the case may be.

(iv) *St Patrick's Institution* This is defined by section 1 of the Criminal Justice Act, 1960 as 'the institution called and known as 'Saint Patrick's' and situate at North Circular Road, Dublin'.

(d) **The financial malpractice exemption** This exemption corresponds with that found in section 30 of the UK Act. If personal data is held by a data controller for the purpose of discharging statutory functions and the Minister for Justice specifies by regulation that those statutory functions are designed to protect the public against financial loss occasioned by

(i) dishonesty, incompetence or malpractice by banking, insurance, investment or other financial service providers, or by the management of companies or similar organisations, or

(ii) the conduct of persons who have at any time been adjudicated bankrupt,

then subject access requests cannot be exercised in respect of that personal data. The financial malpractice exemption seems directed at facilitating confidential investigations into alleged financial sector irregularities. The statutory functions discharged by the Central Bank under the Currency and Central Bank Acts, for example, allow the Central Bank to specify that information must be supplied, when requested, to the bank, by a building society, an industrial or provident society, a credit union, an investment trust company or a unit trust company: see section 18 of the Central Bank Act, 1971 as amended by section 37 of the Central Bank Act, 1989. A complete list of the exempted functions is found in the Schedule to the Data Protection Act, 1988 (section 5(1)(d)) Specification Regulations, 1989[11] which, for the sake of completeness, is set out below in its entirety:

SCHEDULE

Description of function	*Enactments by or under which function conferred*
(1)	(2)
Functions of Central Bank of Ireland	Central Bank Act, 1971 (No. 24 of 1971).

Functions of Director of Consumer Affairs and Fair Trade	Prices Acts, 1958 to 1972. Restrictive Practices Acts, 1972 and 1987. Sale of Goods and Supply of Services Act, 1980 (No. 16 of 1980). Regulations made under the European Communities Acts, 1972 to 1986.
Functions of Minister for Industry and Commerce	Companies Acts, 1963 to 1987. Insurance Act, 1989 (No. 3 of 1989).
Functions of Official Assignee in Bankruptcy	Bankruptcy Act, 1988 (No. 27 of 1988). Rules of the Superior Courts.
Functions of Registrar of Friendly Societies	Industrial and Provident Societies Acts, 1893 to 1978. Friendly Societies Acts, 1896 to 1977. Credit Union Act, 1966 (No. 19 of 1966).

(e) **The international relations exemption** If personal data should be released to a data subject and this would be contrary to the interest of protecting the international relations of the State, section 5(1)(e) permits the data controller to restrict access to that personal data. The exemption is extremely broad: the data controller need not be a government department or a semi-state body, e.g. a private company holding personal data that reveals some irregular behaviour by that company, or some other person or organisation, may conceivably plead this exemption if disclosure to the data subject would be likely to embarrass the State.

In explaining this exemption the Minister for Justice Mr Collins said that the Convention permitted exemptions in respect of 'state security' and that 'state security' was to be interpreted so as to include the protection of the international relations of the state.[12] It is nevertheless an exemption that could be used to stifle any 'freedom of information' kind of application: a data subject who seeks access to personal data in order to verify statements that are likely to appear in a book which deals with a sensitive subject such as marine pollution, acid rain or cross-border smuggling, for example, could have the application turned down under this exemption.

(f) **The insurance claim exemption**   The bill, as initially presented, did not contain this exemption. It was introduced by the Minister for Justice at Committee Stage in Dáil Éireann in a response to a submission made to the Minister by the Irish Insurance Federation. The exemption permits a data controller, who puts on file an estimate of the amount of money that may be needed to meet a claim for damages or compensation, to plead an exemption if the release of that estimate would be prejudicial. The Irish Insurance Federation represented that these 'provisional' estimates are placed on file for financial and management reasons — the company should be able to know approximately what its potential liabilities are — but that if these estimates were disclosed to a data subject it would prove prejudicial for the estimate is also used as the basis upon which a settlement of the claim is negotiated. The professional privilege exemption would not cover all of these provisional estimates because all claims are allocated a provisional estimate shortly after the claim is received and often this will take place long before the legal department is consulted. Although the present writer has dubbed this exemption the insurance claim exemption, section 5(1)(f) is drafted so as to apply also to data controllers who are not insurance companies. For example, if an employer faces a claim for a personal injury suffered by an employee at the workplace and the employer seeks information on a likely settlement figure or compensation award — from the employer's insurance company for example — the employer could refuse to release that data to the employee if it would be likely to prejudicial: the employer could not plead the exemption if the claim has been settled at the time the application is made.

(g) **Legal privilege**   If a claim to privilege in respect of personal data could be maintained in proceedings in court in relation to communications between a client and his professional legal advisers, or between those advisers, the subject access provisions in section 4 are not available in respect of that personal data. In practical terms, this exemption will be of relevance in cases where a legal adviser holds, on an automated system, personal data about a person other than the client of the legal adviser and that non client seeks to exercise subject access rights in respect of that personal data. Because of the difficulties that may arise within the context of legal professional privilege — the law is by no means easy to understand or, in practical terms, apply — it may be prudent for legal advisers to keep personal data which relates to third parties on manual files.

While it is not possible in this book to give a detailed account of the law relating to legal professional privilege it is nevertheless desirable that the central aspects of legal professional privilege be delineated. In this regard the concept of legal professional privilege must be distinguished from the duty of confidence that arises in relation to information imparted by a client to his lawyer, and the claim of privilege in respect of defamation actions.

The basis upon which a claim to legal professional privilege rests was recently discussed by the House of Lords in *Waugh v British Railways Board*.[13] In this case the plaintiff's husband was killed in an accident whilst working in the employment of the defendant. The Board, as was its usual practice, compiled a report on the accident two days after the accident occurred. The report was headed 'for the information of the Board's solicitor'. The report was prepared so as to establish the cause of the accident and facilitate improvements in work practices, and also to allow the Board's solicitor to advise on the litigation that would in all probability result. The report contained statements by witnesses on the events surrounding the accident. The plaintiff's action under the Fatal Accidents Acts required the plaintiff to establish the cause of her husbands death. She sought to obtain discovery of the report in order to assist her in preparing the case. The Board resisted the application on the ground that the report was covered by legal professional privilege. The House of Lords ordered that the report should be made available. In this case, as in many discovery applications, the Court was faced with two conflicting values. The first is the efficient administration of Justice. Because the report was virtually contemporaneous with the accident it provided the best evidence upon which the events surrounding the accident could be established and the due administration of justice is a worthy and important goal. In contrast, it can be argued that the compilation of reports for, and the correspondence between, a lawyer and client should be privileged if done in contemplation of litigation, for an important policy consideration to be advanced is candor and honesty as between these persons. In his speech Lord Wilberforce took the view that legal professional privilege is in part due to the adversarial system of litigation: within certain limits a litigant can refuse to disclose the nature of the case until the trial. The other 'must wait until the card is played and cannot try to see it in the hand.' However, the strongest argument to explain the privilege is a desire to encourage a person who knows facts to state them fully and candidly: if a client is to state the facts fully and candidly, Lord Wilberforce said, the law must allow the communication to be privileged. In the celebrated words of Sir George Jessel, the court, as a matter of policy, deems it necessary that the client should be able to make 'a clean breast of it' to the person the client consults in connection with potential litigation.[14]

However, the plea of privilege is closely scrutinised. For the sake of ease of exposition it can be said that legal professional privilege is normally asserted in two situations. Firstly, if there is a communication of information between a lawyer[15] and a client. Secondly, if there is a disclosure of information to a lawyer by third parties, typically being witnesses or experts consulted by the lawyer. The protection afforded by the Data Protection Act, 1988 does not extend to the areas of sacerdotal privilege,[16] journalistic privilege,[17] or constitutional or executive privilege.[18]

Privilege in communications between lawyer and client The lawyer must refuse to disclose communications made between the lawyer and his client for the purpose of giving and obtaining legal advice about any matter, regardless of whether litigation was contemplated at the time the advice was sought and obtained. While the law at one time seems to have required that litigation be contemplated or in train, this is no longer the case.[19] The communication must have been confidential, that is, a communication made in the course of business.[20] Even if no relationship of lawyer-client exists, the duty is imposed on the lawyer as long as some such relationship was contemplated at the time of the consultation, according to the House of Lords in *Minter v Priest*.[21] Communication between lawyers working for the same client is similarly privileged. Where one lawyer works for two or more clients in respect of the same matter and one client provides information, it is said that the lawyer has a discretion as to whether he may use that information on behalf of the other client.[22] The recent decision of the Court of Appeal in *Buttes Gas & Oil Co. v Hammer (No. 3)*[23] suggests that this remains the case but that the lawyer is duty bound not to disclose this information to third parties who are not clients in respect of that same cause. The protection given is capable of being waived by the client but not the lawyer: see below, p. 79.

Legal professional privilege between lawyer and third parties The balance between encouraging frank communication between a lawyer and his client and allowing information to be freely available within the context of litigation is a delicate one. When the privilege is asserted by a lawyer in the context of information provided by or to a third party — a witness or expert — the courts will generally favour the view that disclosure here is more desirable than is the case where the lawyer communicates with his client. In these third party situations the courts have allowed a plea of privilege only in cases where the communication satisfies the dominant purpose test. This test, articulated by Barwick CJ in *Grant v Downs*,[24] allows a report or communication to be privileged if it is brought into existence wholly or mainly for the purpose of preparing the case. This principle was adopted by the House of Lords in *Waugh v British Railways Board*.[25] The House ruled that because the report was prepared for two equally important purposes, namely, accident avoidance and contemplated litigation, the dominant purpose[26] test could not be satisfied and privilege was therefore refused. Legal professional privilege can also be asserted in respect of communications made by a third party to a lawyer, the intention being that the lawyer should transmit that information to his client. In *Re Sarah C. Getty Trust, Getty v Getty*[27] Mervyn Davies J held that there was no basis for separating a communication made in these circumstances from communications which are generally part of the process of giving and receiving advice.

The limits of legal professional privilege The plea of privilege is a narrow one.[28] Where the communication involves instructions given to the lawyer or the lawyers advice given in a professional capacity to the client, or another lawyer, a plea of privilege will operate. However, the plea of privilege does not operate so as to prevent a lawyer giving evidence or making disclosure of facts that relate to the client, or facts that do not involve the disclosure of information passing between client and lawyer, that information being necessary for the purpose of legal advice.[29] So, in the old Irish case of *Bowles v Stewart*[30] it was held that there is no breach of confidence if a solicitor is called to prove a clients handwriting: the solicitor is bound to do so if called. Similarly, it was held in *O'Gorman v McNamara*[31] that a solicitor can give evidence of having seen a document and provide information on who had the document. Where a solicitor acts in a capacity which does not involve the solicitor in obtaining or giving information or advice then a communication or document will not be privileged. So, in *Kerry County Council v Liverpool Salvage Association*[32] a claim of privilege was rejected when it was established that the documents in question were prepared within the context of a principal and agent relationship, no legal advice being contemplated at that time.

Even information about the nature of the relationship between lawyer and client is outside the privilege in certain circumstances. If a solicitor settles a claim on behalf of a client it should be possible to prove the solicitor's authority to do so on behalf of the client.[33] Instructions given by a client to a solicitor requiring him to collect rents on behalf of the client would be disclosable.[34]

In one recent English case,[35] it was decided that a copy document which comes into existence in order to obtain legal advice on its significance is privileged, even though the original document itself is not within the privilege. However, in *Tromso Sparebank v Beirne, Forde, Grimson and Northern Bank Ltd*[36] Costello J refused to follow the decision. Costello J held that the privilege did not apply to copy documents made for the purpose of obtaining legal advice when the originals were not themselves privileged. Costello J followed Denning MR in *Buttes Gas and Oil Co. v Hammer (No. 3)*, who had doubted that privilege could attach to copy documents of this kind. Costello J declared, after noting the conflict in the English authorities,

> The conclusion I have come to is this: I can see no reason why legal professional privilege should apply to the copy documents with which this case is concerned. Legal professional privilege primarily exists so that a

litigant can have recourse to his legal advisers in circumstances which enable him to have complete confidence that the communications made to him and from him will be kept secret. It is well established that this privilege extends to documents which come into existence after litigation is commenced, either for the purpose of obtaining or giving legal advice (see: *Anderson v Bank of British Columbia* (1876) 2 Ch. 644 at 649). But I cannot see that the protection of the interests of a litigant requires the privilege to be extended to copies of documents which came into existence prior to the contemplation of the litigation, documents which are themselves not privileged and which the other side could probably inspect as a result of a third party discovery order and which they could have produced at the trial pursuant to a subpoena duces tecum. The rules of court are designed to further the rules of justice and they should be construed by the court so that they assist the achievement of this end. If inspection of documents cannot conceivably injure the interests of one party and may well assist the other to ascertain the true facts of the case prior to trial, I do not think that the Court should put a gloss on the rules which would prevent this result and so I will order inspection of the documents.

Exceptions to legal professional privilege

Fraud   If a lawyer provides advice to a client on the best way to commit a crime, or work a fraud, that communication is not privileged: *R v Cox & Railton.*[37] The test is whether the communication can be regarded as being 'in preparation for, or in furtherance or as part of any criminal designs'[38] by the client. Fraud in this context is not limited to cases where a criminal offence or the tort of deceit is the basis of the legal proceedings in which the issue of privilege arises. All instances of fraud and dishonesty such as fraudulent breach of contract and fraudulent conspiracy are included but not the tort of inducing breach of contract. In *Francis & Francis v Special Criminal Court*[39] the House of Lords, by a majority of 3:2, ruled that conveyancing documents held by a solicitor, but which had been intended by a third party to be used in the illegal act of 'laundering' the proceeds of drug trafficking, could not be privileged even though the holder was innocent. While this case appears to turn on the interpretation of UK legislation two members of the majority held that this conclusion was representative of the common law and, as such, this case is of persuasive authority in Ireland.[40]

Evidence to prove the innocence of an accused   Where documents are in the possession or control of a solicitor which, if produced, would help to further the defence of an accused person, no legal professional privilege will attach to these documents. This principle of natural justice[41] is seen as more important than the competing policy of maintaining the confidentiality of information passing between lawyer and client.

Waiver It is difficult for a privileged communication to lose that status, at least where the client or third party retains an interest in maintaining non-disclosure.[42] A recent English case indicates that, in some circumstances the court may waive the privilege if, in a criminal trial, it can be shown that the party relying on the privilege no longer has an interest to protect and the interests of the person standing trail, on balance, outweigh those of the party pleading privilege.[43]

In other circumstances it is for the client to decide whether to waive the privilege or not. Waiver is normally achieved when he client decides to give evidence of the communication. Once this is done the client cannot reassert the privilege unless the part that the client does not tender in evidence is distinct and severable.[44] The courts have drawn a distinction between waiver in the context of general communications between solicitor and client and communications in documentary form which are prepared for the purpose of trial. Waiver is less readily imputed in the second type of situation.[45] If a document is prepared in anticipation of litigation and a copy is sent to a third party unconnected with the litigation, e.g. an MP, this does not remove the privilege.[46]

(h) **The statistics and research exemption** Where data is kept for the purpose of preparing statistics or carrying out research, a subject access exemption is available as long as the data is not used or disclosed for any other purpose and the resulting statistics or research are not made available in a way which allows the data subjects to be identifiable. Section 5(1)(h) stresses that the only disclosure possible is a disclosure made under one of the circumstances set out in section 8. This means, for example, that it is not possible to refuse to allow the data subject, or a person making the request on the data subjects behalf, or a person acting on the data subjects behalf, to have access to the data in question.[47] The exemption therefore is really only of importance in cases where the personal data contains personal data relating to persons other than the data subject (see section 4(4)): the data subject cannot use section 4(4). This permits the statistician or researcher to refuse to make the work generally available to anyone who just happens to be one of the persons included in the data constituting the research.

(i) **The back-up data exemption** Back-up data is excluded from the accuracy principle.

Restriction of subject access rights: section 5(2) and(3) Section 5(2) of the Act empowers the Minister for Justice, by regulation, to direct that specific provisions already in force, which authorise the restriction of information and the withholding of such information, shall prevail as against the subject access rights provided by section 5. By Regulation[48] the Minister has directed that the provisions of section 22(5) of the Adoption Act, 1952 (which relate to the index kept by the Registrar of Births tracing the connection between the entries in the Adopted Children Register and the Register of Births) shall prevail in the interests of the data subjects concerned and other individuals concerned. That regulation also upholds the primacy of section 9 of the Ombudsman Act, 1980 in respect of information obtained by the Ombudsman during the course of an investigation undertaken within the terms of that Act.

SUBJECT ACCESS – RIGHT OF RECTIFICATION OR ERASURE

Once the data subject has exercised subject access rights in relation to personal data held by a data controller, the data subject may establish that there has been a breach of the data protection principles. It will be relatively easy to establish certain kinds of breach: the individual may be able to show that the data is materially inaccurate or has not been kept up to date. The individual may find it relatively easy to establish that the data controller has not obtained the data fairly, e.g. data given by the individual to the data controller for a specific purpose may, in breach of an express undertaking, be used for some other purpose. Other instances of non-observance of the data protection principles may be more difficult to establish: the use and disclosure principle and the security principle for example will present problems for an individual who suspects that personal data has been obtained by a third party from a data controller. If the data controller is not required to register the individual will be unlikely to establish breach of the Act if the data controller simply decides to pass that information on to a third party. If these evidentiary obstacles can be overcome the data subject will be anxious to remedy the situation. Section 6 provides a general right to seek rectification or, in appropriate circumstances, erasure of the personal data kept by the data controller.

A central point to note about section 6 is that these 'rights' do not simply apply to cases where the personal data kept is inaccurate, that is, where the data is incorrect or misleading as to any matter of fact. The UK Act gives rectification or erasure only if the data is inaccurate. The Irish Act gives these rights whenever it is established that there has been a breach of section 2(1). So, any breach of any of the data protection principles can lead to rectification or erasure even if the data in question is accurate. Rectification or erasure is an obvious remedy in cases of inaccuracy and obsolescence, unfair obtaining and processing and where the data is no longer relevant or is no longer necessary for the data controllers legitimate commercial activities. Rectification or erasure are perhaps less obvious remedies where the personal data is accurate but is being disclosed in breach of the provisions in the Act. Nevertheless, the breadth of the rectification or erasure remedy could provide a significant incentive for a data controller to observe the provisions of section 2(1): non observance could conceivably result in loss of a file or files by erasure.

The security principle in section 2(1)(d) could present an interesting problem: suppose an individual knows that data is kept by a data controller but the individual is also aware that lax or inadequate security procedures operate within the data controller's premises. Could the individual assert that the non-observance of section 2(1)(d) by the data controller entitles the data subject to have personal data erased on the ground that the potential for harm to the data subject is such that erasure of personal data is reasonable in these circumstances? It may be that in practical terms this issue will not arise. Section 6 presupposes that it is established that there is a contravention of section 2(1). If the data controller refuses to accept that section 2(1) has not been observed then it will be for the Commissioner, under section 10, to serve an enforcement notice which may require rectification or erasure of any of the data concerned: section 10(3)(a).

However, a section 6 application for rectification or erasure, once a contravention of section 2(1) is established, must be made in writing. The data controller is required to comply with the request not more than 40 days after it has been given or sent to him. If the data is inaccurate or not kept up to date the data controller is permitted to avoid having to rectify or erase if the data controller and the data subject can agree on a statement relating to the matters referred to in the data and that agreed statement is inserted into data. Such a supplementary statement is regarded as deeming the data controller not to be in contravention of the obligations to keep data accurate and up to date.

Section 6(2) is extremely important. Once the request has been complied with, i.e. data has been rectified, erased or supplemented by an agreed statement, the data controller must, within 40 days of compliance, notify the data subject that compliance has occurred. More important still, if the data controller's compliance with the request materially modifies the data concerned, any person to whom the data was disclosed, during the period of 12 months preceding the giving or sending of the request, is also to be notified of the rectification, erasure or supplementary statement. In practical terms it is going to be extremely difficult for a data controller to monitor the disclosure of personal data, much less record the persons to whom disclosure has been made over a given period of time. The data controller is not, it seems, guilty of a criminal offence if the data controller fails, whether knowingly or otherwise, to issue the notice of rectification, erasure or compliance. If the data subject feels that section 6(2) has not been complied with, a complaint under section 10 appears to be the next course of action.

Relying on the exemptions   The distinction between refusing to respond to a subject access request and invoking one of the section 5 exemptions is of importance. When a subject access request is made and the data controller decides that it cannot be complied with because this would prejudice a criminal investigation, or state security for example, the data controller will not respond by informing the data subject that the data controller holds personal data but that it cannot be disclosed in the circumstances. Such information may itself be prejudicial to the wider public interest. In such a situation the data controller will assert that no personal data is held which he is required by law to disclose to the data subject. This opaque reply will not tip off the data subject that he or she may be under investigation.

6

Exemptions

INTRODUCTION

We have considered in the preceding Chapter the subject access exemption provided for in section 5 of the Act. In this Chapter we shall examine those parts of the Act which exclude certain categories of personal data altogether from the remit of the Act. We shall also examine the exemption given by section 8 of the Act *vis-à-vis* the disclosure of personal data, regardless of the unauthorised disclosure principle contained in the data protection principles.

PERSONAL DATA EXCLUDED FROM THE ACT: SECTION 1(4)

Section 1(4) of the Act excludes three categories of personal data from the scope of the Act. In other words, the data protection principles, the registration requirement, the subject access provisions, the duty of care, and the entire enforcement machinery, have no application to these categories of personal data. The categories are:

(a) *personal data that in the opinion of the Minister for Justice, or the Minister for Defence, are, or at any time were, kept for the purpose of safeguarding the security of the State.*

This exemption is extremely broad. Note in particular that it applies to all personal data kept, at any time, for the purpose of safeguarding the security of the State. So, if personal data is held by a Government agency and the relevant Minister makes the necessary judgment, i.e. that the data was kept for the purpose specified, subject access will be denied even if the data no longer has any security implications. Contrast the practice of releasing cabinet papers thirty years after the event: clearly personal data of a one-time sensitive nature is often released once it is clear that no security implications remain. Under this exemption the personal data at no-time becomes amenable to the Data Protection Act, 1988, once it is established to the satisfaction of the Minister that the personal data, at the time of its compilation, was kept for national security purposes. This contrasts sharply with section 27 of the UK Act which requires the personal data to be exempt 'if the exemption is required for the purpose of safeguarding national security'. This formula requires the issue to be tested by reference to the time when the question of the applicability of the Act arises. Although the Registrar's guidelines do not make it clear that the section 27 exemption in the UK can be lost through the effusion of time and the data becoming 'stale', the wording of the Act seems to so direct.

The contrast between the wording of the exemption given in respect of national security under the Irish Act and the UK Act throws up another point. Under the Irish exemption in section 1(4) a difficult problem of interpretation may arise if personal data is kept, e.g., by a private sector employer, but the release of that personal data could compromise national security. The personal data, in such a case, while not arguably 'kept' for national security purposes should in principle be included by this exemption but the wording of the section seems to stop short of achieving this result. One can think of several examples: suppose personal data is held by a company providing goods or services to the defence forces about defence forces personnel. If a breach of security occurs and there is an injury inflicted on a member of the defence forces (e.g. a subversive organisation acquires personal data on military personnel in circumstances which show the data controller has not complied with the section 7 duty of care) the question of the applicability of the Act may arise. Should personal data be 'kept' for purposes other than national security purposes, e.g. payroll, transportation of troops, provision of materials and the like, then the exemption would not appear to be applicable. Conversely, should a data subject seek access to employment records and he is suspected of leaking information contained in his employment records (on logistical or policy matters for example) to a subversive organisation with which he sympathises, it may be a nice point whether such employment records are kept for national security purposes.

The Act however envisages that these distinctions will not prove to be a fruitful area of controversy because the question of whether the national security exemption is available is to be decided by either the Minister for Justice or the Minister for Defence. The opinion of the Minister is not said to be conclusive (contrast section 27(2) of the UK Act) but the Dáil Debate at Committee Stage revealed a consensus amongst all Deputies that, as the Bill was presented, the judiciary have no power to review the decision of the relevant Minister. The Minister for Justice rejected an opposition amendment,[1] moved by Deputy Barrett, which would have permitted the Circuit Court or the Supreme Court, on appeal, to set aside the opinion of the Minister. This amendment, designed to allow a judge to act as an arbitrator in a review procedure,[2] was motivated by a fear that, in certain circumstances, access to personal data with little or no national security content could be restricted on the grounds of national security.[3] Mr Collins rejected the amendment on the ground that even if a judicial review procedure were to apply, personal data with security implications would be available to a greater number of persons and, as such, would increase the danger of information falling into the wrong hands. The balance between injustice to an individual, on the one hand, and loss of life on the other, is a very fine one but, in the Minister's view, in this particular case, the balance must be weighted in favour of protecting life.[4] The Minister repeatedly gave as an illustration the need to prevent a subversive from being able to make subject access requests in order to find out what data is kept about his or her movements and lifestyle.

It is however not clear whether the Constitution will allow the Minister's statement of opinion to be conclusive. The cases on executive privilege[5] indicate that the Irish judiciary take a robust approach to the plea of privilege, when it arises, and it is standard practice, following *Murphy v Dublin Corporation,*[6] for the courts to decide, as a matter of discretion, whether official documents should remain confidential in the public interest. This helps explain why the Irish exemption is drafted very differently to the UK exemption. Where state security is impleaded however the courts will be very slow to intervene and overturn a ministerial decision.[7]

(b) *Personal data which the person keeping the information constituting the data is required by law to make available to the public.*

If personal data has to be disclosed, by law, then there is no need for the individual's right of privacy to be supported via data protection legislation for no privacy can exist in such a context. So, if personal data is kept by a data holder who is obliged to allow the public to have access to this information, the Act is inapplicable. The question is whether the public have a right to obtain access to the information comprising the data, in a form intelligible to members of the public: the issue is not whether the public have a right of access to the data in a processable form.[8] Information that falls into the category of information to which the public has access as of right includes electoral lists and information contained in the companies register. If, however, this information is loaded onto an automatic system by someone other than the person legally charged with the task of making this information available to the public, the exemption does not apply to that person.

(c) *Personal data kept by a individual and concerned only with the management of his personal, family or household affairs or kept by an individual only for recreational purposes.*

This exemption clearly operates only in respect of individual data controllers, regardless of whether they are elected or unelected officials of a recreational or sporting club or simply keeping personal data about household or family members. There are however some important points to note about the exemption. Firstly, if the individual claims an exemption because the data relates to the maintenance of his personal, family or household affairs, the data must be concerned only with such affairs. If the personal data is kept for some ancillary purpose, e.g. writing a literary work such as an autobiography or biography, then the exemption would not apply to personal data so kept. There are no definitions of 'personal, family or household affairs' set out in the Act so it will be for the Registrar to decide whether personal data kept on an *au pair*, on a distant relative, or on persons who provide domestic services to the data controller, come within any of these exemptions. There are obviously many borderline situations: does personal data kept on a person who maintains a company car or a home computer come within the personal or household affairs exemption or does the usage of the vehicle or computer, as the case may be, take the situation into the realm of a commercial or business activity? This question would appear to be answerable in the affirmative for the exemption clearly requires the personal data to be kept exclusively for domestic purposes. If records are kept in order to provide information for an employer, business contacts or the Revenue Commissioners, for example, the exclusivity element in the exemption is not satisfied.

The exemption provided for personal data kept by an individual for recreational purposes is also extremely narrow. If data containing personal data is kept on an automated system — the details of a sporting event or the personal details (e.g. telephone number) of persons participating in a darts ladder or golfing competition — there may be little difficulty in regarding situations of this kind as falling within the Minister for Justice's description of the exemption as being applicable to activities undertaken for 'amusement purposes'.[9] However, personal data held on particular athletes could easily fall outside the exemption: if a club or a representative body keeps personal data on an athlete (using the term athlete in its widest sense) there will be many obvious instances where the exemption will not apply. Personal data on an individual's national origins may be necessary to determine if selection at representative level is possible but it would appear to be outside the exemption. The data controller in such a case would be registerable. Personal data on drug and steroid use by particular athletes would also be data which a representative body could legitimately keep but the exemption would not be applicable.

At Committee Stage[10] an amendment was moved by Deputy Colley to broaden the exemption so as to allow sporting clubs and other organisations of a 'non business' nature to claim an exemption, on the ground that the 'non business' nature of a club or organisation should attract an exemption *vis-à-vis* data held on its members. The Minister for Justice very wisely resisted this amendment. He pointed out that in regard to membership records the bulk of personal data has nothing to do with recreational matters but relate to tangible activities such as membership subscriptions, customer accounts and the like, matters which, in Mr Collins words, 'would not be very different from any other business'.[11] The amendment was withdrawn.

DATA KEPT OR PROCESSED OUTSIDE THE STATE

Data controllers   Where data is kept outside the Republic of Ireland — the Act does not apply to data kept in Northern Ireland — section 23(1) indicates that there is a general exemption from the provisions of the Act. So, generally, a data controller who is resident in the State is not subject to the Act in respect of personal data which is capable of automatic processing if that personal data is kept and controlled in another country. The crucial question then will be whether the data controller kept personal data within the State. Section 23(2)(a) directs that data is deemed to be kept by a data controller in the place where he controls their contents and use. For example, a data controller who keeps data in Belfast or Brussels but who directs the contents and use of that data from an office in Dublin would not be within the exemption: the data controller would be subject to the Act. Conversely, if the data controller stores personal data in Dublin but the contents and use of the personal data is controlled from an office in London, the Irish Act does not apply, unless it is caught by the 'processing' element in section 23.

If the data controller is not resident within the State but personal data is stored or held within the State, specific provision is made in the Act to deal with instances where control over contents and use is exercised by an agent or employee who is situated within the State. In such a case section 23(3) directs that the agent or employee is to be regarded as if he or she were acting on his own account. In other words, the provisions in the Act apply to the agent or employee and the non resident is ignored. The agent or employee then may have to register, just as if the agent or employee were in possession of personal data for his or her own purposes.

Data processing   Section 23(1) directs that, where data is processed outside the State, the Act does not generally apply. The question of where the data is processed is answered by section 23(2)(b) which directs that data is processed in the place where the relevant data equipment is located. So, personal data which is processed in Kerry for an American company, the data being used in its processed form in Detroit, will bring the data processor in Kerry into the Act. Registration will be necessary if processing is to occur lawfully in such a case. Similarly, if there is processing of data within the State for a non resident data processor, e.g. a US company that subcontracts processing work to an Irish company, the agency or employee exception discussed above in relation to data controllers also applies and the US company is not covered by the Act.

Exceptionally however, section 23(4) provides that a data processor who carries on processing wholly outside the State will not be exempt if the data is used or intended to be used within the State. It will therefore be prudent for data processors abroad to register if the data processor is aware that the data controller will use the personal data — possibly for further processing — within Ireland.

THE DUTY OF NON-DISCLOSURE: EXEMPTIONS THERETO

The disclosure principle in section 2(1)(c)(ii) inhibits the right of a data controller to make personal data available to third parties, at least where the data controller is required to register under section 16. In such a case personal data must not be used or disclosed in a manner incompatible with the purpose or purposes for which the data is kept: the entry on the register is to be conclusive on the question of why the data is kept. The use of data for a purpose other than that stated on the register is a criminal offence: section 19(2)(b). Section 19(2)(d) also makes it an offence for the data controller to disclose personal data to a person not described in the entry made in the register against that data controller. Section 19(2)(d) however cross-refers to section 8 and exempts from the offence a disclosure made to a person within the terms provided for in section 8.

(a) *The security of the State exemption* If (in the opinion of a member of the Garda Síochána not below the rank of chief superintendent, or an officer of the permanent defence force who holds an army rank not below that of colonel, and the officer is designated by the Minister for Defence) personal data is required in order to safeguard the security of the State, the data controller may make that personal data available, notwithstanding the non disclosure principle. The data controller does not, under the section, have to comply with the request. It would nevertheless be arguable that the data controller who refuses to comply with a request by the gardaí could be open to a charge of obstruction of a police officer under section 38 of the Offences Against the Person Act, 1861. If the police officer believes that the data controller is obliged to provide the information when the data controller is not, by statute, so obliged, the police officer is not acting in the course of duty by making the request.[12] However, in such a case non compliance with the request does not, it seems, constitute obstruction, despite some dicta in which obstructing has been defined as 'making it more difficult for the police to carry out their duties'.[13] Should the data controller go further and warn the data subject that the police and security forces have been enquiring about the data subject and believe[14] or suspect[15] that an offence has been committed, obstruction may take place.

The effect of section 8(a) is to provide the data controller with a defence should the data subject claim in a section 7 tort action that the data protection principles have been broken. It is envisaged that if the data controller has doubts about the legitimacy of the request, the data controller should ask for the necessary statement to be given, in writing. In cases of urgency the data controller should seek confirmation from the chief superintendent, by telephone. If this is forthcoming the data controller should be immune from liability under section 7,[16] even if the courts should subsequently determine that the chief superintendent, or defence forces officer, as the case may be, could not reasonably hold that opinion.

(b) *The offences and fiscal interests of the State exemption* If personal data is required for the purpose of preventing, detecting or investigating offences, apprehending or prosecuting offenders, or assessing or collecting any tax, duty or other moneys owed or payable to the State, a local authority or a health board, then the data controller may disclose that personal data, as long as a refusal to do so would be likely to be prejudicial to those proceedings and activities. Again, the data controller is not obliged to comply with a request to furnish personal data. It is likely that data controllers who are approached by State agencies under this provision will be mindful of the industrial relations implications of too readily disclosing personal data and, in such a case, it would be prudent for the employer to make disclosure under section 8(e), where applicable, rather than under 8(b). The following example, given by the Minister for Justice, stresses that under section 8(e) the information may be required in circumstances where no fiscal interests are concerned.

> An example would be where the Gardaí get a tip-off that a mans life has been threatened and that an attack against him is being planned. They might approach the individual's employer to ascertain his address for the purpose of alerting him. If that information is held on a computer it would be difficult to justify withholding it either because the data controller has not registered the the Gardaí's disclosures or where the employer is not required to register because such disclosure would not be compatible with the purposes for which the data is kept. Here again it is up to the data controller to disclose the information or otherwise.[17]

It is also possible to view such situations as falling within the exemption provided for in section 8(d) above.

(c) *The international relations exemption* The restrictions on disclosure of personal data are inapplicable if disclosure is in the interest of protecting the international relations of the State. This exemption is seen as a part of the State Security exemption. The derogation permitted by Article 9 of the Convention in respect of state security is regarded as having a particularly wide ambit and can embrace matters touching international relations with other states. It is therefore open to data controllers to disclose information 'to the proper authority'[18] if the disclosure of personal data would best serve this important aspect of public policy.

(d) *The injury or damage to property exemption* The restrictions on disclosure of personal data are inapplicable if disclosure is required urgently to prevent injury or other damage to the health of a person, or serious loss of, or damage to, property. For example, if personal data is needed in order to trace persons who have purchased defective products (e.g. defective motor vehicles or medicines that are potentially dangerous), the data controller could release the data without being liable for breach of the non disclosure principle. This of course raises the question of what the liability of a data controller would be if the data controller refuses to provide the data sought and the data subject suffers death or injury. The possibility of criminal or tortious liability for an act of omission, would make it prudent for the data controller to provide the personal data requested, once the data controller is reasonably satisfied that the information is 'required urgently'.

(e) *The legal compulsion rule* If the personal data is required by or under any enactment or by way of a rule of law or order of a court, the restrictions on unauthorised disclosure do not apply. An example of personal data kept which would have to be disclosed under statute is provided by the Social Welfare (Consolidation) Act, 1981. Section 114(3) of that Act gives inspectors the power to demand registers, cards, wages sheets records of wages and other documents as the inspector may reasonably require.' This section would probably apply to computer held records, and certainly in respect of hard copy. An example of personal data required by a rule of law would cover the personal data an applicant is required to disclose to an insurance company (under the utmost good faith principle of *uberrima fides*) at the time the application for insurance is made, or at the time renewal of the policy is sought. An applicant for insurance is obliged to disclose personal data that would affect a prudent insurer's decision to accept the proposal or which would affect the terms upon which acceptance is forthcoming. Medical health, criminal convictions, national origins and even family circumstances are to be disclosed under this principle. However, within the context of the 1988 Act the data controller has a discretion about whether to make the personal data available. In *Murphy v PMPA Insurance*[19] the High Court upheld the view that personal data provided to an insurance company on a proposal form may not be disclosable to the Garda Síochána, even on foot of a statutory provision, where disclosure would be contrary to natural justice. The complainant, a garda inspector, sought information from the Insurance Company about an insured, the information being sought in respect of a disciplinary hearing against the insured who was himself a member of the gardai. There was a statutory basis for this request but the insurance company declined to provide the data because, the insurer argued, it was given in the context of a duty of utmost good faith, a duty which exists on both sides.[20] The insurance company were convicted of an offence: on appeal, Doyle J quashed the conviction. In the circumstances of this case the disclosure of personal information to an employer would be potentially prejudicial and contrary to natural justice. The insurer was entitled to exercise a discretion in the matter. The exception in section 8(d) confirms that the data controller retains such a discretion under the Data Protection Act. Indeed, *Murphy* itself implies that where an utmost good faith obligation exists the data controller should exercise careful judgment before disclosing the data sought in case the duty of utmost good faith is breached by the insurer.

Personal data required to be disclosed by order of a court would include instances where such data is required under the terms of an order for discovery of documents.

(f) *The legal advice or legal proceedings exemption*   Personal data required for the purpose of obtaining legal advice, or for the purposes of, or in the course of, legal proceedings, is exempt from the non disclosure principle. The legal advice exemption is broader than the legal professional privilege exemption in section 5 because, at this preliminary stage, legal proceedings are not always contemplated and, as we have seen, the legal professional privilege generally requires the communication for which privilege is sought to be proximate to litigation. If the personal data kept is sought in respect of legal proceedings, the disclosure only comes within the exemption if the person making the disclosure is a party or a witness in regard to those proceedings.

(g) *The data subject or a person acting on his behalf exemption*   Disclosure of personal data to the data subject or someone acting on the data subject's behalf is exempt from the non disclosure provision. If the data controller is not prepared to take reasonable steps to verify that the person to who disclosure is proposed to be made is the data subject, or is acting on behalf of the data subject, the data controller will be unwise to provide the data; it would clearly leave the data controller open to a section 7 tort action if the data is disclosed to an imposter. The exemption could be used, for example, where the data controller discloses to a social worker personal details about the social worker's client when those details are at variance with the information provided by the client to the social worker. The exemption would operate and the only issue to remain would be whether the personal data kept by the data controller is accurate within section 2. This provision will obviously be used when a data controller is asked to provide personal data to another, the data relating to an employee or customer of the data controller. For example, when details of an employees salary are requested by a lending institution in connection with a loan application made by the data subject.

(h) *The data subject makes the request exemption*   If the data subject requests personal data from the data controller, the disclosure of this personal data is not a breach of the non disclosure principle. Similarly, if the request is made by a person acting for the data subject, compliance with the request does not infringe the Act. Presumably this exemption is directed at allowing professional advisers and even parents to obtain personal data about a data subject. Trade union officials could presumably use this provision in order to obtain personal data about members of the union[21] but perhaps not about members of the workforce who are not members of that trade union.[22] However, where the data is personal data relating to the physical or mental health of the data subject, or is social work data, specific provisions governing disclosure to the data subject have been provided for by statutory instrument.[23]

7

Registration requirements

INTRODUCTION

Ireland has benefited from the fact that other States have had data protection legislation in place for several years.[1] The experience of other states has been very influential in shaping the Irish Act: this is particularly evident on the question of registration. Some states such as Sweden and Norway have imposed a requirement that, before an automated data file which holds personal data can be established, it is necessary to obtain a licence from the controlling authority. The workload and bureaucracy such provisions engender were clearly unacceptable to a Government that is dedicated to reducing public expenditure and the size of the Public Service. Similar considerations made the model of universal registration of data controllers and processors unacceptable. It was decided to follow a trend established in other countries, most notably Finland, towards a less complicated method of control and supervision. So called 'second generation' data protection legislation eschews universal registration but instead imposes registration requirements on large scale controllers and on data processors and those requirements on large scale controllers and on data processors and those controllers, who, regardless of size and activity, hold or keep sensitive personal data. Indeed, in the United Kingdom, where universal registration was imposed, it has not proved successful. In his fifth Annual Report (June 1989) the UK Registrar has declared that the law should be amended so as to impose registration requirements on a limited number of data users, chiefly public sector organisations, government departments, the police, personal financial service entities, and holders of sensitive personal data. A complementary feature of the new approach favoured in Ireland is to build into the legislation much simpler and less time consuming compulsory registration procedures. The Irish Act is also intended to stimulate a high degree of self regulation amongst data controllers, particularly through the emphasis placed on section 13 on codes of practice.

WHO MUST REGISTER?

Section 16(2) of the Act imposes upon the Commissioner the statutory duty to establish and maintain a register of persons, who are obliged to be entered on the register if they are to lawfully process or keep personal data on an automated information system. The compulsory registration system is applicable to the following persons.

(a) **Data controllers, being public authorities, bodies and persons referred to in the Third Schedule**   These authorities, bodies and persons are

(1) the Government
(2) a Minister of the Government
(3) the Attorney General
(4) the Comptroller and Auditor General
(5) a local authority, health board and any other body (other then the Garda Síochána and the Defence Forces) established (i) by or under any enactment (other than the Companies Acts, 1963 to 1987), or (ii) under the Companies Acts, 1963 to 1987, in pursuance of powers conferred by or under any other enactment, and financed wholly or partly by moneys or loans made or guaranteed by a Minister or by the issue of shares held by or on behalf of a Minister, or a body subsidiary thereto
(6) a company the majority of the shares in which are held by or on behalf of a Minister
(7) a body (other than one in categories 5 and 6 above) appointed by the Government or a Minister
(8) an individual, other than one remunerated by a body mentioned in categories 5, 6 or 7, above, or in relation to whom the Government or a Minister is the appropriate authority,[2] who is appointed by the Government or a Minister of the Government to an office established by or under any enactment.
(9) Any other public authority, body or person standing prescribed for the time being and financed or remunerated wholly or partly out of moneys provided by the Oireachtas.

Essentially then, all Public Sector departments, agencies, semi-state companies and persons, appointed by the Government and financed out of public funds, must register, under section 16(1)(a) and (2), except for the Garda Síochána and the Defence Forces.

(b) **Data controllers being financial institutions, insurance companies direct marketing agencies, credit reference and debt collection businesses**

The following points should be noted about this miscellaneous category. Firstly, the Bill, as originally introduced, did not define the phrase, financial institution. As a vague and somewhat modish expression it was later seen as essential that a definition be provided, for, despite the fact that it appears in other legislation (see section 90 of the Central Bank Act, 1989 for example) it is nowhere uniformly defined in Irish law. The Bill was amended at the Committee Stage in Dáil Éireann. A financial institution, for the purpose of the Data Protection Act, 1988 is now defined in section 1(1) of the Act as

(a) a person who holds or has held a licence under section 9 of the Central Bank Act, 1971, or

(b) a person referred to in section 7(4) of that Act.

Thus, under (a) above, the Associated Banks are registrable. Under (b), the Agricultural Credit Corporation, the Industrial Credit Company, trustee savings banks certified under the Trustee Savings, Bank Acts, 1863 to 1965, a building society, an industrial and provident society, a society, a credit union, an investment trust company or the manager under a unit trust scheme, are all registrable in respect of their activities.

Secondly, the insurance company classification is quite specific and applies to persons holding authorisations under the European Communities (Non Life) Insurance Regulations 1976.[3] Any non life insurance undertaking carrying on business in Ireland, whether from a head office, branch or agency established in Ireland, must be authorised if the undertaking is to carry on business in Ireland. The Department of Industry and Commerce is the supervisory authority. The classification also extends to persons holding authorisations under the European Communities (Life Assurance) Regulations, 1984.[4] Any Life Assurance head office, branch or agency established in Ireland must be authorised if the undertaking is to carry on business in Ireland. The Department of Industry and Commerce is the supervisory authority.

Thirdly, direct marketing is defined by section 1(1) as including direct mailing.

Fourthly, the final category, that is, persons engaged wholly or mainly in collecting debts, is open-ended. While it was pointed out in the Dáil[5] that some solicitors do collect debts this would not seem to bring many solicitors within this category of registrable persons for the average practice would not involve the solicitor being engaged 'wholly or mainly' in this activity. There may be solicitors who have a specialist debt collection practice who may, on the facts, fall within this category.

(c) Other data controllers who keep personal data relating to the following:

(i) *Racial origin* While some English case law[6] provides a narrow definition of racial (the phrase racial origin would perhaps exclude groups that are ethnically distinct[7] or are nationally distinct[8]) the phrase racial origin, as interpreted by the European Court of Human Rights under the Human Rights Convention,[9] would seem to require the adoption of a broader interpretation. Whether racial origin can be used to encompass persons with distinctive cultural characteristics or life patterns is by no means clear. It would clearly be contrary to the spirit of the Data Protection Convention to allow uncontrolled processing or keeping of data in Ireland on travellers, for example, even though persons included in such groups are not always racially or ethnically distinct.

(ii) *Political opinions or religious or other beliefs*   The European Convention on Human Rights, in Article 9, guarantees freedom of thought, conscience and religion. The Data Protection Convention uses the phrase, political opinions or religious or other beliefs. Clearly the fact that data controller keeps personal data relating to membership of a political party would bring that data controller within the registration requirement. However, the notion of 'political opinion' is broader than this and could, for example, include membership of a pressure group or association that seeks to advance a particular position, e.g. reform of the law of censorship, pornography and the like, by parliamentary or even extra-parliamentary means. An anti-extradition enthusiast or pro-divorce agitation group member would hold 'political opinions'. It is submitted 'religious or other beliefs' must similarly receive a broad interpretation. While the law of charities does not recognise that a non-theistic or humanist philosophy which rejects the existence of God, is a religion,[10] a person who subscribes to a set of values, ethics, or philosophy would certainly be within the phrase 'other beliefs'. Indeed, the High Court of Australia, for tax purposes at least, has held in *The Church of the New Faith v The Commissioner of Pay Roll Tax*[11] that the Church of Scientology is a religion. The Court held that the concept of a religion is not to be confined to theistic religions.

(iii) *Physical or mental health (other than any such data reasonably kept by them in relation to the physical or mental health of their employees in the ordinary course of personnel administration and not used or disclosed for any other purpose)*   The notion of data which is reasonably kept coincides with the data protection principles themselves. It may not be reasonable to keep personal details of an illness or condition that has occurred some time in the past, especially if there is no chance of recurrence.

(iv) *Sexual life*   This would clearly cover sexual activities of any kind. Data which indicates that a person has undergone a sex change operation would presumably also be covered.

(v) *Criminal convictions*   It should be noted that Ireland does not have legislation which allows a convicted person, as part of the rehabilitation process, the right to have a criminal record expunged.[12]

General comment

It is important that the full significance of this category of registrable data controller is appreciated. Many organisations, professions and individuals may at some time keep personal data on an automated information system. It may be, for example, that an employer has details about employees or former employees on a mainframe or other computer. The employee's name, address, religious affiliation, next of kin, date, place of birth, accident record and details about performance or demeanour in the job, are all legitimate matters for an employer to keep. The employer however becomes registrable because, in this example, details about religion and personal health are kept. A Church that keeps records on computer about members or parishioners — e.g. suppose details on the date of baptism and the like are kept — would similarly be registrable. While the Act contains an exemption in respect of personal data which is kept on a computer simply for word processing[13] this exemption is very narrow. The retention of data, either for recording purposes or for further use or processing, clearly takes the situation outside the exemption and if the data kept is sensitive personal data, then registration is necessary. Any number of examples come to mind. A doctor, hospital, nursing home or other medical or para-medical agency or individual prepares a medical report and keeps it on an automated system. A solicitor or barrister prepares an opinion, file note or pleadings in respect of an individual who has been injured in a road accident; the opinion, note or pleadings refer to the medical condition of the individual. If these details are kept on the automated system the data controller is registrable. A marriage bureau or marriage guidance counsellor who keeps details about clients who are having sexual difficulties would also be registrable if such details are stored on a automated system. An association which provides assistance and support to prisoners and their families, disabled or infirm persons, or sensitive data on persons with a history of mental illness, becomes registrable if such information on members or clients is held on an automated system.

(d) **Data processors whose business consists wholly or partly in processing personal data on behalf of data controllers** If the owner of a personal computer keeps personal data for another person — an employee for example, this would not automatically mean the owner has to register. The issue becomes, does the owner do this as part of a business activity?

(e) **Prescribed categories of data controllers and data processors** This provision is aimed mainly, but not exclusively, at data controllers who are not otherwise registrable under section 16 but, nevertheless, the Commissioner feels that supervision by way of registration is necessary. This will be particularly appropriate in cases where an enforcement notice, prohibition notice or information notice has been duly served and no valid appeal is extant.

General comment

It is evident from the above that not every data controller has to register. However, if a data controller also processes data, registration *qua* processing will be necessary. Although these categories of registrable data controller are generally easy to understand (save for the lack of definition in (c) above) there is one particular difficulty that should be clarified. The relationship between the excluded categories in section 16(1)(a) — Garda Síochána and Defence Forces — and section 16(1)(c) is not set out. Surely if the Garda Síochána hold sensitive personal data, as they do, on an automated system (which may not be the case), the organisation is registrable under section 16(1)(c), notwithstanding section 16(1)(a) and the Third Schedule of the 1988 Act.

THE REGISTER

Once the register is established, the Commissioner is under a statutory duty to maintain the register. The Commissioner is required to make an entry or entries in the register once the Commissioner accepts an application for registration.[14] The register is to be available for inspection by members of the public, at all reasonable times, free of charge. The public may also take copies of, or extracts from the register, free of charge.[15] Upon payment of a fee of £2[16] a member of the public may obtain a certified copy of, or an extract from, any entry on the register.[17] Such a certified copy is evidence of the entry or extract and a document purporting to be a copy is deemed to be a copy unless the contract is proved.[18] The Commissioner may also furnish a no entry certificate but no fee is payable where such a certificate is given: this no entry certificate is also given evidentiary value by the Act.[19]

It is arguable, it is submitted, that the Commissioner may be liable in negligence if the register, or the documents issued by him in respect of a registration have been carelessly compiled and cause financial loss. Although there is an understandable reluctance on the part of the courts to establish that a duty of care is owed by public officials to the world at large, it is possible that where applicants for registration are concerned, a duty of care may be owed to members of such a class, so that, if loss results from negligence, the Commissioner may be liable in damages. It may however be difficult to envisage circumstances in which such loss can occur.

By statutory instrument[20] it is provided that the entry on the register in respect of a registrable data controller shall be

(a) name and address,

(b) purpose(s) for which data is kept,

(c) description of data,

(d) persons or categories thereof to whom data may be disclosed (save for Section 8 disclosures),

(e) countries or territories to which data may be directly or indirectly transferred,

(f) should the Commissioner request disclosure of the source of the data or information, the persons or categories of persons who are sources thereof,

(g) name or job status of person to whom the subject access request may be made,

(h) date on which the entry, or continuance of entry, on the register was made,

(i) a cross reference to any other entry on the register relating to the data controller.

The same statutory instrument[21] provides that, where the entry relates to a data processor whose business consists wholly or partly in processing personal data for others, and the data processor is not also registrable under section 16, the particulars to be included in the entry shall be his name and address.

It should be noted that, while the application for registration requires the applicant to indicate the technical and physical security measures in place, the entry on the register will not, for obvious reasons, disclose what those security measures are.

APPLICATIONS FOR REGISTRATION

The legislation recognises that five kinds of registration may be involved and, as such, there are specific provisions which govern the procedure to be followed, and details that must be disclosed by the applicant, as well as the fees that must be paid before registration will be accepted.

1. First application for registration as a data controller or a data processor and data controller A person wishing to be registered must make an application, in writing, to the Commissioner. The applicant must provide the Commissioner with such information as is prescribed and any other information the Commissioner may require.[22] Both the form and the information required is generally prescribed by statutory instrument.[23] The form DPA1 is found in the Schedule to the statutory instrument in question,[24] and that form, or a form to like effect[25] must be used. The form prescribes the information required but, additionally, the Commissioner may request additional information. The Commissioner may require this additional information to be furnished as a supplementary document to DPA1.[26]

There are differences between the information that must be provided to the Commissioner on the application form and the information that must appear on the register. The application form requires information on ten points. These are

(i) *Name and address*[27]   A partnership is registrable as a person and the application must state the name and address of each partner. If the application is made in respect of a company the address of the registered office must be given. It is therefore not necessary for the data controller — in this context the phrase means applicant for registration — to name all employees who control the contents and use of the data file. If the applicant is neither a partnership or company — a club, unincorporated association or church group for example — the address of the principal place of business (i.e. activity) must be provided.

(ii) *Name or job status of the person to whom access requests must be directed*
The Act does not require an employer to appoint a subject access supervisor but it is prudent to do so at an early stage. Indeed, the subject access supervisor should ideally be the person who carried out the data survey prior to registration. If the person is not named the job title should be given, e.g. data manager, company secretary. If that person's address is different from that provided in response to question (i), this other address must be given.

(iii) *Purposes for which data is kept*   A distinction is drawn between data kept for the purposes of a business, trade, profession or public service, and data kept for other purposes. A general but comprehensive statement of purpose or purposes must be given in respect of the first category. In any other case, it is necessary to specify the purpose or purposes for which data is kept or used.

(iv) *Description of all personal data kept or used*   It is necessary to (a) describe the applications and data normally associated with such applications, (b) give full details of personal data which is not associated with any of the applications in (a).

(v) *Persons or bodies to whom the personal data may be disclosed (other than section 8 disclosures)*

(vi) *Countries or territories to which it is intended to transfer data, a description of the data and the purpose of transfer*

(vii) *Sensitive personal data*   If the applicant keeps sensitive personal data, i.e. relating to racial origin, political opinions, religious or other beliefs, physical or mental health (other than data relating to employees only) sexual life or criminal convictions, the applicant must provide information to the Commissioner. The applicant must

- (a) state what kind or kinds of personal data is kept,
- (b) specify what applications this data is put to,
- (c) specify the physical and technical safeguards in place to protect the privacy of data subjects concerned.

(viii) *Public disclosure*   If the personal data kept by the applicant is information that the applicant is required by law to make available to the public, the applicant is required to give details.

(ix) *Data processing*   The applicant is asked if the business operated consists wholly or partly in processing personal data for others. If so, the data processor is required to specify the countries or territories, if any, to which data is transferred or it is intended to transfer, for processing, directly or indirectly.

(x) *Name or job status of data protection supervisor within the organsiation*
While the Act does not specifically require the appointment of a data protection supervisor, it will not only be prudent, in an efficiency sense, to do so, it will also be problematical if this is not done. A failure to answer this question, as well as question (ii), relating to subject access requests, could allow the Commissioner to refuse to accept the application for registration on the ground that the prescribed information has not been provided.

The applicant is required to sign the DPA1 form. The applicant certifies that the information is correct and is advised that knowingly to furnish false or misleading information is an offence.[28] The applicant must furnish the fee at the time of making the application. The fee for first registration is £100.[29]

In general, the submission of an application is subject to a positive vetting procedure. Section 17(2) provides that the Commissioner *shall* accept an application made in the prescribed manner, if the prescribed fee has been paid, and if made by an eligible data controller or person who is both a data controller and data processor, unless the information provided is insufficient for inclusion in the entry on the register, or the applicant is likely to contravene the provisions of the Act: this refers to contravention of the data protection principles. Particular safeguards are built into the Act in respect of data controllers who keep sensitive personal data under section 16(1)(c). The Commissioner *shall not accept* the application unless he is of the opinion that appropriate safeguards for the protection of the privacy of the data subject or subjects concerned are, and will continue to be, in place.[30] Should the application be refused the Commissioner is obliged, as soon as may be, to notify the applicant in writing of the decision. The notification must specify the reasons for the refusal and inform the applicant of the applicant's section 26 rights of appeal to the Circuit Court. The appeal must be lodged within 21 days of receipt of the notification of refusal of the application.[31] In cases where the Commissioner, by virtue of special circumstances (e.g. flagrant non-observance of the data protection principles) is of the opinion that the refusal of an application should 'take effect urgently' the Commissioner may include a statement to this effect in the notification. The effect of such notification is to reduce the period within which an appeal can be lodged to 7 days instead of 21 days.[32] If an appeal is brought within that 7-day period the lodgment of notice of appeal does not prevent section 19 from operating. In other words, the applicant cannot keep, use, compile, disclose or transfer automated special circumstances notice simply by lodging an appeal. Only if the Circuit Court appeal is successful and registration is ordered can the applicant avoid committing a section 19(1) offence, that is, keep personal data, in respect of which the data controller is registrable, when there is no entry in the register concerning the data controller. This is however subject to section 26(4) which permits the Circuit Court, on application, to direct, *inter alia*, that contravention of section 19 shall not constitute an offence. Once registration takes place the registration is to last for one year — the prescribed period by statutory instrument.[33] The period begins to run from the data on which the relevant entry was made on the register.[34] Upon expiry of that period the entry is to be removed unless the registration is continued.[35] While the Commissioner is obliged to continue with the registration during the prescribed period[36] the Commissioner may, at any time, remove the entry from the register if so requested by the person to whom the entry relates.[37]

2. **Application for separate registration**   Section 17(1)(b) provides that, where a data controller intends to keep personal data for two or more purposes, he may make an application for separate registration in respect of any of those purposes. Separate entries shall be made in the register in respect of those multiple applications. The decision on whether to opt for multiple registration is partly an organisational one. Where separate divisions of an organisation, performing separate tasks are run in different locations, with different personnel involved in controlling, processing and supervising automated data activities, separate registrations may be prudent although separate registrations will require the disbursement of more than one registration fee. The form used to make an application for separate registration is form DPA2, or a form to like effect.[38] The applicant provides the same information as that required to effect

a first registration, discussed above, but additionally, the applicant is also asked to specify the number of separate registrations made: this presumably means the number of registrations in place and the number of applications made. The prescribed fee[39] of £100 must accompany the application. In all other respects the application for separate registration is governed by the rules that apply in respect of an individual application for first registration as a data controller or data controller/processor, discussed above, at 1.

3. Application for registration as a data processor only Where the application is made for registration as a data processor by a person whose business consists wholly or partly in processing personal data on behalf of data controllers, the application must be made on form DPA3, or a form to like effect.[40] Form DPA3 requires the name and address of the applicant be given. A partnership application must state the name and address of each partner. An application in respect of a company must state the address of the registered office. In the case of any other business, the address of the principal place of business must be given. The applicant must also disclose the countries or territories (if any) to which the applicant transfers or intends to transfer personal data for processing, directly or indirectly. The prescribed fee of £100[41] must accompany the application. The processing of the application is governed by the rules discussed above at 1, in respect of an individual application for first registration as a data controller or data controller/processor.

4. Application for continuance of registration Section 18(1) provides that registration is to last for a prescribed period. That period is set at one year[42] commencing on the data of entry onto the register. An application for continuance of registration must be made at the expiry of the prescribed period. Failing such an application for continuance the entry must be removed from the register. The legislation is silent on the question of the proximity to the expiry date that an application for continuance should be made within and it remains to be seen whether applications for continuance are processed within days of receipt of the application. The application for continuance is to be made on form DPA4, or a form to like effect. The form is short and requires the applicant to give the name and address and registration number of the previous application. If the applicant simply seeks to continue the same particulars, without change, he specifies this, returning a statement of the previous entry to the Commissioner.[43] If any changes are required, the particulars of those changes must be given in the statement. The application for continuance of registration must be accompanied by the prescribed fee of £100.[44] In Dáil Éireann the Minister for Justice Mr Collins gave an undertaking to review the fees charged.[45] It is submitted that £100 is a rather high figure to charge, particularly when the administrative costs of continuance of a registration will not be as substantial as those involved in vetting a first time registration.

Once a registration is continued the prescribed period of one year runs from the date of continuance, not the date of application or the date of expiry of the previous registration. The procedure for such applications is that applicable to first data controller applications: section 17(7).

5. Application for alteration of registration particulars   If, in the course of the period of registration a change of address occurs, the data controller or data processor is obliged to notify the Commissioner of that change of address. No fee is payable if the change relates to such a change of address.[46] However, if the data controller undertakes a new sphere of activity, e.g. obtains data from new sources or discloses data to new categories of person, it will be necessary to change the entry if the data controller is not to commit an offence under section 19(2). Surprisingly, if a data processor, during the currency of an entry on the register, begins to transfer personal data to a country or territory for processing and that entry is therefore inaccurate, there seems to be no basis for charging the data processor with a criminal offence. Indeed, there is no statutory obligation on the data processor to amend the entry on the register for the only offence the data processor may commit is the processing of data without there being an entry on the register in respect of him.[47]

The application by the data controller for alteration of registration particulars must be made by use of form DPA5, or a form to like effect.[48] The applicant must give his name, address and registration number and a statement of the amended particulars. The prescribed fee is £50.[49] The procedure for such applications is that applicable to first data controller applications: section 17(7).

EFFECT OF REGISTRATION

A data controller who keeps personal data without there being an entry on the register in respect of himself commits a criminal offence if, of course, the data controller is a person specified in section 16(1) as being obliged to register.[50] A data processor who is also within section 16(1) also commits an offence by processing data without an entry on the register in respect of him.[51] Even if a data controller is registered the entry must be kept accurate and up to date for section 19(2) and 19(6) makes it an offence to knowingly, use, obtain, disclose or transfer personal data in a manner not stated in the entry. These obligations extend to employees and agents (other than data processors) of the data controller. This emphasis on self regulation provides a very efficient method of control, as long as the Commissioner has the resources to investigate and verify the accuracy of entries on the register.

8

The Commissioner
and enforcement of the Act

INTRODUCTION

The Council of Europe Convention provides in Article 10 that 'each party undertakes to establish appropriate sanctions and remedies for violations of provisions of domestic law giving effect to the basic principles for data protection', as set out in Chapter 2 of the Convention. The Convention does not specifically require the appointment of a supervisory agency but most countries have established an official or tribunal to oversee the effective implementation of domestic law. In Ireland, the provision of sanctions and remedies through the criminal law and the civil law of tort is complimented by the establishment of a new body, the Commissioner for Data Protection,[1] who is a body corporate and is independent in the performance of his functions.[2] Ultimately, the Commissioner depends on the criminal law to counter any breach of the Act for the Commissioner had no power to order, or even recommend, the payment of compensation to data subjects effected by non-observance of the Act.

THE COMMISSIONER

Section 9(1) provides that there shall be a person, the Coimisinéir Cosanta Sonraí, in english the Data Protection Commissioner, who shall perform the functions laid down for him in the Act. The Second Schedule to the Act[3] makes specific provision for the workings of the office of Commissioner for Data Protection. The Commissioner is to be a body corporate and shall be independent in the performance of his functions.[4] This means, for example, that the Commissioner is to be seen as a quasi-judicial officer who is to be free and unrestricted by ministerial control in the discharge of his functions under the Act, even though the Commissioner is appointed by the Government and holds office upon such terms as the Government shall determine.[5] As a quasi-judicial officer the Commissioner must act fairly and impartially, without regard to factors or pressures which are extraneous to the requirements of both the Constitution and the Data Protection Act, 1988.[6]

The Commissioner must not hold any other office or employment in respect of which emoluments are payable to the holder.[7] The term of office of the Commissioner shall be a period not exceeding five years. That period is to be specified at the time of appointment and the Commissioner is eligible for reappointment unless the Second Schedule contains a provision which disqualifies the Commissioner from office.[8] On 22 July 1988 Donal C. Linehan was appointed to the office of Commissioner until 7 June 1993.[9]

The Commissioner may resign at any time, by letter addressed to the Secretary of the Government. The Government may at any time remove the Commissioner from office on the ground that ill-health prevents him from effectively performing his functions, or if he has committed stated misbehaviour.[10] In any case the Commissioner is to vacate the office upon reaching 65 years of age.[11] If the Commissioner is nominated to be a member of Seanad Eireann, elected as a member of either House of the Oireachtas, the European Parliament, a local authority, or is deemed elected to the European Parliament so as to fill a vacancy therein, he shall thereupon cease to be the Commissioner.[12]

The Second Schedule to the Act makes the usual provisions in respect of the financing of the office of Commissioner. Remuneration and allowances for expenses shall be paid by the Minister for Justice. The Minister for Justice must seek the consent of the Minister for Finance in respect of the amount to be paid to the Commissioner to defray these costs.[13] The budgetary allocation for the Commissioner does not appear as a separate item under Part II of the Schedule to the Appropriation Act, 1988 in the way that the costs of defraying similar offices do: the salaries and expenses of the office of the Ombudsman for example appear as separate items in that Act. The link with the Department of Justice and the Minister for Justice is quite substantial.[14] For example, the Minister for Justice is to provide pensions, gratuities and other allowances on the retirement or death of the Commissioner for Data Protection. The Minister for Justice is to appoint the staff of the Commissioner. The staff of the Commissioner have been deployed from the Department of Justice and other parts of the Civil Service.[15] The Minister for Justice, indeed, may delegate certain of his statutory powers[16] to the Commissioner. Similarly, in case of temporary absence, e.g. illness or while attending meetings of the mutual assistance committee of the Council of Europe, the Commissioner may designate a member of his staff to perform the Commissioner's functions during the absence of the Commissioner.[17] The Second Schedule also provides for proper and usual accounts to be kept by the Commissioner and for an auditing procedure.[18]

Functions of the Commissioner   In general terms, the functions of the Commissioner can be summarised thus: the Commissioner is to ensure that there is compliance by data controllers and data processors with the obligations imposed on them by the provisions of the Act. The Commissioner has the statutory power to initiate investigations, either on his own behalf or following the receipt of a complaint,[19] and he has certain statutory powers which may compel compliance, under threat of the criminal law, if voluntary compliance is not forthcoming. However, the Minister for Justice Mr Collins advised Dáil Éireann that he saw the role of the Commissioner as that of a 'mediator' in disputed cases.[20]

The methods by which the Commissioner may compel performance, principally by the issue of enforcement, prohibition and information notices, are discussed extensively later in this chapter. It is necessary to provide some indication of the specific issues that come within the Commissioner's remit, as well as those issues that the Commissioner seems to have no jurisdiction over. These issues involve the discharge of rights, the scope of some discretionary powers, as well as duties, imposed under Statute.

(1) *The section 2 data protection principles* This is the most obvious and most important aspect of the Commissioner's functions under the Act. Because non-observance of these principles does not, as such, constitute a criminal offence, the intervention of the Commissioner is an essential part of the enforcement mechanism contained in the Act.

(2) *The applicability of the Act* The Commissioner could investigate, and rule on, issues of demarcation. For example, a data controller may argue that data kept by him is outside the scope of the Act because it is required by law to be made public, or it is concerned only with the management of personal or family affairs, or is kept for recreational purposes.[21] It is possible for the Commissioner to rule on issues of this kind.

(3) *Section 3 personal data requests* If a data controller or data processor refuses to accede to a section 3 request, e.g. by responding that he does not keep automated personal data, a statement that the person who made the request disputes, the Commissioner may investigate.[22]

(4) *Section 4 subject access requests* This is another important provision. The Commissioner has an important role to play in ensuring that data controllers do not frustrate or obstruct data subjects who seek access to data relating to the data subject. For example, the Commissioner can rule on whether the fee charged under section 4(1)(c) is reasonable or whether the data controller is acting reasonably in refusing to give personal data because insufficient evidence of identity has been provided.[23] The Commissioner is of course able to investigate written notifications of refusal of a subject access request.

(5) *Section 5 subject access restrictions* It is possible, it is submitted, for the Commissioner to look into certain grounds for refusal to grant access to personal data. For example, if a subject access request is refused on the ground that disclosure would materially prejudice a criminal investigation, it is within

the power of the Commissioner to investigate this assertion.[24] However, it is not likely that the Commissioner could look behind the opinion of the Minister of Justice should the Minister declare that some personal data is kept in respect of financial malpractice and is not to be disclosed, under section 5(1)(d). The operation of section 5 and the role of the Commissioner in respect thereof will only be clarified by the Commissioner when he investigates complaints about non-access being unjustified under section 5.

(6) *Section 6 rectification requests*   Should the data controller fail to comply with the data subject's section 6 request to rectify or erase allegedly inaccurate data, or make the supplementary statement referred to in the proviso to section 6(1), the Commissioner may investigate under section 10.

(7) *Section 8 non-disclosure exceptions*   Like paragraph (5) above, the power of the Commissioner in regard to disclosure within section 8 is far from clear. The Commissioner may, in investigating an unauthorised disclosure complaint within section 2(1)(c)(ii), be faced with an argument which claims that disclosure was lawful because it was made within section 8. It is possible, it is submitted, for the Commissioner to rule on whether disclosure was authorised within section 8 in certain instances, e.g. the Commissioner could investigate and rule that disclosure was or was not needed for legal proceedings[25] or to avoid injury to a person or damage to property.[26] However, should a Garda chief superintendent[27] assert that information is needed for safeguarding the Security of the State, this cannot, it seems, be investigated or second-guessed by the Commissioner.

(8) *Section 10 notices*   The Commissioner is authorised under the statute to issue notices requiring persons to comply with the Act. These notices are discussed in detail below.

(9) *Codes of Practice*   The Commissioner has a statutory duty to encourage trade associations and other representative bodies of data controllers to prepare codes of practice, to be complied with by data controllers concerned in the activity in question.[28] This duty is discussed later in this chapter.

(10) *The Annual Report*   The Commission must prepare an annual report detailing his activities and cause the report to be laid before each House of the Oireachtas.[29]

(11) *The Convention*   The Council of Europe Convention for the Protection of Individuals with Regard to the Automatic Processing of Personal Data, obliges Parties to the Convention, under Chapter 4 'Mutual Assistance', to designate one or more authorities to advance mutual cooperation within the Convention area. The authority so designated is required to provide details to other contracting parties on law and administrative practice in the field of data protection, and afford assistance to data subjects resident abroad who seek to exercise rights given under the law to such foreign residents. Section 15(1) of the Act provides that the Data Protection Commissioner is the designated

authority in Ireland for the purpose of the relevant part of the Convention. Section 15(2) gives the Minister for Justice the power to make any regulations he considers necessary or expedient for the purpose of enabling the mutual cooperation provisions of the Convention to have full effect.

(12) *Registration* The Commissioner's obligation to establish and maintain a register[30] is one of the cardinal duties imposed upon him under the Act. Registration, and ancillary issues, is considered in detail in chapter 7.

(13) *The Commissioner's officers* The Commissioner is empowered to authorise persons, in writing, to exercise certain powers of entry, inspection, investigation and seizure.[31] These powers are discussed later in this chapter.

(14) *Proceedings* The Commissioner is given a power to bring and prosecute proceedings of a summary nature in respect of offences under the Act.[32] These powers are discussed later in this chapter.

(15) *Law-making* Apart from the indirect power to foster codes of practice and initiate the procedure whereby an approved code of practice within section 13 can acquire the force of law, the Commissioner can, under the operation of the delegation of powers provisions contained in paragraph 8(4) of the Second Schedule, with the consent of the Minister for Justice, make provision for certain matters which arise out of the Act. For example, The Data Protection (Registration Period) Regulations, 1988[33] and the Data Protection (Registration) Regulations, 1988[34] were both made under this power.

ENFORCEMENT OF THE ACT

Introduction In this part of the chapter we shall consider the circumstances in which non-observance of the obligations imposed by the Act on a data controller may be rectified. We have already considered in detail the power of the data subject to implement the self-help provisions found in sections 3 to 6. If the subject access provisions in sections 3 to 6 do not produce a satisfactory outcome for the data subject, it will be necessary for the data subject to consider other avenues. In cases where the data controller has refused to respond, cooperate or adjust the personal data kept in respect of that data subject, the most obvious response will be to alert the Commissioner to the possibility that a data controller is keeping personal data in circumstances where non-compliance with the Act is a very real possibility. The data subject may also consider an action against the data controller in tort, either for breach of a common law duty of care or breach of the section 7 statutory duty of care.

The role of the Commissioner Section 9(1) of the Act directs that there shall be appointed a person, to be known as the Data Protection Commissioner:[35] the Commissioner shall perform the functions conferred upon him by the Act. Section 10 draws a distinction between cases where the Commissioner *may* investigate, or cause to be investigated, possible contraventions of the Act, and cases where the Commissioner *shall* investigate possible contraventions of the Act. The permissive provision applies to circumstances in which contravention of the Act, by either a data controller or a data processor, may have occurred in respect of an individual data subject. Section 10(1)(a) allows the Commissioner to investigate, or cause to be investigated, whether provisions of the Act have or are being contravened, either on the Commissioners own initiative or following a complaint by the data subject affected by the alleged contravention. While the Act does not expressly recognise that others may have the *locus standi* to complain,[36] it is of course possible for a third party, e.g. an employee or former employee of a data controller or data processor, to inform the Commissioner of an alleged contravention and, given the discretionary nature of the Commissioner's own powers to initiate an investigation, the complaint can be investigated. However, despite the terms of section 10(1)(a) the Commissioner's discretion is immediately qualified in section 10(1)(b) by a direction that the complaint 'shall' be investigated where the complainant is a person who complains that personal data about him is being kept or processed in breach of the Act, or where the Commissioner is of the opinion that a contravention has or may be taking place. The Commissioner's discretion is thus considerably circumscribed by section 10(1)(b).

However, if the Commissioner is of the opinion that the complaint is frivolous or vexatious, the Commissioner is obliged to reject the complaint and decline to investigate or cause the complaint to be investigated. There are English cases in which pleadings have been struck out on the ground that the pleadings or the defence indicate that the action is frivolous or vexatious. The rule followed in relation to cases of pleadings which indicate that the cause of action is frivolous was stated by Jeune P in *Young v Holloway* to be, 'is the case now intended to be set up . . . so clearly frivolous that to put it forward would be an abuse of the process of the Court?'[37] If, for example, the claim by the complainant is vague or tentative then there is authority in the House of Lords to justify striking out pleadings as frivolous and and vexatious, particularly when allegations of fraud or dishonesty are made without any particularity in the allegations.[38] The decision to refuse to allow the action to proceed must not however be taken lightly[39] and should not be exercised simply because the allegation seems improbable.[40] If the complaint sets out facts that are garbled[41] and seem to have no possible chance of a remedy being given then the complaint may be frivolous or vexatious.[42] Should the Commissioner refuse to initiate the investigation sought, the individual concerned is to be notified, in writing, by the Commissioner of the decision. The individual may appeal to the Circuit Court within 21 days of receipt of the letter of notification.

The enforcement notice   If the Commissioner is of the opinion that a data controller or data processor is contravening or has contravened a provision of the Act, which is not of itself designated to result in criminal liability, the Commissioner may issue an enforcement notice.[43] The most obvious examples of provisions which are not criminal offences, as such, are the data protection principles in section 2, the existence of personal data obligation in section 3, the access right provisions in sections 4 and 5, and the rectification or erasure right given to a data subject by section 6.[44] The enforcement notice must be in writing and it must be served on the person acting in contravention of the Act. The notice states that the person served must follow such steps as are specified in the notice, within the time specified in the notice, if the Act is to be complied with. If the data controller has contravened section 2(1) of the Act then the enforcement notice may specify that the data controller is required to rectify or erase any of the data concerned, or insert a supplementary statement approved by the Commissioner.[45] If the personal data is complained of because it is inaccurate or not kept up to date, the insertion of a supplementary statement will result in the data controller being deemed not to be in breach of section 2(1)(b). The enforcement notice shall specify which provision in the Act the Commissioner regards as having been contravened and the reasons which have led him to form this opinion.[46] The person served with the enforcement notice could presumably make informal representations to the Commissioner in the hope that the Commissioner would be prepared to exercise his power under section 10(8) to cancel the notice. If this fails, the person served with the enforcement notice may appeal to the Circuit Court against the requirement specified in the enforcement notice within 21 days of service of the notice.

Section 11 makes specific provision for the time limits that must be satisfied following service of an enforcement notice. The Commissioner must not specify that compliance with the requirement stated in the enforcement notice must occur within 21 days of service of the notice: this will allow the person served the time to consider lodging an appeal before compliance must be effected. If an appeal is lodged then the requirement stipulated need not be complied with,[47] pending the outcome of the appeal. However, if the Commissioner certifies that, by reason of special circumstances, he is of the opinion that the requirement specified should be complied with immediately, and the enforcement notice contains a statement to that effect, the 21-day period within which an appeal may be lodged, and the dispensation from compliance with the specified requirement, do not operate.[48] Obviously the Commissioner will exercise this power in cases where a continuing infringement is likely to have serious and exceptional consequences for the data subject, e.g. possible loss of employment or a privilege such as the opportunity to adopt or foster a child, because personal data held is inaccurate. Once the enforcement notice contains the urgency and exceptional circumstances statement the appeal period is 21 days since service of the enforcement notice: the appeal is governed by section 26 and it is necessary under the Act for the Commissioner to summarise the section 26 appeals mechanism[49] in the enforcement notice if the Commissioner includes an urgency and exceptional circumstances statement in the enforcement notice. The important aspect of the serving of the urgency and exceptional circumstances statement is that the Commissioner can avoid the general rule, that is, that lodging an appeal will effect a stay on compliance with the requirement in the enforcement notice until the appeal is heard. The Commissioner can insist that the enforcement notice be complied with even pending the hearing of the appeal in the Circuit Court although the Commissioner must give the person served with the enforcement notice at least seven days, starting from the date of service, within which to comply with the requirement specified in the enforcement notice. There is no statutory maximum period within which compliance must be insisted upon under the urgency and exceptional circumstances exception permitted by section 10(6), but the time stipulated is likely to be seven days in most cases, for there would not be a great deal of point in invoking section 10(6) and then allowing the data controller or data processor an extended period of time to comply with the enforcement notice. There is no right of appeal against the decision of the Commissioner to include an urgency and exceptional circumstances statement in the enforcement notice but, under section 26(4), an application can be brought by the appellant to the Circuit Court, and, if the Court so determines, the Court may direct that non-compliance during the period the appeal is outstanding shall not constitute an offence. Thus, section 26(4) requires a person served with an enforcement notice to lodge an appeal and then bring an application to have the section 10(6) urgency and exceptional circumstances statement limited, or effectively suspended, by the Circuit Court. One can only speculate on whether the Circuit Court will require the appellant to show a *prima facie* case, or whether the Circuit Court will accede to an application simply upon proof that the business of the data controller or data processor would be disrupted by compliance. The interests of the data subject should not be ignored and the section 26(4) power should be sparingly exercised, in this writer's view.

If the enforcement notice relates to a section 2(1) contravention — i.e. the data protection principles have not been observed, and the Commissioner, under section 10(3), has insisted on rectification, erasure or a supplementary statement being added to the data — the data controller must do more than merely comply with the enforcement notice. Within 40 days of compliance the data controller must notify the data subject, and, if compliance materially alters the data, any person to whom the data was disclosed in the period beginning 12 months before service of the notice and ending immediately before the date of compliance.[50] This is subject to the lodgment of a Circuit Court appeal against the enforcement notice, (the effect of which is to suspend the requirement to comply until the appeal is heard)[51] and subject to the power of the Circuit Court to grant an application against an urgency and special circumstances certificate under section 26(4). It is an offence under section 10(9) to fail or refuse, without reasonable excuse, to comply with a requirement specified in an enforcement notice.

The prohibition notice In some respects, the interests that the prohibition notice procedure attempts to protect are central to the whole Act. Because of the truly international nature of trade, and in particular business activities that require the transmission and processing of financial data, a state has a legitimate interest in protecting its citizens from the effects of data being exported to other jurisdictions, where it may be used in a way which is unfairly prejudicial to the citizen, whether by reason of its inaccuracy or otherwise. The state cannot intervene once the data has left its jurisdiction but it is perhaps entitled to make the export of personal data to so called 'data havens' difficult, if not impossible. On the other hand, the business community may legitimately point to the competing principle of freedom of information, as well as a kind of international utilitarianism, in order to insist on a more balanced approach to resolving the conflict between individual human rights and commercial expediency. The Council of Europe Convention attempts to resolve this conflict in Article 12. The central element in Article 12 is found in paragraph 2:

> A Party shall not, for the sole purpose of the protection of privacy, prohibit or subject to special authorisation transborder flows of personal data going to the territory of another Party.

While this Article seems to indicate that the balance is tilted in favour of commercial expediency, and while this Article forms part of the Irish Act, the role of the Commissioner in regulating the exportability of personal data from Ireland, by way of the prohibition notice, is made all the more important when it is noted that the Council of Europe Convention does not require Contracting Parties to appoint a Commissioner or someone discharging the functions of a Commissioner. Nevertheless, it is difficult to see how the provisions of Article 12 and the domestic law provisions in sections 11 and 12 of the Irish Act which implement Article 12 could be expected to work effectively, but for the supervisory activities of the Commissioner.

Section 11(1) provides that the Commissioner may, subject to the provisions in the section, prohibit the transfer of personal data from the State to a place outside the State. Section 11(1) therefore makes it clear that what is feared is not a transgression that takes place within the State by persons situated with Ireland. Section 11(1) also makes it clear that the Commissioner is closely controlled by the provisions in section 11: the Commissioner does not have a broad discretion on the issue of whether personal data may be exported. Section

11(2) specifically directs that, in considering whether to prohibit a proposed transfer of personal data from the State to a place in a state bound by the Convention (a Convention country), the Commissioner 'shall have regard' to the provisions of Article 12. However, section 11(2) goes on to build upon this distinction between the transfer of personal data to a Convention country and the transfer of personal data to a non-Convention country. Article 12.3. itself permits derogations:

> a. where the 'exporting' state has national laws that provide specific protection for certain categories of personal data (e.g. sensitive personal data on race or religion) or certain categories of automated data files, unless the recipient Convention state provides equivalent protection,
> b. Where the transfer is made to a non contracting state via the intermediary of another Convention state. Clearly such practices would result in circumvention of the legislation of a Convention country.

On the sensitive question of transborder data flows, the Irish Act provides an example of legislation that is designed to pre-empt another Convention state from refusing to allow the transmission of personal data to Ireland under derogation (a). Section 2(6) allows the Minister, by regulations, to provide additional safeguards *vis-à-vis* sensitive personal data, in order to preclude the possibility of another Convention country refusing to permit the transfer of data to Ireland. The thinking behind section 2(6) is that if another convention country proposes to block the transfer of data to Ireland, regulations will be adopted in order to make the derogation in Article 12.3.a. inapplicable. Section 11 does not, strangely enough, build directly on the wording of Article 12. Rather, the reference in section 11(2) of the Act to Article 12 itself may incorporate Article 12 into Irish law, insofar as the State to which personal data is sent is a Convention state. 'Shall have regard' however is an ambivalent phrase. The Convention permits a contracting party to adopt national laws that allow the unimpeded transfer of personal data across national frontiers if the contracting party so desires. It follows that if a data subject objects to transmission of personal data about the data subject to another Convention state, but the Commissioner refuses to prohibit such a transfer after the Commissioner has taken account of Article 12 of the Convention, the data subject has no remedy in certiorari or any of the other prerogative or state-side orders, even if the personal data is sensitive in the extreme.

Where the data controller proposes to transmit personal data[52] to a state which is not a Convention country, the situation is governed by section 11(3). Section 11(2) permits the transfer of data to Convention countries even if the data protection principles are not going to be observed in the reception state: nothing in that section *requires* the Commissioner to block such a transfer. Section 11(3) provides even less protection to a data subject. The Commissioner is under a statutory duty *not* to prevent the transfer of personal data unless he is of the opinion that the transfer, if the recipient state were a Convention state, would lead to a contravention of the principles for data protection set out in Chapter II of the Convention. This does not mean that the Commissioner may block the transfer of personal data when a serious infringement of rights of privacy will or may result from the transfer of personal data to a non-Convention country.

The ultimate factor the Commissioner must consider, in deciding whether to prohibit the transfer of personal data under section 11 (whether the recipient state is a convention or non-convention state) involves a question of balance. Section 11(4) states that the Commissioner

> shall also consider whether the transfer would be likely to cause damage or distress to any person and have regard to the desirability of facilitating international transfers of data.

Should the Commissioner consider, that, on balance, the data should be exported, there is no realistic prospect of the data subject affected being able to challenge the decision by way of judicial review: section 26 does not confer a right of appeal against the refusal by the Commissioner to grant a prohibition notice.

While section 11 considerably restricts the power of the Commissioner to prohibit a transfer of data, section 11(10) prevents the Commissioner from prohibiting the transfer of data if the transfer of the data or the information therein is required or authorised under any enactment, or a convention, or any other instrument imposing an international obligation on the State. Examples of these obligations exist in the field of international co-operation in social security matters, as well as European Community law generally. Should the Commissioner, notwithstanding the considerable practical and legal constraints imposed, decide that a transfer should be prohibited, this is effected by serving a prohibition notice on the person proposing to transfer the data: section 11(5). The notice must prohibit the transfer absolutely or until specified steps are complied with. These steps must be directed at protecting the interests of the data subject concerned. The notice must specify both the time the notice is to take effect and the grounds for the prohibition. The notice must also state the existence of rights of appeal to the Circuit Court, under section 26, within 21 days of service of the prohibition notice.[53] The prohibition notice must not be drafted so as to expire before the end of the 21 days following service of the prohibition notice, thereby enabling the person served to consider whether to lodge an appeal, without in that time being prejudiced by implementation of the prohibition notice. However, this provision, found in section 11(7), is immediately conditioned by subsection (8) which allows the prohibition notice to take effect at any time after seven days following service of the prohibition notice if the Commissioner is of the opinion that, by reason of special circumstances, a prohibition in the prohibition notice should be complied with urgently, and the prohibition notice carries a statement to this effect. Where the prohibition notice contains such a special circumstance/urgency statement, the notice must also contain a summary of the effect of section 26.[54] There is a specific right of appeal to the Circuit Court against a prohibition specified in a prohibition notice under the terms of section 26(1)(b). Once the appeal is entered, it is possible to have the special circumstances/urgency aspect of the prohibition notice varied by the Circuit Court for the time the appeal is pending, until it is withdrawn, or for such period as the Circuit Court may direct. In such a case, non-observance of the prohibition notice is not an offence under section 19.

Section 11(13) provides that, a person, who, without reasonable excuse, fails or refuses to comply with a prohibition specified in a prohibition notice shall be guilty of an offence. What will constitute a 'reasonable excuse' is unclear but this is discussed in chapter 9.

The definition of data transfer   This is an extremely broad concept and it is not limited to instances where personal data exists in a form in which it can be automatically processed. The Commissioner's *Guide* provides an indication of the range of situations envisaged to include a data transfer

> Data can be transferred abroad in various forms. They can be in plain text or encoded or can be stored on magnetic tape, disk, punched card, punched tape, paper etc. They can be transported physically or by post or tele-communications link (circuit-switched or packet-switched). They can be transferred from one country to another either directly or via another country and the transfers can be within an organisation or between different organisations or persons.

It is not clear whether the transmission of personal data by electronic mail or telex is included. In the absence of a definition there seems no reason to exclude personal data exported across national frontiers by such a means for the above statement seems to envisage that printed paper, once posted abroad, can come within the concept of a data transfer.

Jurisdictional problems   Enforcement of section 11 is problematical in the extreme. The Commissioner will be aware of precisely how data protection laws in other countries function, not least because the Commissioner, as the designated mutual assistance authority under Chapter IV of the Convention,[55] will be able to call on other designated authorities abroad to provide information on its law and administrative practice in relation to data protection. However, it is evident that the Commissioner will have to obtain the cooperation of industry generally if the Commissioner is to obtain information about the kind of data that is transferred, or is about to be transferred, outside the State. The registration procedure is going to be the only conceivable source of information: while holders of sensitive personal data and the other categories of registerable data controller will provide this information as part of the registration process, categories of data controller who are not perhaps obliged to register, e.g. trade unions, employers associations, for example, may be more difficult to supervise. Note also that a data subject may have some difficulty in complaining about a transborder data flow which potentially concerns the data subject, for section 11 does not confer upon data subjects a right to complain. Section 10 may not be relevant because section 10 relates to a breach of the provisions in the Act. In this situation the Act is not always relevant because non-observance of the data protection principles will occur outside Ireland. In practical terms however, a section 10 complaint about a data transfer abroad could not be ignored by the Commissioner but the data subject, like the Commissioner, faces the difficulty of finding out what unregistered data controllers keep by way of personal data, and the purposes for which it is kept. In the time a section 3 or section 4 request is satisfied personal data may often be effectively transferred to a jurisdiction where rectification or erasure may be a difficult right to exercise. An enforcement notice in Ireland cannot be issued in respect of personal data situated in another state if that data is not accessible in Ireland.

Information notices Section 12 of the Act permits the Commissioner, by notice in writing served on a person, to require that person to furnish the Commissioner, in writing within a specified time, with such information as is specified in the notice, as is necessary or expedient for the performance of the Commissioner's functions. This notice, the information notice, is not so much a method of enforcing the provisions in the Act but, rather, it is an essential method of gathering information. Note in particular that the power is not limited to data controllers, data processors or data subjects. Employers, Government Departments, the Gardai, for example, are required to make the disclosure specified. The information need not be held in any particular form: information retained by the person served by way of that person's memory is just as amenable to this procedure as material held on computer or in manual files. The information sought must however be provided to the Commissioner in writing.

The Commissioner is also entitled to side-step many of the exclusions and limitations that confront the data subject: section 12(4)(a), for example, provides that no enactment or rule of law which prohibits or restricts the disclosure of information shall preclude the person served from providing the Commissioner with the information sought, if it is necessary or expedient for the performance by the Commissioner of his functions. Examples of enactments which limit the power of an information holder to make disclosure would include the Industrial Development Act 1986, section 43 of which prohibits the disclosure of information given to a person whilst that person was a member of the IDA or an employee of the IDA. A similar provision is set out in section 14 of the Agriculture (Research, Training and (Advice) Act, 1988. Certain rules of law inhibit a persons freedom to disclose information: the law of confidence,[56] the implied contractual duty that employees owe *vis-à-vis* an employers trade secrets, as well as contractual undertakings[57] not to disclose information, are all well established, but they are subordinate to section 12(4)(a). The only circumstances in which the Commissioner cannot insist on obtaining information are set out in section 12(4)(a). Firstly, if information is, or at any time was, in the opinion of the Minister for Justice or the Minister for Defence, kept for the purpose of safeguarding the security of the State, that information need no be disclosed under an information notice. Similarly, if information is privileged from disclosure, in proceedings in any court, then section 12(4)(b) does not apply.

The information notice is served and reviewed in much the same way as the enforcement notices and prohibition notices served under sections 10 and 11 respectively. The notice, once served, must state that the person served has, for 21 days, a right of appeal to the Circuit Court under section 26 of the Act. The notice must not be expressed to expire before the elapse of the 21 days in which the appeal can be lodged.[58] However, if an appeal is lodged within that 21-day period the requirement in the information notice need not be met until the appeal is determined or withdrawn.[59] Should the Commissioner however state in the information notice that, by virtue of special circumstances the information sought is urgently needed, compliance with the notice, not less than seven days after service, may be required. However, the notice will also contain a summary of the rights of appeal to the Circuit Court under section 26 and it is possible that once an appeal is lodged the Circuit Court may, on application, vary the requirement in the information notice under section 26(4). Section 12(5) of the Act provides that a person who, without reasonable excuse, fails or refuses to comply with a requirement in an information notice, or who, in purported compliance furnishes information that the person knows to be false or misleading in a material respect, shall be guilty of an offence. Both parts of this offence are qualified somewhat. Non-compliance, while not expressly[60] requiring *mens rea* for an offence to be committed, contains a defence of 'reasonable excuse'. Furnishing false information which is known to be false or misleading is also not *per se* an offence: it must be shown that the information was known to be false or misleading in some material[61] respect.

The power of the Commissioner to require information under section 12 may overlap with other provisions in the Act, particularly sections 17(1)(a) and 20 relating to information sought in respect of registration.

Powers of investigation and prosecution held by the Commissioner Section 24 of the Act confers extensive powers of entry, inspection and examination on 'authorised officers'. These powers can be exercised generally by authorised officers without the need for an application to any judge or judicial authority: indeed, as the Bill initially stood, the power of the Commissioner to bring about the exercise of these powers was in no way subject to judicial control. As we shall see, the Act was amended at Committee stage in Dáil Éireann, as a result of lobbying from financial institutions, and there is a significant impediment to the exercise of the powers of authorised officers where financial institutions are concerned.

Section 24(1) defines an authorised officer as a person authorised in writing by the Commissioner to exercise, for the purposes of the Act, the powers conferred under section 24. A general authorisation will suffice: it is not necessary for the authorised officer to be specifically authorised to enter a certain premises. Nor must the authorised officer show the authorisation as a condition precedent to exercising these powers: the authorised officer need only produce the authorisation if so required. The section seems to indicate that if the authorisation is requested but is not then produced, entry and subsequent actions on the part of the officer will not be lawful. Both the search and any evidence obtained will be illegal and, as we shall see, this may prove to be fatal to any subsequent prosecutions. Indeed, illegal search and seizure may themselves be the subject of a civil action for trespass or infringement of Constitutional rights. Section 24(2) directs that the authorised officer may exercise the powers set out in section 24 for the purpose of obtaining any information that is necessary or expedient for the performance, by the Commissioner, of his functions. This is extremely broad. The section is not limited to the investigation of criminal offences or the enforcement of the data protection principles. The 'functions' of the Commissioner are not specifically enumerated in the Act. If the Commissioner is empowered or required to do something under the Act then that is a function. So, the authorised officer could conceivably enter premises and carry out investigations for the purpose of assisting in preparing the annual report[62] or gather information for the discharge of mutual assistance obligations in respect of automatic processing in Ireland.[63] These provisions differ radically from those found in the UK Act. In the UK powers of entry and inspection must be authorised by a warrant obtained by way of judicial proceedings, upon sworn affidavit by the Register, when he suspects that an offence has been, or is being committed, or the data protection principles have been or are being contravened.[64] There are however some safeguards in the Irish Act against abuse. These are inherent in the powers specified in section 24(2). Section 24(2) provides that the authorised officer may

(a) at all reasonable times enter premises that he reasonably believes to be occupied by a data controller or a data processor, inspect the premises and any data therein [other than data kept at any time, in the opinion of the Minister for Justice or Defence for safeguarding the security of the State or which is privileged from disclosure in court proceedings] and inspect, examine, operate and test any data equipment therein.

Some aspects of section 24(2)(a) deserve closer examination. Firstly, it is not clear what is meant by 'at all reasonable times.' Because of the disruption and inconvenience that may result from the exercise of powers of entry, it can be argued that the authorised officer should give a period of notice of his intention to enter premises and inspect them. It may not be reasonable for an officer to arrive at office premises during office hours on a particular day and insist that the activities of the data controller or data processor immediately cease in order to facilitate the inspection of premises, data and equipment. The UK Act specifically provides for a period of seven days notice to have been served on the occupier as a *sine qua non* to obtaining a warrant.[65] Secondly, while the section is clearly intended to provide for entry to be exercised during reasonable hours, e.g. an office premises should be entered and searched during office hours, the application of the 'reasonable times' provision to domestic premises may be problematical. Suppose data is kept or controlled in a domestic residence. It is arguable that the authorised officer should not be able to exercise powers of entry and inspection during the evenings or at weekends. Further, if the same data is kept at both office premises and a domestic residence the powers should be exercisable, in the first instance, in respect of the office premises. The authorised officer is obliged to establish that he reasonably believes the premises to be occupied by a data controller or data processor. 'Occupied' is not defined in the Act. It does not however seem that the authorised officer has to establish that at the time of entry or inspection the data controller or data processor was physically present. It should also be noted that there is no requirement that the authorised officer establish a reasonable belief that the Act or the data protection principles have been contravened. Thirdly, 'data equipment' is defined in section 1(1) as 'equipment for processing data'. Machinery which does not process data such as an information retrieval system or recording equipment is therefore not to be inspected, examined, operated, or tested under section 24(2)(a).

Section 24(2)(b) relates to the power of the authorised officer to obtain disclosure of data and data material. A person who is on the premises and who is a data controller, data processor or an employee thereof, is required to disclose data or data material which is in that person's power or control. The subsection also permits the authorised officer to seek disclosure of such information as he may reasonably require in regard to the data or data material. Section 24(2)(d) also requires the person, being a data controller, data processor or employee thereof, to provide information which is reasonably required and relates to compliance procedures, data sources, the purposes for which data is kept, the persons to whom data is disclosed, as well as information on data equipment situated on the premises.

Section 24(2)(c) allows the authorised officer to inspect and copy and take extracts from data, or take information from the data. Examination, inspection and extraction may take place on the premises, or some other place.

There are some limits however on what the authorised officer can do. It is unlikely that the officer can insist on interviewing a data controller or data processor when that person is on premises which are not being used for keeping data (e.g. the home of the data processor). There is clearly no power to interview the data processor or controller when in the street, or to order the data processor or controller to attend at a designated place to answer questions. It is important to establish precisely the powers of the authorised officer for section 24(6) creates a criminal offence in respect of subsection (2). Section 24(6) provides:

> A person who obstructs or impedes an authorised officer in the exercise of a power, or, without reasonable excuse, does not comply with a requirement under this section or who in purported compliance with such a requirement gives information to an authorised officer that he knows to be false or misleading in a material respect shall be guilty of an offence.

The financial institution exception   When the Commissioner is of the view that it is necessary or expedient for the performance by him of his functions that an authorised officer be able to exercise the powers of entry and search set out in subsection 2, in relation to a financial institution,[66] the Commissioner must apply to the High Court for an order.[67] The High Court will make the order if the Court is satisfied that it is reasonable to do so and 'the exigencies of the common good' warrant that the order be made. The order will allow the authorised officer to exercise those powers set out in subsection (2) but the High Court may set such conditions as it thinks proper and specify the conditions in the order made. The order will obviously in these circumstances limit the powers of entry, inspection and examination, e.g. a certain time may be set. Data may be excluded or limited in terms of access. The Government moved a late amendment to the Bill in Dáil Éireann following lobbying by the financial services sector. It is arguable that the amendment makes effective investigation of the institutions covered by the amendment virtually impossible. The onus of proving that it is reasonable to make the order and that the common good requires the order to be made rests on the Commissioner. The difficulty of discharging the onus is not made any easier by the inherent vagueness of the criteria.

Section 24 and illegally obtained evidence   There is a considerable volume of Irish case law which indicates that evidence obtained following and illegal search, examination and seizure operation by the Gardai is not admissible in evidence against an accused person. The protection afforded by the Constitution is discussed extensively by O'Connor in an article, "The Admissibility of Unconstitutionally Obtained Evidence in Irish Law".[68]

Prosecution of offences   The offences created by specific sections of the Act can be prosecuted by way of summary proceedings, or upon indictment. Section 30(1) provides that summary proceedings may be brought and prosecuted by the Commissioner. Summary proceedings can of course be brought and prosecuted by the Gardaí. However, it is anticipated that enforcement in general by summary proceedings is to be within the remit of the Commissioner. The general provision in section 10(4) of the Petty Sessions (Ireland) Act, 1851 requires proceedings to be instituted within 6 months of the alleged offence. Section 31(2) of the Data Protection Act, 1988 extends the period for institution of proceedings to one year from the date of the alleged offence. Section 28 provides for *in camera* hearings by conferring upon the court a discretion to hear the whole or any part of the proceedings without the public being admitted. Obviously this discretion will be relevant to proceedings which will require sensitive personal data to be discussed during the course of the proceedings. Should the proceedings involve questions involving assertions that personal data is or was kept for the purpose of safeguarding the security of the State, a certificate signed by either the Minister for Justice or the Minister for Defence which states that the material was, in the opinion of that Minister, so kept, is under section 27(1)(a) evidence of that opinion.[69] Such a statement may *inter alia*, be relevant to a prosecution for an offence under section 24(6) because the authorised officer's rights of entry, search and examination are not exercisable in respect of personal data kept for State security purposes. Section 27(2) however creates an exclusionary rule of evidence in respect of information provided under section 3 — the right to establish the existence of personal data section — and also under section 4 — the subject access request section. Information supplied in compliance with section 3 or section 4 obligations are not admissible in evidence against the supplier or the supplier's spouse when an offence under the Act has been charged.

Self-regulation and codes of practice   One of the features of Irish data protection legislation that marks a significant departure from the legislation adopted in the United Kingdom relates to the degree of self-regulation that is possible under the Irish Act. Both the UK Act and the Irish Act require the Registrar and the Commissioner respectively to prompt trade associations and other representative bodies to prepare codes of practice. Section 13(1) of the

Irish Act does not allow the Commissioner to draft a code of practice and present it to a sector of industry. Section 13(1) directs that trade associations and bodies representing categories of data controllers are to be encouraged to prepare codes of practice, to be complied with by those categories of data controller in dealing with personal data. However, there are significant advantages which may result from undertaking work on preparing a code of practice: any association or representative body will have a significant opportunity to establish the standards that are to apply within the sector in question and this standard will be of crucial importance in civil actions for breach of a duty of care.

Once a code is prepared, it may be presented to the Commissioner for scrutiny. If the Commissioner is of the opinion that the code provides safeguards for data subjects that conform to the right to establish the existence of personal data,[70] the data protection principles found in section 2, the subject access rights in section 4,[71] and the rectification and erasure remedies in section 6, the Commissioner may approve of the code.

The Commissioner is then required by section 13(2) to encourage dissemination of the code to data controllers concerned. Additionally, once it is approved the code may be laid by the Minister for Justice before each House of the Oireachtas and, if approved by resolution of each House, the code will have the force of law in regard to personal data held by the categories of personal data controller affected. Section 13(3)(a)(ii) goes even further and directs that any code which has the force of law is to be read with the sections in question.[72] The code is also deemed by section 13(3)(b) to be a statutory instrument. The UK Act has nothing that resembles section 13(3); the net effect of section 13 is to allow an association to expand upon the bare bones of the data protection principles, subject access rights and rectification and erasure remedies. If the code is approved by the Commissioner, the Minister and then the Oireachtas, the code will help to determine the standard by which the conduct of the data controller involved in the activity in question is judged. The question whether a data controllers actions meet the standards set by the code of practice will be of vital importance in cases where the section 7 duty of care is involved. A code of practice in the area of personnel management, insurance, or some other homogeneous activity will be of considerable assistance to a court that is required to decide if a data controller has broken the duty of care owed to a data subject. If the data controller can show compliance with a code that has not been approved by the Commissioner, or has been approved but not laid before the Oireachtas, these factors will provide some indicators to a court on the issue of breach of duty. Indeed, if the code has not been approved, it may be that the court may seek further information from the Commissioner on the reasons why approval was withheld. Should the code be accorded the status of a statutory instrument this will presumably be conclusive on the issue of breach of duty. If the code is satisfied, no breach of sections 2 to 6 can be established by a data subject. In explaining this provision to the Seanad, Mr Collins gave a further explanation for section 13(3), the approval of each House procedure, and its consequences. If the code were purely voluntary the codes would be binding, in practice if not in law, on members of the body that had drawn the code up. The code could not apply to non-members. The section 13 approval procedures, if satisfied, will result in the code being enforceable, in the same way as the data protection principles are,[73] even if the data controller is not a member of any trade association or representative body, as long as he is a participant in the sphere of activity covered by the code of practice in question.

Section 13(4) applies the provisions relating to codes of practice to data processors as well as data controllers. The only part of section 2 that is relevant to data processors is the obligation to take appropriate security measures against unauthorised access, alteration, disclosure or destruction of personal data, and against accidental loss or destruction of that data.

9

Criminal and civil liability
under the Act

CRIMINAL LIABILITY

While the intention behind the creation of an independent supervisory agency, the Data Protection Commissioner, is directed at ensuring that compliance with the Act is achieved through a process of education and mediation, it is clear that the most straightforward method of ensuring compliance with the Act is through the imposition of criminal sanctions following a successful prosecution for infringement of the statutory offences laid down in the Act. The criminal penalties are quite substantial: on summary conviction a fine not exceeding £1,000 can be imposed. On conviction on indictment a fine not exceeding £50,000 can be imposed.[1] The court may also, following conviction, order any data material which appears to the court to be connected with the commission of the offence to be forfeited or destroyed and any relevant data to be erased.[2] If, however, another person owns or is otherwise interested in the data material, the data material is not to be forfeited, destroyed or erased unless steps have been taken to notify that person, giving him the opportunity to show cause why the order should not be made.

These sanctions are necessary under Article 10 of the Council of Europe Convention which requires contracting parties to establish 'appropriate sanctions and remedies for violations of provisions of domestic law giving effect to the basic principles for data protection.' It should be noted that the Article mentions 'sanctions and remedies'. It is arguable that the remedies available to data subjects under the Irish Act are not adequate given the failure of the Act to provide a power to recommend or award compensation to data subjects prejudiced by violations of the Act, regardless of whether such a power be exercisable by the Commissioner or the courts.

Contravention of the provisions of the Act and section 10 Some provisions in the Act are not obligations in the sense that a direct sanction is imposed if the obligation is not complied with. This is illustrated by reference to the section 2 data protection principles. Non-observance of these principles is a serious matter but no criminal offence is committed by the data controller in question.

Only when the Commissioner issues an enforcement notice in which he specifies the provision which he is of the opinion is not being observed is there an obligation to comply: failure to do so within 21 days (7 days in urgency cases) means that a person who fails to comply with an enforcement notice, without reasonable excuse, shall be guilty of an offence.[3] We have considered the enforcement, prohibition and information notice procedures in Chapter 8. The provisions in the Act that appear to raise the possibility that the Commissioner may issue enforcement notices in respect thereto are also set out in Chapter 8 above.

Similar provisions apply in respect of prohibition notices — orders prohibiting the transfer of personal data outside the State — and information notices. If a prohibition notice or information notice is not issued or the notice is defective, no prosecution for an offence is possible in respect of a prohibition notice[4] or an information notice.[5] A conviction may not be entered if the accused shows that he had a reasonable excuse for not observing the enforce- ment notice, the prohibition notice or the information notice, as the case may be.

Offences

Registration offences   Section 19 creates a series of criminal offences which may be committed by registrable data controllers. Section 19(1) directs that a data controller who is registrable shall not keep personal data unless there is for the time being an entry in the register in respect of him. Section 19(2) directs that a data controller in respect of whom there is an entry on the register shall not

   (a) keep personal data of any description other than that specified in the entry [on the Register]
   (b) keep or use personal data for a purpose other than the purpose or purposes described in the entry,
   (c) if the source from which such data, and any information intended for inclusion in such data is required to be described in the entry, to obtain such data or information from a source that is not so described,
   (d) disclose personal data to a person not described in the entry [other than a person mentioned in the section 8 exception]
   (e) directly or indirectly transfer such data to a place outside the State other than a place named or described in the entry.

Section 19(3) imposes these section 19(2) duties on employees and agents (other than data processors) of the data controller. Data processors are required to register under section 16: section 19(4) obliges data processors not to process personal data unless there is for the time being an entry in the register in respect of him.

A registered data processor or data controller who changes his address must notify the Commissioner of the change.[6] Section 20(1)(b) provides that there may be prescribed, by regulations, the information required to be furnished to the Commissioner by applicants for registration, continuance of registration or alteration of registration particulars. Section 20(2) makes it an offence for such a person to furnish the Commissioner with information that the person knows to be false or misleading in a material respect.

Disclosure offences Apart from the offence stated by section 19(1)(d), mentioned above, namely, the disclosure of personal data to a person not described on the relevant entry on the register, there are two important offences which attempt to discourage the authorised disclosure of personal data to third parties. Firstly, section 21(1) directs that personal data processed by a data processor shall not be disclosed by him, or by an employee or agent of his, without the prior authority of the data controller on behalf of whom the data are processed. To knowingly do so makes the person who contravenes this provision guilty of an offence.[7] Secondly, section 22(1) directs that a person who obtains access to personal data, or obtains any information constituting such data, without the prior authority of the data controller or data processor by whom the data are kept, and, that person discloses the data or information to another person, shall be guilty of an offence. Section 22(2) provides that a section 22(1) offence is not to apply to a person who is an employee or agent of the data controller or data processor concerned.

As the Commissioner's *Guide to the Act* acknowledges, the Act therefore has no direct criminal sanction where an employee of a non-registrable data controller discloses personal data for a purpose which is incompatible with the purposes for which the data are kept. The *Guide* continues:

> It would be unreasonable to make it an offence for an employee to make an 'incompatible' disclosure when it is not an offence for the employer himself to do so. The only remedy against an employer in such a situation is for the Commissioner to issue an enforcement notice requiring him to take steps to comply with the Act. There is no power to issue an enforcement notice to an employee nor would such a power be appropriate as it is the employer, as data controller, who is responsible for complying with the data protection provisions and seeing that his employees do so too. Breach of an enforcement notice is an offence.

There is thus no direct or immediate sanction on the staff of unregistered data controllers in the event of their disclosing personal data in any manner incompatible with the purposes for which the data are kept. However, the Commissioner, with the consent of the Minister for Justice, is specifically empowered by section 16(1) to make regulations requiring registration of all unregistered data controllers who have had enforcement notices issued against them. That would make employees of those controllers liable to criminal sanctions for irregular disclosures of data in the future.

Obstruction of authorised officers   Section 25(6) provides for a series of offences in regard to the discharge by an authorised officer of the Commissioner of his powers and duties. It is an offence to obstruct or impede an authorised officer in the exercise of a power. It is an offence, without reasonable exercise, to fail to comply with a requirement under section 25 (e.g. fail to allow an officer at a reasonable time to enter premises believed to be occupied by a data controller or data processor or provide information). It is also an offence to, in purported compliance with the section, give information to the officer that is known to be false or misleading in a material respect.

Mens rea   The offences stated in the Act provide difficulties in regard to the writer who seeks to provide clear guidance on the constituent elements of the offence. The sections state what the person charged must do in order to come within the offences set out therein — the *actus reus* of the offence. In some marginal cases it is conceivable that the outcome of a case may turn on the question of whether a person keeps personal data or whether disclosure has taken place. It is also conceivable that as the provisions of the Act are set out, considerable uncertainty may arise on the question of whether all the offences are *mens rea* offences, that is, offences in respect of which the prosecution must establish a guilty mind, or whether some may be absolute or strict liability offences. It is submitted that there are three distinct problems.

Our analysis must start from the proposition that is a central element in the common law, that is, that where it is alleged that a criminal offence has been committed, it is necessary to establish that the accused intended those actions constituting the *actus reus* of the crime or was reckless in respect of the circumstances and consequences of his actions. While the requirement of *mens rea* can vary as between common law crimes, particularly murder and manslaughter, and while there are considered to be exceptions to the rule, even at common law, the requirement that the accused intend, or be reckless as to, the consequences of his actions is long established. However, where offences are statutory in nature the language of the statute may lead to different results. There are cases which indicate that a person may be convicted of a statutory offence because the statute is considered to have dispensed with the need to establish *mens rea*. The leading cases are *Prince*[8] and *Cundy v Le Coq*.[9]

In *Cundy v Le Coq* the defendant was convicted of selling intoxicating liquor to a drunken person, a statutory offence under section 13 of the Licensing Act 1872. The defendant did not know the person was drunk and it was established that the person had not displayed signs of drunkenness. Some sections of the Act contained the word 'knowingly'. Section 13 did not. It was held that the defendant was guilty. Cases of this kind are sometimes used to advance the view that if the words of a particular section in an Act use the word knowingly, or some other formula, there is a presumption that sections in the Act that also create offences, but which do not employ that word or formula, are strict liability offences. This view is now unacceptable.[10] If the offence is created by statute there is a presumption in favour of the view that *mens rea* must be proved. The words of the statute are likely to displace that presumption, when the words of the statute are viewed in the light of the subject matter with which it deals. In such a case the Courts consider whether the action proscribed is not so much criminal in any real sense but is such that it is in the public interest to prohibit under a penalty. Classical illustrations of such public interest statutory offences include food and drugs legislation[11] and building safety legislation,[12] the rationale being that such criminal liability will lead to the conviction of careless and inefficient persons who endanger a large number of persons. It is accepted that this approach is simplistic and some recent English cases demonstrate a retreat from strict liability,[13] particularly where it is shown that the imposition of strict liability would be unjust, as is the case where the defendant could not have ordered his affairs in a way which would promote observance of the statute. In *Gammon (Hong Kong) Ltd. v A.G. of Hong Kong*[14] the Judicial Committee of the Privy Council stated the law thus

> (1) there is a presumption of law that *mens rea* is required before a person can be held guilty of a criminal offence; (2) the presumption is particularly strong where the offence is "truly criminal" in character; (3) the presumption applies to statutory offences, and can be displaced only if this is clearly or by necessary implication the effect of the statute; (4) the only situation in which the presumption can be displaced is where the statute is concerned with an issue of social concern; public safety is such an issue; (5) even where a statute is concerned with such an issue, the presumption of *mens rea* stands unless it can also be shown that the creation of strict liability will be effective to promote the objects of the statute by encouraging greater vigilance to prevent the commission of the prohibited act.[15]

If we apply the above principles to the statutory offences set out in the Data Protection Act, 1988 then it appears to follow that all statutory offences require *mens rea*. Firstly, the sections 19(2) and (3), 20(1), 21(1) offences require *mens rea*. The offences require that the accused must 'knowingly' do the thing proscribed. As Devlin J said in *Roper v Taylor's Garage*,[16] '[a]ll that the word "knowingly" does is to say expressly what is normally implied.' Secondly, those statutory offences that do not use the word 'knowingly' or some other formula are not strict liability offences. The presumption in favour of a *mens rea* requirement is not displaced. So, the section 22(1) offence is not committed by accessing data or information and disclosing it to another person: an intention or recklessness must also be proved.[17] Thirdly, despite the reasoning in *Cundy v Le Coq*, it is not likely that the section 19(1), (4) and (5) offences are strict liability offences despite the existence of section 19(6), the subsection that designates certain section 19 offences (namely section 19(2) and (3) offences) to be expressly *mens rea* offences. The words of the Statute and the offences in question, that is, keeping or processing data while not registered as the Act requires, or failing to provide a change of address, are obviously issues of public concern but no more so than the other offences set out in the legislation. On the other hand, it can be argued that the position disclosed by section 19(6) of the Data Protection Act, 1988 is stronger than *Cundy v Le Coq* because section 19(6) distinguishes between offences in one section of the Act rather than as between different sections in the same Act. It could be further argued that any interpretation other than that the section 19(1), (4) and (5) offences are strict liability offences, while section 19(2) and (3) offences are *mens rea* offences, makes a nonsense of the section.

This argument is indirectly buttressed by the fact that some persons may escape criminal liability for offences under the Act by showing that they had reasonable cause for not observing the provisions of the Act. The section 10(9) enforcement notice provision, the section 11(13) prohibition notice provision and the section 12(5) information notice provision, as well as the section 24(6) offence of non compliance with the instructions of an authorised officer provision, give a defence of 'reasonable excuse'. On balance, however, the present writer feels that all offences in the Act are *mens rea* offences.

'Without reasonable excuse' The defence of 'reasonable excuse' has been considered in some English cases, particularly in the areas of planning law, public health law enforcement and landlord and tenant law. It is established by *A Lambert Flat Management Ltd v Lomas*[18] that a statutory notice requiring the person served to comply with the instructions therein is not to be challenged under a defence of 'reasonable excuse' by alleging that the notice was invalid. Such statutory defences are 'designed to provide a defence to a criminal charge where he had some reasonable excuse, such as some special difficulty in relation to compliance with the notice. It does not provide an opportunity, when prosecuted, to challenge the correctness and justification of the notice where the defendant has not availed himself of his statutory opportunity to do this by way of appeal'.[19] If this is good law in Ireland it means that a person charged with an offence which contains the reasonable excuse defence, where the offence relates to non-observance of an enforcement notice, prohibition notice,

or information notice, cannot allege during the prosecution that the notice is invalid. The statutory right of appeal under section 26 is the appropriate mechanism for relief in such cases.[20] Should the court find that there was evidence to support the view that the accused had a reasonable excuse for not complying with the notice, and if there is some evidence to support this, the defence may be made out.[20a] If however the law is unclear, or the law has been misstated by an official, it is probable that a defence of 'reasonable excuse' will be more difficult to establish.

Despite the maxim, *ignorantia iuris neminem excusat*, Ashworth[21] argues that the strength of the maxim has been sapped by the proliferation of statutory defences which provide a defence for the accused: the failure of the courts to provide guidance on reasonable excuse, he argues, makes reliance on official advice on the law, that advice being erroneous, perilous. Such a case should fall within the statutory defence. If this argument be correct, misinformation or a misinterpretation emanating from the Commissioner would be within the defence, but it is problematical whether incorrect advice from one's lawyer or accountant would be a 'reasonable excuse' for non-compliance with the order in question.

Offences by bodies corporate Section 29(1) provides that where an offence has been committed by a body corporate (e.g. the body corporate is a financial institution which has not registered but nevertheless it keeps automated personal data), and it is proved that the offence has been committed with the consent, connivance or is attributable to any neglect on the part of a person, being a director, manager, secretary or other officer of that body corporate, or a person purporting to act in that capacity, that person as well as the body corporate shall be guilty of an offence. The person is liable to be proceeded against and punished accordingly. Section 29(2) makes the same provision applicable to organisations run by members, e.g. co-operatives. If members are similarly culpable they too can be proceeded against separately.

This kind of provision is a common provision[22] and it can be most often seen in relation to certain offences contained in the Social Welfare Acts. Because all legal persons act via intermediaries it is thought necessary to broaden the class of those who may be potentially liable under the criminal law in order to encourage corporate officers to intervene so as to prevent the commission of a criminal offence by 'the corporation'. One way of ensuring this is to make collusion, negligence or passive acquiescence by an officer something for which the officer is to be criminally liable.

CIVIL LIABILITY

Civil liability under section 7 In the opening chapter of this book we considered some of the ways in which the infringement of a citizen's privacy may produce liability, either under the terms of the Constitution, the law of torts, confidence and other related forms of action, including statute law. It is conceivable that where the data protection principles in particular are not observed the data subject may avail of some of these causes of action. Indeed, in the following chapter we mention the possibility of an employer being liable in contract if the employer fails to observe the requirements of the Act and this failure is brought within the duty of trust and confidence which the employer owes to an employee. This is illustrative of the fact that the imaginative use of existing legal rights, concepts and remedies, can provide a data subject with reasonably optimistic prospects of compensation for loss caused by others who abuse the facilities afforded by information technology. However, we will now consider the cause of action conferred upon data subjects by section 7 of the Data Protection Act, 1988. Section 7 of the Act provides:

> for the purposes of the law of torts and to the extent that that law does not so provide, a person, being a data controller or a data processor, shall, so far as regards the collection by him of personal data or information, intended for inclusion in such data or his dealing with such data, owe a duty of care to the data subject concerned.

This part of section 7 establishes a statutory duty of care but it does so really by way of declaration rather than elucidation. Clearly, many information holders owe a duty of care to persons who use that information. The development of the law of torts has, in the twentieth century, been primarily concerned with establishing the extent to which liability for physical and then economic or purely economic loss can be kept within manageable boundaries. It is evident that the law of tort implicitly recognises that a data controller owes a duty of care in respect of data subjects concerned, under the ordinary law of tort. It is also probable that a data processor owes a duty of care to data controllers, as well as data subjects. If data is processed or controlled negligently the data subject affected would be proximate enough to the data processor or data controller to establish a remedy in tort. In *Lawton v BOC Transhield Ltd*[23] the plaintiff had been made redundant by the defendants. He had worked for the defendants for ten years. The plaintiff applied for other employment and gave the defendants name as a reference. The plaintiff was offered temporary employment by another company but before the job was made permanent the references were taken up. The reference given by the defendants was unfavourable and the plaintiff even lost his temporary job. The plaintiff was subsequently unemployed for two years: he brought an action alleging that this loss had been caused by the defendants negligently providing an inaccurate or unfair reference. In the High Court, Tudor-Evans J found for the plaintiff and awarded damages of £7,550, representing the loss of wages he would have earned in employment. The central issue before the court was not whether the reference was misleading or unfair — it was clearly compiled without due care and attention being exercised by the defendants — but whether a duty of care existed. On these facts Tudor-Evans J held that the duty existed. The defendants knew a reference was required for employment purposes. They knew or ought to have known that they were being relied on to provide an accurate reference or a reference that a prudent employer would give. On these facts it was also foreseeable that if the duty was broken then financial loss would result for the plaintiff.

The importance of section 7 must not be overlooked. The statute closes the issue of proximity in favour of the plaintiff by declaring that the duty of care exists *vis-à-vis* all data subjects who are in some way concerned by the activities of data controllers and data processors. This however seems to refer to the data subject in respect of whom personal data is kept or processed by the data controller or data processor. Members of the data subject's family do not seem to come within the section 7 duty of care. We can illustrate this by an example. Suppose a data controller provides information on X, a relative of Y, as part of a security clearance exercise directed at establishing whether Y is a suitable appointee to employment which brings Y within contact with information possessing profound national security implications. The data controller wrongly indicates that X has a long history of subversive or criminal activities. Y does not get the job because of the security risk. Y cannot, it seems, bring an action under section 7. X may bring an action in defamation, and if nervous shock or emotional distress is caused, X could probably recover damages in negligence against the data controller, but this is hardly of relevance to Y.

Section 7 may also be of limited utility in cases where economic loss is caused, not to the data subject, but to some other party who, in an appropriate case, may decide to bring an action in tort for negligence or negligent mis-statement. If we return to the facts of *Lawton v BOC Transhield Ltd* (*supra*) and adapt them slightly, a credible tort action can be devised. Suppose the reference is given in respect of a former employee who happens to be a specialist in a particular field. The reference is requested by a company, that company representing the only realistic chance the former employee has of finding suitable employment because of that persons degree of specialisation. The reference is compiled by reference to an automated file which holds personal data which is stale or inaccurate. The reference is unfavourable so the post is not filled. Because it remains vacant, loss to the company results. When the inaccurate nature of the reference comes to light, could the data subject and the prospective employer both sue for damages in negligence (or conceivably fraud) and thereby recover their loss of salary and lost expenditure/profits respectively? Such a cause of action may be open via the law of negligence but it cannot be predicated on a section 7 cause of action.

The basis of section 7   The basis for section 7 seems to be, in part, the Lindop Report.[24] In Lindop's view the promulgation of codes of practice, the power of an enforcement agency to require compliance with data protection laws, as well as the emphasis on producing an enlightened and educated population of data users, were of primary importance: 'data protection law should be preventative rather than remedial: it should seek to ensure that things did not go wrong in the first place.' Lindop however accepted that where data subjects are harmed by a data user who fails to observe a code of practice, a civil remedy under the Act is to be available, in addition to any contractual or tortious remedy already available.[25] The role of the code of practice was central to this suggestion. If the code was being observed the statutory civil remedy was not available.

The point of contact between Lindop and the Data Protection Act, 1988 is as follows. The Act gives a new civil remedy, in addition to any existing contract or tort liability, as Lindop recommended. However, if a code of practice is being observed in Ireland by a data controller or data processor, that code, having the force of law under section 13, it is unlikely that an Irish court would hold that the section 7 duty of care has been broken. While sections 7 and 13 are silent on this point, adherence to such a code of practice is going to provide compelling, if not conclusive, evidence that the duty of care is satisfied.[26]

However, even in the UK the Lindop recommendation was not followed on the issue of compensation. The White Paper[27] and the UK Data Protection Act 1984 follow Lindop to the extent that a right to compensation for harm caused by inaccurate data[28] or data that is lost or disclosed in an unauthorised manner.[29] The Act however does not extend to codes of practice the authoritative quality envisaged by Lindop. The UK law however does seem to provide a much more straightforward statutory cause of action although it does not give the Registrar any role in securing compensation for the data subject.

The section 7 duty of care is, it is submitted, quite unsatisfactory in several respects. Firstly, the data subject is required to prove negligence and, as such, the difficulties of proof may be considerable. The Act provides no clear guidance to the data subject on whether the Commissioner's investigative reports, if any, are to be available and what evidentiary value such a report is to have. The data subject is obliged to fund orthodox litigation, a very problematical state of affairs for a person of modest means, particularly when civil legal aid in tort cases is not readily available. At least one submission to the Oireachtas Committee on Data Protection and Freedom of Information suggested that the statutory agency charged with supervision of data protection law be given the power to order, or at least recommend, the payment of compensation to data subjects as being a necessary part of an effective enforcement mechanism. Like the Registrar in the UK, the Commissioner in Ireland has no such power, discretionary or otherwise. This, it is submitted, is a very substantial shortcoming in the 1988 Act.

An interesting variation on the choice between a straightforward criminal sanction and an action in contract or tort for personal injury, loss or damage is provided by the Consumer Information Act, 1978. Following a summary prosecution for an offence under that Act, it is possible for a person who appears as witness and who has suffered personal injury, loss or damage, to bring an application[30] for payment of the fine, or a specified part thereof, as compensation in respect of the injury loss or damage. Such an application under the Data Protection Act, 1988, at the time a data controller is prosecuted under section 19, for example, may be a very pragmatic way of compensating a complainant under section 10. It is also pertinent to point out that some quasi-judicial bodies have a power to recommend the payment of compensation to persons who have complained about an infringement of rights, whether the right be a common law or statutory right. The role of the Rights Commissioner and the Labour Court, for example,[31] as statutory bodies that can recommend or order the payment of compensation illustrate the point that there is no obvious constitutional impediment to conferring a power to recommend or award compensation to an administrative agency or body, especially when that body is under statute, independent. The reason why no such power was taken under the Data Protection Act, 1988 seems to be financial rather than one of legal principle. If the Commissioner were to be empowered to make recommendations or awards there would have to be a substantial increase in the resources made available to the Commissioner, not least of which would be in the area of manpower.

The proviso The relationship between the section 7 duty of care and the tort of negligence is further underlined by the proviso to section 7. Under the proviso a data controller is deemed to have complied with section 2(1)(b) of the Act, that is, the obligation to keep accurate data and keep it up-to-date, if the data controller has, and continues to have, an accurate record of data or other informa- tion received by the data controller from the data subject or a third party. If the data is disclosed the disclosure must be accompanied by a statement stating that the information constituting the data was received in this manner and, where appropriate, the disclosure must set out that the data subject has informed the data controller that the data subject regards the data as inaccurate and not up to date, as well as any supplementary statement appended under section 6.

It is conceivable that any independent cause of action — negligent misstatement, breach of contract or breach of confidence — could still result in a data controller who meets the section 7 proviso being liable in damages. The proviso clearly states that the defence is only available for the purpose of section 7 actions only and the section 2(1)(b) data protection principle. If data is inaccurate and the data controller could have, or, with reasonable diligence would have been able to see that the data is obviously incorrect, the negligent misstatement action is likely to result in an award of damages against the data controller. The proviso has no relevance to any situation in which personal data is improperly used. If the data subject suffers loss because data has been improperly disclosed, within the terms of section 2(1)(c) for example, the proviso is irrelevant, even in a section 7 tort action.

Damages If damages are awarded the measure of damages may be substantial. While pure economic loss is problematical — the defendant should always take the point that pure economic loss is too remote in order to take advantage of the considerable uncertainty that surrounds this issue in English law at least,[32] the plaintiff who can establish emotional distress, nervous shock, and ill-health is likely to be awarded damages to compensate for these heads of loss. If the plaintiff can establish that data was obtained by an invasion of privacy such as physical intrusion into the home of the plaintiff it is possible that aggravated, exemplary or punitive damages may be awarded.[33] This is particularly likely in cases where the defendant is a state agency or a public authority. A supplementary claim for damages for conspiracy to infringe the Constitutional rights of a citizen may also be possible in an appropriate case. For recent cases concerning the measure of damages for tortious misrepresentation see Burrows, *Remedies for Torts and Breach of Contract*.[34]

10

The Data Protection Act in the workplace

INTRODUCTION

The Act was, to all intents and purposes, in force on 19 April 1989. In order to appreciate the impact the legislation will have in respect of commercial activities generally, it is, for illustrative purposes, useful to reflect on the effect the Act will have on the employment relationship. Indeed, experience in the UK after over one year of the Act being in operation indicates that employees are the most likely group of persons to seek to access personal data. The question of subject access rights in the workplace is only one of several significant matters that the Act addresses. In this chapter we will consider these matters under the following headings:

the data protection principles

subject access rights

contractual and tortious remedies available to the employee

statutory duties and the employee

vicarious liability .

THE DATA PROTECTION PRINCIPLES

In the normal course of the employment relationship a considerable amount of information may be obtained and stored about an employee and indeed the employee's family. If that data is disposed of, or is kept on a manual filing system, then there is not much likelihood of the Act being relevant to these operations. However, if personal data is kept on an automated system then the data protection principles set out in the Act are applicable, regardless of whether registration is necessary. If the employer does not want the employee to have access to this data, or if he does not want to take care to collect, revise and dispose of data,[1] it should be transferred to a manual filing system. This is not always practicable when an automated system is already in use so most employers will be obliged to observe the provisions of the Act. Why? The use of information technology has inherent dangers. The prospects of data being corrupted, accessed by others, or disclosed to others, are generally greater than where manual files are used. Where the data is sensitive data the probability of the data subject being harmed or prejudiced are substantial. Even if the data is accurate the individual may still be entitled to feel that the unauthorised use of such data is wrongful in both a moral and a legal sense. To this end, the Act sets out certain standards of conduct the data controller must seek to observe.

A moments reflection may indicate the range of information an employer may hold on an employee. The employee's age, address, marital status will probably be known. If paid by standing order the employees bank account will be known. His trade union affiliation, if any, may be known. If the employee is a member of an occupational pension scheme or has been absent from work due to illness the employer may have access to medical data. The employer may have details about the employees past — place of birth, previous employment or details about criminal convictions and periods of detention, e.g. internment in the 1940s, and 50s. This information may have been given in confidence. At the time of disclosure it may have been pertinent to the employment relationship but should the employer hold onto this information for ever? Section 2 sets out the data protection principles which seek to address issues of this kind.

(i) **The fairly obtaining and processing principle**   Suppose the employee provides information to the employer for a limited purpose but the employer has misled the employee. The information will be used for a quite distinct purpose. The employee may complain that the information has not been obtained fairly, e.g. the employee was told the information would be used in connection with an occupational pension scheme when in fact the employer intends to use it for direct mailing purposes. The employer, if he is to meet the requirements of the Act must observe certain rules:

- the employee should be told why the information is needed.
- the employee should be given an explanation of the use to which information is to be put and whether any other use is contemplated.
- the information should not be used for any other purpose. Additionally, the word fairly, as used in the Act, comprehends lawfully too. The interception of mail or telephone conversations in order to gain information is clearly unlawful. However, the compilation of data by reference to other sources — e.g. obtaining data from colleagues or trade union officials is not unlawful[2] but it is hardly good industrial relations practice.

A prudent employer, in the first instance, will seek information from the employee. Where the employee is being evaluated by a colleague or foreman and a report is produced, this is of course permissible.[3] The disgruntled employee's remedy is under the subject access provision in section 4.

(ii) **Data shall be accurate and kept up to date** The Act obliges the employer to take care in relation to the compilation and the upkeep of personal data. Information that is inaccurate is as likely to cause damage to the data as information that is used for some uncontemplated purpose. Statements about a workers' job performance, time-keeping and the like must be revised and reviewed.[4] Back-up data need only be kept up to date[5] if it is at some stage used by the data controller.

(iii) **Data shall be kept for specified and lawful purposes** This means that if data is kept for some other purpose, a complaint to, and investigation by, the Commissioner may result in prosecution under section 19. The possibility that some disgruntled former employee, who is aware of data being kept in breach of this principle, is a real one. The employer should make sure that the entry on the register is kept up to date in order to minimize the prospects of breach of this requirement, a requirement which directly leads to criminal prosecution. If the purpose is not lawful, e.g. personal data is used to incite racial hatred, registration is unlikely to take place. Employment blacklists are also not likely to be acceptable to the Commissioner but the entry on the register will not always be enough to disclose this specific purpose, e.g. 'recruitment', would be an adequate description for the purpose of effecting a registration.

(iv) **Data will not be used or disclosed in any manner incompatible with those purposes** Once the register states the use or disclosure purposes, the entry is conclusive. For example, data kept on employees is not to be used for direct mailing unless the entry specifies this. This principle however is not going to inhibit the transmission of personal data within an organisation. The entry on the register (see question 3 on the DPA1 form) and the description (see question 4 on the DPA1 form) is not misleading if, for example, data for 'payroll', or 'worker competency assessment' or the like is stipulated. 'Recruitment' or 'welfare fund' or some other description will also be adequate.[6]

(v) **Data shall be adequate, relevant and not excessive in relation to that purpose** This principle directs that a rule of proportionality in respect of the keeping of personal data is required. Some details may be quite irrelevant. Questions about a person's religion are likely to be irrelevant to most kinds of employment. Questions about the employee's marital state, are also unlikely to be relevant. Details about a person's employment record in the distant past, or scholastic achievements, may also be suspect under the proportionality rule.

(vi) **Data must not be kept for longer than is necessary**   Data about an employee's criminal past may be relevant at the time of recruitment. But what if the employee serves conscientiously for many years? At some stage that data will be stale or irrelevant. Because of the danger that could follow from this data being accessed by fellow employees it should be deleted. Subject access searches will throw up cases of this kind.

(viii) **The security principle**   This principle is probably the principle that will have the most impact on work practices within an organisation. Because data controllers and data processors are required by the Act to initiate and maintain appropriate security measures against unauthorised access to, alteration, disclosure or destruction of personal data, as well as against accidental loss or destruction of personal data, there will be significant cost and practical implications. Firstly, the questions on DPA1 for data controllers indicate that the Commissioner will require evidence of physical restrictions and technical obstacles to be in place. For example, is access to computer equipment and personal data open access? Could members of the public gain entry to a building where data is accessible? Can all employees gain access to data, e.g. personnel records on other employees, with minimal effort? At the technical level, how effective are internal security measures? Are passwords exchanged within an organisation? Are passwords discontinued, e.g. when an employee leaves the organisation or a particular department? Is particular care directed at protecting sensitive personal data like medical records?

Note also that these questions must be honestly addressed by data controllers and processors. Providing false information at the time of registration is a criminal offence under section 20(2).

THE EMPLOYER'S COURSE OF ACTION

It is vital that an employer is provided by his employees, independent contractors or persons who are affiliated to the employer in some way, (e.g. a consultant or researcher employed by someone else but who has access to personal data) with a comprehensive statement on the use to which equipment is put, the extent to which persons access or indeed use data held by the employer, and the extent to which this data is made available to others. Without this kind of cooperation it is not going to be possible to adhere to the Act and it is likely that an offence will be committed by both the data controller as well as the employee or other person who acts in this way. Obviously, if an employee is going to use an employer's facilities and data for an unauthorised purpose (e.g. compile a mailing list to solicit orders for a private activity that benefits that employee) the employee is not always going to cooperate. This leads onto the crucial point. An employer must train and educate. If the employer is unambiguous about the Act, and this is brought home to employees, then any serious departure should be regarded as a breach of contract, specifically breach of the employee's duty to serve the employer honestly and faithfully. Disciplinary action such as transfer to some other department, withdrawal of access rights, or even dismissal, will be necessary.

SUBJECT ACCESS RIGHTS

An employee is entitled to obtain access to personal data which relates to himself. The subject access rights in section 4 are exercisable by employees. The remedies given in sections 6 and 7 are also available. The question of how the employer responds to a subject access request will throw up a number of issues.

Firstly, how should the employer cope with subject access requests? It may be desirable for the employer to encourage the workforce to make subject access requests at a particular time, e.g. gear up the data processing, the personnel division, or whatever department holds or controls personal data, to respond during a given week. This is sometimes achieved by circular or by agreement with unions. On the question of the fee some UK companies have insisted on employees paying the prescribed fee. This has caused industrial relations problems. It may be prudent for an employer to use the fee as an incentive, e.g. waive the fee if an employee makes a subject access request at a particular time. Other organisations may insist on charging the fee as a method of deterring employees from making subject access requests altogether.

When a subject access request is made, all personal data held must be disclosed. The Irish Act does not follow the UK Act in exempting statements of opinion (e.g. 'In my view this employee lacks initiative'.). Delicate issues may arise, e.g. where an unfavourable report on an employee has been compiled. The data controller may seek to exclude the identity of the author of the report. This can be achieved under section 4(4).

EMPLOYEE RIGHTS AND REMEDIES

A data controller who fails to take reasonable care in regard to the collection and use of personal data may be liable in tort to a data subject who suffers loss as a result of breach of that duty to take reasonable care. Obvious examples include:

(i) obtaining or using personal data from a source without taking reasonable steps to verify the accuracy of the data or the reliability of the source, e.g. incorrectly state in a reference that X has a prison record and may therefore not be reliable.

(ii) failure to take reasonable steps to prevent unauthorised disclosure.

(iii) failure to delete stale or inaccurate data which is made available to others, whether authorised or not.

(iv) failure to install adequate security systems and procedures allowing hackers to access personal data, particularly sensitive data.

A data controller who provides data which is incorrect and which is damaging to the reputation of another, e.g. an employer gives a very unflattering or hostile reference — 'Jones is a thief but I can't prove it' — could be liable in the tort of defamation. Similarly, an employer who intercepts mail or telephone conversations is possibly liable for breach of the citizens constitutional right to privacy.[7]

If the employer fails to safeguard personal data or makes public his views about an employee, this could possibly result in contractual liability. At the level of general principle it must be noted that the courts have recognised that a degree of trust and confidence must exist between employers and employees and, further, that there are obligations on both parties that should be observed. In *Robinson v Crompton Parkinson Ltd*[8] it was stated:

> In a contract of employment, and in conditions of employment, there has to be mutual trust and confidence between master and servant. Although most of the reported cases deal with the master seeking a remedy against a servant or former servant for acting in breach of confidence or breach of trust, that action can only be upon the basis that trust and confidence is mutual. Consequently where a man says of his employer, 'I claim you have broken your contract because you have clearly shown you have no confidence in me, and you behaved in a way which is contrary to that mutual trust, which ought to exist between master and servant', he is entitled in those circumstances, it seems to us, to say that there is conduct which amounts to a repudiation of the contract.[9]

While the cases in which this proposition has been specifically tested[10] concern the question of whether it is a repudiatory breach of contract for an employer to arbitrarily and capriciously refuse to grant a pay increase to one particular employee, while improving the pay rates for other workers, this principle has not been rejected in any subsequent English case-law. It would appear to be arguable that where a worker discovers that an employer has unfairly singled out an employee for an unfavourable evaluation, the above principle is infringed. If, for example, an employee finds out that information has been passed on to others which is harmful to that employee and the employer can be said to be acting arbitrarily or capriciously, that conduct is a repudiatory breach of contract. However in *Murco Petroleum Ltd v Forge*[11] Kilner Brown J held that a critical and probably unfair assessment of an employee does not constitute arbitrary or capricious behaviour: if the evaluation is made and it leads to an unfavourable decision (e.g. lack of promotion or no salary increase) the decision, even if unreasonable, is not necessarily arbitrary or capricious. It would be arbitrary or capricious, it is submitted, for an employer to produce an evaluation of the workforce and, acting upon that evaluation, refuse promotion to some unfavourably assessed workers while promoting others who receive a similar assessment. Indeed, there is very oblique authority for the proposition that conduct which represents a departure from good industrial relations practice may constitute a breach of contract.[12] Apart from the possibility of disclosure of personal data given to an employer in confidence having the effect of producing civil liability, via the law of confidence,[13] the careless use of information in respect of employees or even former employees will be actionable under *Hedley Byrne. Lawton v BOC Transhield Ltd*[14] establishes that a carelessly compiled reference in respect of a former employee, which is to be used by a third party in order to assist in evaluating that former employee, may result in liability to that former employee. The principle clearly governs similar references when the subject remains in the employment of the compiler of the reference.

LEGAL DUTIES FOR EMPLOYEES

(i) **Registration** The Act imposes duties on employees, even if the employee is not a data controller or data processor. It must be emphasised that employees may, in certain cases, be registrable or must respond, as individuals, to subject access requests. An employee who uses data equipment at home in order to perform certain work related tasks is likely to be a data controller in his own right. In the majority of cases such a data controller is not going to have to register but this does not deflect attention from the basic fact that there remains a likelihood that the Act is applicable. A personnel manager who maintains an automated data file at home on employees is likely to be registrable. A consultant surgeon employed by a hospital who maintains medical records at home on a p.c. is also likely to be registrable. In any event, such a person much respond to section 3 and 4 requests, when made by data subjects.

(ii) **The disclosure principle** An employer who informs a colleague about details relating to a data subject may, in certain circumstances, be held to have infringed the disclosure principle. For example, employee X comes across personal data about Z; X informs A, Z's neighbour, about this as a matter of idle gossip. X infringes the disclosure principle. However, disclosure that takes place in order to allow an employee or agent to carry out his or her duties is not a disclosure under section 1(1). The question of one employee passing on information to a fellow employee is not dealt with in the Act but an employee, while not a data controller, should be able to pass on personal data to another employee for employment purposes without infringing the disclosure principle. Even if breach of the disclosure principle takes place, the non-registrable data controller is subject to the enforcement procedure mechanism under sections 10(2) and (3).

(iii) **Enforcement procedures** An employee could be identified via the registration process as the person responsible under the Act for failure to meet the requirements of the Act in section 2. Should the enforcement notice or information notice procedure be used and the notice requires that employee to respond, failure to do so, without a reasonable excuse, could result in criminal liability under section 10(9).

(iv) **Registrable data controllers — offences** Note that the registration process requires a data controller to nominate a person to whom inquiries are to be addressed. If the Act is to be observed within the organisation this should be a person of authority and expertise. There is no point in nominating a minor clerical assistant. That employee or officer must be aware of what the Act requires or difficulties will follow. The employee must possess sufficient status to be able to exert pressure on senior personnel to comply with the Act.

The restrictions on use, source, disclosure or transfer of data,[15] apply to employees or agents of a registrable data controller. Contravention of section 19 results in liability for any person who contravenes. This means that the data controller commits an offence and the employee in question also commits an offence. Note that section 19 relates to registrable data controller and employees only. Non-observance of section 2(1) by non-registrable data controllers and employees is not *per se* criminal. Non-compliance with enforcement notices and prohibition notices will result in criminal liability under sections 10 and 12.

Section 21 of the Act provides for a criminal offence in providing mis-information at time of registration. The offence is very broad. An employer who instructs an employee to provide materially false or misleading information will commit a criminal offence. So will the employee providing the incorrect information. Note that the employee does not have a defence of 'reasonable excuse' — e.g. coercion by the employer — and a defence of duress is not likely to succeed in such circumstance.[16]

(v) Data processors — offences All data processors are registrable. Processing personal data when there is no entry in respect of their processor is an offence. Employees who do this, with knowledge of non registration also it seems commit offences. The section 21 misinformation offence applies to data processors and employees also.

(vi) Miscellaneous criminal offences The section 22 offence is potentially of enormous impact and it can be seen as reinforcing the security principle in section 2(1), as well as the tort duty of care provision in section 7. If personal data is accessed without the prior authority of the data controller, or data processor, by whom the data is kept and it is disclosed to another person, the person obtaining and disclosing commits an offence. While the offence can only be committed by someone breaking into an information system, e.g. hacking into personal data, when the hacker is not an employee[17] the dangers of allowing an independent contract or contractor, or someone else's employee, access to personal data in respect of which he is not authorised, and that person then disclosing to another, are substantial. It would of course be arguable that such facts would point up a failure to implement an effective security policy which would give rise to breach of section 2(1)(d) which in turn would raise the spectre of tort liability via the principle of vicarious liability.

The section 24 obstruction offence is also important. An employer who, through ignorance of the law, refuses to comply with an authorised officer's request could be criminally liable. Education of personnel and other employees is essential if the employee is not to perhaps, unwittingly, commit an offence.

The section 29 offence is also of vital importance. A company officer who does not actually commit the offence, e.g. does not provide false information (section 21) or obstruct the authorised officer (section 24) can nevertheless be personally guilty of an offence in criminal proceedings. An officer of the company who turns a blind eye to the shortcomings of the company is liable to conviction as well as the company and, presumably, the employee in question.

VICARIOUS LIABILITY

This phrase describes two basic situations which may arise in such a way as to create liability for an employer in respect of acts committed by an employee, or perhaps an independent contractor. Firstly, the employer, A, may incur liability to a member of the public, C, for negligent or other tortious[18] acts committed by an employee, B. It is not a condition of A's liability that A participate in any way in procuring the commission of the tort. As long as A stands in a relationship to B that makes it reasonable to fix A with liability, or perhaps more accurately, give C, the victim, the choice of seeking redress from either, or both, A and B, a case of true vicarious liability will arise. The second sense in which the phrase vicarious liability is used is, in reality, a case where the employer, A, incurs liability to C because A has chosen to discharge contractual or tortious duties that A owed to C via B, an intermediary. For example, if A owes a duty to C but, e.g., he negligently selects B, an employee or independent contractor, to perform that duty on A's behalf, an act or default by B creates direct or primary liability for A *vis-à-vis* C.[19]

Liability is visited upon the employer as long as a breach of duty can be established on the part of the employer, the employee or, in some cases, an independent contractor.

In the context of the Data Protection Act, 1988 it would be pertinent to speculate on the kind of events that could possibly occur. An employee may carry out contractual duties in a way which infringes the data protection principles: the employee may, for example, provide information which is inaccurate or misleading about an individual and thereby causes loss or distress. The employee may divulge personal data to an unauthorised disclosee. The issue that arises is whether the person prejudiced by this may sue the employer for the tortious or even criminal conduct of that person's servant, even if the employer was not negligent or the act committed was in no way advantageous to the employer. The concept of vicarious liability has expanded considerably over the centuries. In the seventeenth century liability was extended from cases where a master gave express instructions to a servant and applied also to cases of implied commands, the issue of whether an implied command had been given being tested by reference to the general authority conferred on the servant by the master.[20]

The course of employment   On the issue of the vicarious liability of employers and its evolution from the concept of an employers primary liability, the eighteenth century saw the judges asking whether a relationship existed which made it possible or desirable to visit the carelessness of a servant at the door of the master, and the answer to this question began to centre on whether the wrong could be said to have occurred 'in the course of employment'.

If we accept that the relationship of employer and employee exists between the person who has committed the wrong (the tortfeasor) and the employer, the central issue becomes whether the act occurred in the course of employment. The issue is not simply whether the wrong committed was expressly or impliedly authorised.[21] Additionally, the issue can be tested by considering whether the employee has done an authorised thing in an unauthorised manner or has done something necessarily incidental to that which the employee is authorised to do. Thus, cases where an employee is expressly prohibited from doing a thing, rather than merely being prohibited from doing that thing in a particular manner, may lead to the employer being able to avoid vicarious liability. For example, if a data controller expressly prohibited employees from keeping sensitive personal data on either manual or automated files, but in breach of this instruction an employee negligently compiles an automated file holding sensitive personal data, that file in some way leading to economic loss for a data subject, then vicarious liability may be avoided. the prohibition in such an example is directed at the sphere of employment itself rather than the manner in which the employment task is performed.[22]

Wilful acts of no benefit to the employer   It is also clear that the employer may be liable for fraudulent acts committed by an employee, even if the act was not intended to benefit the employer but, for example, was intended to be of sole benefit to the employee or another. In *United Africa Co. v Owoade*[23] the appellants had given goods for carriage into the custody of the respondents employees, at the request of the respondent, in order to enable the goods to be transported. The employees stole the goods. The Privy Council held the employer liable for the servant's fraud, perpetrated in the course of the respondents' business, regardless of whether the fraud was for the employers benefit or not. The leading case, *Lloyd v Grace Smith & Co.*,[24] has been followed in Ireland, at least in cases where the tortious act is fraudulent conversion by the employee and it occurs in the course of employment.[25] Instances in which the employee steps outside the course of his employment can be found in the Irish reports[26] although these cases, which involve the transport industry or the manufacturing industry, are of little immediate relevance to the data processing industry.

Where the facts of a case indicate a wilful and deliberate attempt to breach or repudiate the contract of employment, the guiding principle already mentioned, namely, the doing of an authorised act in an unauthorised manner[27] cannot always be relied upon, as the recent case of *General Engineering Services Ltd v Kingston and St Andrew Corporation*[28] illustrates. A fire broke out in the appellant's premises in Kingston, Jamaica. The local fire brigade were called. Normally the journey from the station to the premises would take three and a half minutes. The firemen, as part of industrial action in support of a pay claim, worked a go-slow, i.e. they drove the fire engine forward, stopped, then proceeded forward again, and so on. It took seventeen minutes to reach the fire. The premises had completely burnt down because of the delay caused by this industrial action. The appellant brought an action against the fire authority alleging the authority was vicariously responsible. The Privy Council, upholding the decision of the Jamaica Court of Appeal, held that this could not be regarded as an unauthorised method of performing an authorised act. Lord Ackner giving the judgment of the Board said

the members of the fire brigade were not acting in the course of their

employment when they, by their conduct . . . permitted the destruction of
the building and its contents. Their unauthorised and wrongful act was so
to prolong the time taken by the journey to the scene of the fire, as to ensure
that they did not arrive in time to extinguish it, before the building and its
contents were destroyed. Their mode and manner of driving, the slow
progression of stopping and starting, was not so connected with the
authorised act, that is, driving to the scene of the fire as expeditiously as
reasonably possible, as to be a mode of performing that act.

For all the practical difference it would have made, they might . . . just
as well have waited in the fire station, until they were confident that the
building and its contents were beyond saving.[29]

The fire authority were held not vicariously liable for the tortious acts of their
employees.

In these cases the analysis is directed at whether the wrongful act is committed for a purpose which is quite outside the purpose for which the employer
has engaged the employee. It is necessary to establish some nexus between the
act (particularly in cases of criminal acts) committed by the employee and the
circumstances of the employment.[30] In *Heasmans (a firm) v Clarity Cleaning
Co.*[31] the Court of Appeal stressed that because employment creates for an
employee the opportunity to commit wrongful or criminal acts, this will not
necessarily lead to liability for an employer. Clarity Cleaning Co. provided
office cleaning services to the plaintiffs. The cleaners, engaged under a contract
of employment, were allowed after hours access to the plaintiffs building. One
employee was required to dust and disinfect telephones. The employee used the
telephones to make calls, thereby incurring large charges to the plaintiffs. In an
action the plaintiffs sought to make Clarity Cleaning Co. liable for the wrongful
acts of their employee. It was accepted on all sides that the defendants had not
been negligent in engaging this particular employee. The Court of Appeal found
the employer not liable. The authorised act, cleaning of telephones, could not
be considered to have been done in an unauthorised manner. The use of the
telephone could not be regarded as cleaning: it was another and entirely separate
act. The Irish courts[32] have been particularly slow to extend the vicarious
liability concept to cover criminal acts by an employee on the ground that no
employer, expressly or impliedly, would authorise such an act. However,
because the test is not so much whether the act is authorised but whether the
employer exercises a degree of control over that other person,[33] vicarious
liability can arise in cases of delegation. Egan J has recently held that an
employer will be vicariously liable for the wrongful, even criminal acts,
committed by the delegate. In *Johnson and Johnson (Ireland) Ltd v C.P.
Security Ltd*[34] the defendants, a specialist security firm who contracted to
provide a service to the plaintiff, were held vicariously liable for the theft of

property owned by the plaintiffs, the property being stolen by an employee of the defendants employed to safeguard property such as this. The employee in question was convicted of having taken the goods in question. Egan J, following English authorities,[35] awarded damages to the plaintiffs against the defendant for the criminal conduct of the defendant's employee because the defendants had been specifically engaged to safeguard the plaintiff's property.

These elementary principles allow us to provide some guidance on possible issues of vicarious liability that the Act may throw up. Firstly, a person employed to collate or compile data, or to use information extracted from data, will produce vicarious liability if this is done negligently. Even if that employee, for example, uses information for his own purposes (e.g. to defame another, to embezzle funds) vicarious liability may result, although it is a nice question of degree as to whether an authorised act may be done in such a way as to be outside the scope of the employment, as in the Jamaican fire brigade case.[36] On the other hand, if the wrongful act is done by an employee who has not enjoyed direct contact with the data processing or data holding activities of the employer, vicarious liability will be difficult to establish. Perhaps a security guard or an equipment maintenance engineer who accesses and divulges personal data to another would not create vicarious liability on the ground that there is no nexus between the act and the circumstances of the employment tasks which are properly discharged by such an employee.[37] If the employee commits a criminal offence which is also wrongful or tortious in the sense that a data subject suffers actionable loss as a result thereof, it is clear that the fact that a criminal offence has been committed will not prevent vicarious liability for attaching. For example, should an employee of a data controller be convicted of a section 19(3) offence, e.g. keeping personal data whilst not registered, vicarious liability may result for the data controller even if, for example, the data controller is not convicted of a section 19(2) offence. Note however that some criminal offences in the Act cannot be committed by employees or agents.[38]

SI No. 347 of 1988: Data Protection (Fees) Regulations, 1988

I, GERARD COLLINS, Minister for Justice, in exercise of the powers conferred on me by sections 4, 16 and 17 of the Data Protection Act, 1988 (No. 25 of 1988), hereby, with the consent of the Minister for Finance, make the following regulations:

1. These Regulations may be cited as the Data Protection (Fees) Regulations, 1988.
2. In these Regulations 'the Act' means the Data Protection Act, 1988 (No. 25 of 1988).
3. An amount of £5 is hereby prescribed for the purposes of section 4(1)(c)(i) of the Act.
4. A fee of £2 is hereby prescribed for the purpose of section 16(3)(b) of the Act.
5. A fee of £100 is hereby prescribed for the purposes of section 17(2) of the Act in respect of an application for registration.
6. (1) A fee of £100 is hereby prescribed for the purposes of section 17(7) of the Act in respect of an application for continuance of registration.
    (2) A fee of £50 is hereby prescribed for the purposes of section 17(7) of the Act in respect of an application for alteration of the particulars in an entry in the register.

Given under my Official Seal,
this 16 day of December 1988.

GERARD COLLINS
Minister for Justice

The Minister for Finance consents to the making of the foregoing regulations.

Given under the Official Seal
of the Minister for Finance,
this 16 day of December, 1988.

ALBERT REYNOLDS
Minister for Finance

Explanatory Note
(This note is not part of the Instrument and does not purport to be a legal interpretation.)
These regulations prescribe the various fees payable under the Data Protection Act 1988: £5 (Maximum) for obtaining access to data kept in relation to an individual; £2 for obtaining a certified copy of particulars in an entry in the register maintained under the Act; £100 for each registration of a person who is required to register or for continuing a registration; and £50 for altering particulars in an entry in the register.

SI No. 349 of 1988: Data Protection Act, 1988
(Commencement) Order, 1988

I, GERARD COLLINS, Minister for Justice, in exercise of the powers conferred on me by section 35 of the Data Protection Act, 1988 (No. 25 of 1988), hereby make the following order:
1. This Order may be cited as the Data Protection Act, 1988 (Commencement) Order, 1988.
2. In this Order 'the Act' means the Data Protection Act, 1988 (No. 25 of 1988).
3. The 9th day of January, 1989, is hereby fixed as the day on which the following provisions of the Act shall come into operation, namely:
    (a) sections 1, 9, 16 (other than subsection (3)), 17, 28, 20, 26 (other than paragraphs (a),
        (b) and (d) of subsection (1) and subsection (4)), 32, to 35, and
    (b) the Second and Third Schedules.
4. The 19th day of April, 1989, is hereby fixed as the day on which the Act (other than sections 6(2)(b) and 10(7)(b) and the provisions specified in Regulation 3 of these Regulations) shall come into operation.

Given under my Official Seal
this 19 day of December, 1988.

GERARD COLLINS
Minister for Justice

Explanatory Note
(This note is not part of the Instrument and does not purport to be a legal interpretation.)
This order brings the registration provisions of the Data Protection Act 1988 into operation on 9 January 1989. It brings the remainder of the Act, with the exception of sections 6(2)(b) and 10(7)(b), into operation on 19 April 1989. The excepted provisions require individuals or firms who have to correct or erase inaccurate personal data pursuant to the Act to notify the correction of erasure to anyone to whom the data were disclosed within the preceding twelve months.

SI No. 350 of 1988: Data Protection (Registration Period)
Regulations, 1988

I, DONAL C. LINEHAN, Data Protection Commissioner, in exercise of the powers conferred on me by section 18 of the Data Protection Act, 1988 (No. 25 of 1988), hereby, with the consent of the Minister for Justice, make the following regulations:
1. These Regulations may be cited as the Data Protection (Registration Period) Regulations, 1988.
2. A period of one year is hereby prescribed for the purposes of Section 18(1) of the Data Protection Act, 1988 (No. 25 of 1988).

Given under my hand
this 15 day of December, 1988.

DONAL C. LINEHAN
Data Protection Commissioner

The Minister for Justice hereby consents to the making of the foregoing Regulations.

Given under the Official Seal
of the Minister for Justice,
this 19 day of December, 1988.

GERARD COLLINS
Minister for Justice

Explanatory Note
(This note is not part of the Instrument and does not purport to be a legal interpretation.)
These regulations provide that the duration of a registration under the Data Protection Act 1988
(whether it is an initial registration or a continued registration) shall be one year.

SI No. 351 of 1988: Data Protection (Registration) Regulations, 1988

I, Donal C. Linehan, Data Protection Comissioner, by virtue of the powers conferred on me by
section 20 of the Data Protection Act, 1988 (No. 25 of 1988), hereby, with the consent of the
Minister for Justice, make the following regulations:

1. These Regulations may be cited as the Data Protection (Registration) Regulations, 1988.
2. These Regulations shall come into force on the 9th day of January, 1989.
3. In these Regulations 'the Act' means the Data Protection Act, 1988.
4. An application by a person wishing to be registered in the register established and
   maintained by the Data Protection Commissioner under section 16(2) of the Act or to have
   a registration continued under section 18 of the Act or to have particulars in an entry in the
   register altered shall be made by completing the appropriate form specified in the Schedule
   to these Regulations or a form to the like effect.
5. The information required to be furnished to the Data Protection Commissioner by a person
   referred to in Regulation 4 shall be that specified in the appropriate form and any other
   information that the Commissioner may require to enable him to deal either with a
   particular application or with applications generally (in which case he may require the
   information to be furnished by way of an addition to the appropriate form).
6. The particulars to be included in an entry in the register in relation to a data controller to
   whom section 16 of the Act shall be:
   (a) name and address;
   (b) purpose or purposes for which he keeps or uses personal data;
   (c) description of the data;
   (d) persons or categories of persons (other than persons to whom data are disclosed
       pursuant to section 8 of the Act) to whom the data may be disclosed;
   (e) countries or territories to which the data may be directly or indirectly transferred;
   (f) if the source from which the data, and any information intended for inclusion in the
       data, are obtained is required by the Commissioner to be described in the entry, the
       persons or categories of persons from whom the data and information are obtained;
   (g) if the data controller is not the person to whom requests for information under section
       4(1)(a) of the Act should be addressed, the name or job status and address of that
       person;
   (h) date on which the entry was made or, as the case may be, from which the relevant
       registration was continued;

(i) a reference to any other entry in the register relating to the data controller.

7. In the case of a data processor whose business consists wholly or partly in processing personal data on behalf of data controllers and who is not himself a data controller to whom section 16 of the Act applies, the particulars to be included in the relevant entry in the register shall be his name and address.

8. (a) In the case of a partnership which has applied to be registered in the register, the name of the partnership and of each of the partners shall be included in the entry in the register.

(b) In the case of a company (within the meaning of the Companies Acts, 1963 to 1987) which has so applied, the address to be so included shall be that of its registered office.

(c) In the case of a person (other than such a company) carrying on a business who has so applied, the address shall be that of his principal place of business.

SCHEDULE

Data Protection (Registration) Regulations, 1988

FORM DPA 1
Application for registration as a data controller (or as both a data controller and a data processor)

1. Name and Address:
(If a partnership, state its name and name of each partner; if a company, give the address of the registered office; in the case of any other business, give the address of the principal place of business.)

2. Name or job status of person to whom applications for access to personal data should be sent:
(Give address also if different from above.)
Note: Paragraph 3 to 7 do not apply to personal data processed on behalf of another.

3. *Purpose(s) for which you keep or use personal data:*
(If the personal data are kept for the purposes of a business, trade, profession or public service, state in general (but comprehensive) terms the purpose(s) for which it is carried on. In any other case, specify the purpose(s) for which the data are kept or used.)

4. *Description of all personal data so kept or used:*
(a) *The personal data normally associated with each of the following applications, namely:*
(Describe briefly, but adequately, the various applications.)
(b) *Personal data not normally associated with any of the applications specified at (a) above:*
(Give full details.)

5. Persons or bodies (or categories of them) to whom the personal data may be disclosed (other than persons or bodies to whom a disclosure may be made in the circumstances in section 8 of the Act):
Note: A disclosure of any personal data or body specified above must not be made in any manner incompatible with the purpose(s) for which those data are kept. Otherwise the disclosure will be in contravention of section 2(1)(c)(ii) of the Act.

6. Countries or territories (if any) to which you transfer, or intend to transfer, personal data directly or indirectly:
(State countries or territories concerned, description of data to be transferred and purpose of transfer.)

Note: This paragraph relates only to personal information when transferred abroad in automated form.

7. If you keep personal data relating to (a) racial origin, (b) political opinions, (c) religious or (d) other beliefs, (e) physical or mental health (other than any such data reasonably kept by you in relation to the physical or mental health of your employees and not used or disclosed for any other purpose), (f) sexual life or (g) criminal convictions —
    (a) state which of these kinds of personal data you keep;
    (b) state for which of the applications specified at 4 above each of these kinds of data is kept;
    (c) specify under the following headings the safeguards in operation for the protection of the privacy of the data subjects concerned:
        1. physical safeguards,
        2. technical safeguards.
8. (a) Does any of the personal data kept by you consist of information that you are required by law to make available to the public? *Yes/*No
    (b) If the answer is 'Yes', give details:
9. (a) Are you a data processor who is required to register (i.e. you are a person whose business consists wholly or partly in processing personal data on behalf of others)? . . . . . . *Yes/*No
    (b) If the answer is 'Yes', state the countries or territories (if any) to which you transfer, or intend to transfer, such data for processing directly or indirectly:
10. Name or job status of individual (if any) who will supervise the application of the Act within your organisation:

I certify that the above information is correct and complete and apply to be registered in the register maintained pursuant to section 16(2) of the Data Protection Act 1988.

I enclose the prescribed fee (£100).

Signature_____ Date_____
   *authorised to sign on behalf of applicant
   *Applicant

Notes:
1. Knowingly to furnish false of misleading information is an offence.
2. It is also an offence knowingly (a) to keep or use personal data for any purpose not described at 3 above, (b) to keep personal data not specified at 4 above, (c) to disclose personal data to any person or body not described at 5 above or (d) to transfer personal data to a country or territory not named at 6 above.
*Delete whichever is applicable.

Data Protection (Registration) Regulations, 1988

FORM DPA 2
Application for separate registration

1. Name and address: . . . .
    (In the case of a partnership, state its name and the name of each partner; if a company, give the address of the registered office; in the case of any other business, give the address of the principal place of business.)

2. Name or job status of person to whom applications for access to the personal data with which this application for separate registration is concerned should be sent:
    (Give address also if different from above.)
    Note: Paragraph 3 to 7 do not apply to personal data processed on behalf of another.
3. Purpose(s) for which you keep or use the personal data with which this application for separate registration is concerned:
    (State the particular purpose or purposes you wish to have separately registered.)
4. Description of personal data kept or used for the purpose of purposes mentioned in preceding paragraph:
    (a) *The personal data normally associated with each of the following applications, namely:*
        (Describe briefly, but adequately, the applications with which this application for separate registration is concerned.)
    (b) *Personal data not normally associated with any of the applications specified at (a) above*:
        (Give full details.)
5. Persons or bodies (or categories of them) to whom the personal data with which this application for separate registration is concerned may be disclosed (other than persons or bodies to whom a disclosure may be made in the circumstances specified in section 8 of the Act):
    Note: A disclosure of any personal data to a person specified above must not be made in any manner incompatible with the purpose(s) for which those data are kept. Otherwise the disclosure will be in contravention of section 2(1)(c)(ii) of the Act.
6. Counties or territories (if any) to which you transfer, or intend to transfer, the personal data with which this application for separate registration is concerned directly or indirectly:
    (State countries or territories concerned, description of data to be transferred and purpose of transfer.)
    Note: This paragraph relates only to personal information when transferred abroad in automated form.
7. If the personal data with which this application for separate registration is concerned relate to (a) racial origin, (b) political opinions, (c) religious or (d) other beliefs, (e) physical or mental health (other than any such data reasonably kept by you in relation to the physical or mental health of your employees and not use or disclosed for any other purpose), (f) sexual life or (g) criminal convictions —
    (a) state which of these kinds of personal data you keep;
    (b) state for which of the applications specified at 4 above each of these kinds of data is kept;
    (c) specify under the following headings the safeguards in operation for the protection of the privacy of the data subjects concerned:
        1. physical safeguards,
        2. technical safeguards.
8. (a) Does any of the personal data kept by you consist of information that you are required by law to make available to the public? *Yes/*No
    (b) If the answer is 'Yes', give details:
9. Are you a data processor who is required to register (i.e. are you a person whose business consist wholly or partly in processing personal data on behalf of others)? *Yes/*No
    (b) [*sic*] If the answer is 'Yes', state the countries or territories (if any) to which you transfer, or intend to transfer, such data for processing directly or indirectly:
10. Name or job status of individual (if any) who will supervise the application of the Act within your organisation in relation to the personal data with which this application for separate registration is concerned:

11. Number of separate registrations:

I certify that the above information is correct and complete and apply to be separately registered in the register maintained under section 16(2) of the Data Protection Act 1988 in respect of the purpose(s) specified at 3 above.
I enclose the prescribed free (£100).

Signature_____ Date_____
     *authorised to sign on behalf of applicant
     *Applicant

Notes:
1. Knowingly to furnish false of misleading information is an offence.
2. It is also an offence knowingly (a) to keep personal data not specified in your applications, (b) to keep or use personal data for any purpose, or disclose personal data to any person or body, not described in those applications or (c) to transfer personal data to a country or territory not named at 6 above.
*Delete whichever is inapplicable.

Date Protection (Registration) Regulations, 1988

FORM DPA 3
Application for registration as a data processor

1.   Name and address:
    (If a partnership, state its name and the name of each partner; if a company, give the address of the registered office; in the case of any other business, give the address of the principal place of business.)
2.   Counties or territories (if any) to which you transfer, or intend to transfer, personal data for processing directly or indirectly:
    I apply to be registered in the register maintained pursuant to Section 16(2) of the Data Protection Act 1988.
    My business consists *wholly/*partly in processing personal data on behalf of data controllers.
    *I do not control the contents and use of any personal data.
    *I control the contents and use of personal data but I am not a data controller who is required by section 16 of the Act to register in that capacity.
    I enclose the prescribed fee (£100).

Signature_____ Date_____
     *authorised to sign on behalf of applicant
     *Applicant

Note: Knowingly to furnish false of misleading information is an offence.
*Delete whichever is applicable.

Data Protection (Registration) Regulations, 1988

FORM DPA 4
Application for continuance of registration

1. Name and address:
2. Registration No.
    I apply to have my registration continued under section 18 of the Data Protection Act 1988.
    I enclose a statement[+] containing —
    >   A: the particulars in the entry relating to me under the above registration number, and
    >   B: certain other particulars concerning the personal data to which the entry relates

*The particulars in the entry, as set out at A of the enclosed statement[+], do not require amendment.

*The particulars in the entry, as set out at A of the enclosed statement[+], require amendment in the following respects: —
*The particulars set out at B of the enclosed statement[+] do not require amendment.
*The particulars set out at B of the enclosed statement[+] require amendment in the following respects:
I certify that the above information is correct.
I enclose the prescribed fee (£100).

Signature_____ Date _____
>   *authorised to sign on behalf of applicant
>   *Applicant

Note: Knowlingly to furnish false or misleading information is an offence.

[+]A copy of the statement is available on request from the Office of the Data Protection Commissioner.
*Delete whichever is inapplicable.

Data Protection (Registration) Regulations, 1988

FORM DPA 5
Application for alteration in registration particulars

1. Name and address:
2. Registration No.
    I apply to have the particulars in the entry in the register relating to me under the above registration number altered as follows:
    I certify that the above information is correct.
    I enclose the prescribed fee (£50).

Signature_____ Date _____
>   *authorised to sign on behalf of applicant
>   *Applicant

Note: Knowingly to furnish false or misleading information is an offence.

*Delete which is inapplicable.

Given under my hand,
this 15 day of December, 1988.

DONAL C. LINEHAN
Data Protection Commissioner

The Minister for Justice consents to the making of the foregoing Regulations.

Given under the Offical Seal of
the Minster for Justice,
this 19 day of December, 1988.

GERARD COLLINS
Minister for Justice

Explanatory Note
(This note is not part of the Instrument and does not purport to be a legal interpretation.)
These Regulations prescribe (a) the procedure to be followed in relation to registration in the register established under the Data Protection Act 1988; (b) the information required by the Data Protection Commissioner to be furnished in that regard and (c) the particulars to be included in entries in the register.

SI No. 81 of 1989: Data Protection Act, 1988
(Restriction of Section 4) Regulations, 1989

I, GERARD COLLINS, Minister for Justice, being of opinion that the prohibitions and restrictions on the disclosure, and the authorisations of the withholding, of information contained in the provisions of the enactments specified in the Schedule to these Regulations ought to prevail in the interests of the data subjects concerned and any other individuals concerned, hereby, in exercise of the powers conferred on my by subsections (2) and (3)(b) of section 5 of the Data Protection Act, 1988 (No. 25 of 1988), and after consultation with the other Ministers of the Government, make the following Regulations:

1. These Regulations may be cited as the Data Protection Act, 1988 (Restriction of Section 4) Regulations, 1989.
2. These Regulations shall come into operation on the 19th day of April, 1989.
3. The prohibition and restrictions on the disclosure, and the authorisations of the withholding, of information contained in the provisions of the enactments specified in the Schedule to these Regulations shall prevail in the interests of the data subjects concerned and any other individuals concerned.

SCHEDULE

Section 22(5) of the Adoption Act, 1952 (No. 25 of 1952)
Section 9 of the Ombudsman Act, 1980 (No. 26 of 1980).

Given under my Official Seal,
this 19 day of April, 1989.

GERARD COLLINS
Minister for Justice

Explanatory Note
(This is not part of the instrument and does not purport to be a legal interpretation.)

These regulations provide that certain existing enactments that prohibit or restrict the disclosure of information, or authorise it to be withheld, will continue to prevail notwithstanding the right of access to personal data conferred by section 4 of the Data Protection Act 1988. The enactments relate to (1) the index kept by the Registrar of Births tracing the connection between entries in the Adopted Children Register and the register of births and (2) to information obtained by the Ombudsman during an investigation under the Ombudsman Act 1980.

SI No. 82 of 1989: Data Protection (Access Modification) (Health) Regulations, 1989

I, GERARD COLLINS, Minister for Justice, considering it desirable in the interests of data subjects, hereby, in exercise of the powers conferred on my by section 4(8) of the Data Protection Act, 1988 (No. 25 of 1988), and after consultation with the Minister for Health, the Minister for Finance, the Minister for Education, the Minister for Social Welfare, the Minister for Defence and the Minister for Labour, make the following Regulations:

1. These Regulations may be cited as the Data Protection (Access Modification) (Health) Regulations, 1989.
2. These Regulations shall come into operation on the 19th day of April, 1989.
3. In these Regulations —
    'the Act' means the Data Protection Act, 1988 (No. 25 of 1988);
    'care' includes examination, investigation and diagnosis;
    'health data' means personal data relating to physical or mental health;
    'health professional' means —
    (a) a person who is a medical practitioner, dentist, optician, pharmaceutical chemist, nurse or midwife and who is registered under the enactments governing his profession, and
    (b) a chiropodist, dietician, occupational therapist, orthoptist, physiotheraptist, psychologist, child psychotherapist or speech therapist.
4. (1) Information constituting health data shall not be supplied by or on behalf of a data controller to the data subject concerned in response to a request under section 4(1)(a) of the Act if it would be likely to cause serious harm to the physical or mental health of the data subject.
    (2) Nothing in paragraph (1) of this Regulation excuses a data controller from supplying

so much of the information sought by the request as can be supplied without causing the harm referred to in that paragraph.

5.   (1) A data controller who is not a health professional shall not —

(a) supply information constituting health data in response to a request under the said section 4(1)(a), or

(b) withhold any such information on the grounds specified in Regulation 4(1) of these Regulations,

unless he has first consulted the person who appears to him to be the appropriate health professional.

(2) In this Regulation 'the appropriate health professional' means —

(a) the person who is the registered medical practitioner, within the meaning of the Medical Practitioners Act, 1978 (No. 4 of 1978), or registered dentist, within the meaning of the Dentists Act, 1985 (No. 9 of 1985), currently or most recently responsible for the clinincal care of the data subject in connection with the matters to which the information, the subject of the request, relates,

(b) where there is more than one such person, the person who is the most suitable to advise on those matters,

(c) where there is no person available falling within either subparagraph (a) or (b) of this paragraph, a health professional who has the necessary experience and qualifications to advise on those matters.

6.   Section 4(4) of the Act shall not apply in relation to personal data relating to an individual other than the data controller or data subject concerned if that individual is a health professional who has been involved in the care of the data subject and the data relate to him in his capacity as such.

Given under my Official Seal,
this 19 day of April, 1989

GERARD COLLINS
Minister for Justice

Explanatory Note
(This note is not part of the instrument and does not purport to be a legal interpretation.)

These regulations prohibit the supply of health data to a patient in response to a request for access if that would cause serious harm to his or her physical or mental health. They provide also that such data is to be communicated only by, or after consultation with, an appropriate 'health professional' — normally the patient's own doctor.

SI No. 83 of 1989: Data Protection (Access Modification) (Social Work) Regulations, 1989

I, GERARD COLLINS, Minister for Justice, considering it desirable in the interests of data subjects, hereby, in exercising of the powers conferred on my by section 4(8) of the Data Protection Act, 1988 (No. 25 of 1988) and after consultation with the Minister for Health, the

Minister for Education, the Minister for the Environment, the Minister for Social Welfare and the Minister for Labour, make the following Regulations:

1. These Regulations may be cited as the Data Protection (Access Modification) (Social Work) Regulations, 1989.

2. These Regulations shall come into operation on the 19th day of April, 1989.

3. In these Regulations —

   'the Act' means the Data Protection Act, 1988 (No. 25 of 1988);

   'social work data' means personal data kept for, or obtained in the course of, carrying out social work by a Minister of the Government, a local authority, a health board, or a voluntary organisation or other body which carries out social work and is in receipt of moneys provided by such a Minister, authority or board, but excludes any health data within the meaning of the Data Protection (Access Modification) (Health) Regulations, 1989 (SI No. 82 of 1989), and 'social work' shall be construed accordingly.

4. (1) Information constituting social work data shall not be supplied by or on behalf of a data controller to the data subject concerned in response to a request under section 4(1)(a) of the Act if it would be likely to cause serious harm to the physical or mental health or emotional condition of the data subject.

   (2) Nothing in paragraph (1) of this Regulation excuses a data controller from supplying so much of the information sought by the request as can be supplied without causing the harm referred to in that paragraph.

   (3) If the social work data include information supplied to a data controller by an individual (other than an employee or agent of the data controller) while carrying out social work, the data controller shall not supply that information to the data subject under section 4(1)(a) of the Act without first consulting that individual.

5. Section 4(4) of the Act shall not apply in relation to social work data relating to an individual other than the data controller or data subject concerned if that individual is engaged in carrying out social work and the data relate to him in that capacity.

6. These Regulations are without prejudice to the power of a court to withhold from a data subject social work data kept by it and constituting information provided in a report supplied to it in any proceedings.

Given under my Official Seal,
this 19 day of April, 1989

GERARD COLLINS
Minister for Justice.

Explanatory Note
(This not is not part of the instrument and does not purport to be a legal interpretation.)

These regulations prohibit the supply of personal data obtained in the course of carrying on social work if that would cause serious harm to the health or emotional condition of the data subject concerned. The regulations apply to social work carried on by Minister, local authorities, health boards or any such bodies receiving financial assistance from public funds.

SI No. 84 of 1989: Data Protection Act, 1988 (Section 5(1)(d)) (Specification) Regulations, 1989

I, GERARD COLLINS, Minister for Justice, being of opinion that the functions described in Column I of the Schedule to these Regulations, being functions conferred by or under the enactments specified in column 2 of that Schedule, are designed to protect members of the public against the financial loss referred to in subsection (1)(d) of Section 5 of the Data Proptection Act, 1988 (No. 25 of 1988), hereby, in exercise of the powers conferred on my by subsections (1)(d) and (2) of that section, and after consultation with the other Ministers of the Government, make the following Regulations:

1. These Regulations may be cited as the Data Protection Act, 1988 (Section 5(1)(d) (Specification) Regulations, 1989.
2. These Regulations shall come into operation on the 19th day of April, 1989.
3. (a) The functions described in column 1 of the Schedule to these Regulations, being functions conferred by or under the enactments specified in column 2 thereof, are, in so far as they are designed to protect members of the public against the financial loss referred to in section 5(1)(d) of the Data Protection Act, 1988 (No. 25 of 1988), hereby specified for the purposes of the said Section 5(1)(d).
   (b) In paragraph (1) of this Regulation 'enactments' includes rules and regulations and the reference to the enactments specified in the Schedule to these Regulations is a reference to these enactments as amended or extended by any enactment passed or made after the making of these Regulations.

SCHEDULE

Description of function (1)	Enactments by or under which function conferred (2)
Functions of Central Bank of Ireland	Central Bank Act, 1971 (No. 24 of 1971).
Functions of Director of Consumer Affairs and Fair Trade	Prices Acts, 1958 to 1972. Restrictive Practices Acts, 1972 and 1987. Sale of Goods and Supply of Services Act, 1980 (No. 16 of 1980). Regulations made under the European Communities Acts, 1972 to 1986.
Functions of Minister for Industry and Commerce	Companies Acts, 1963 to 1987. Insurance Act, 1989 (No. 3 of 1989).
Functions of Official Assignee in Bankruptcy	Bankruptcy Act, 1988 (No. 27 of 1988). Rules of the Superior Courts.

Functions of Registrar of
Friendly Societies

Industrial and Provident
Societies Acts, 1893 to 1978.
Friendly Societies Acts, 1896 to
1977.
Credit Union Act, 1966
No. 19 of 1966).

Given under my Official Seal,
this 19 day of April, 1989.

GERARD COLLINS
Minister for Justice

Explanatory Note
(This note is not part of the instrument and does not purport to be a legal interpretation.)

These regulations restrict access to personal data kept by Ministers or statutory bodies with regulatory functions designed to prevent financial loss to members of the public through (a) dishonesty, incompetence or malpractice on the provision of financial services or the management of companies or (b) the conduct of persons who have been adjudicated bankrupt. The restriction applies only where access to the data would be likely to prejudice the proper performance of those functions.

Notes

CHAPTER ONE

1. *Malone v Metropolitan Police Commissioner* [1979] 2 WLR 700: see generally Burns, 'Privacy and the Common Law' in *Aspects of Privacy Law* ed. Gibson (Butterworths, London,1980) and *Privacy*, ed. Jones (David & Charles, Newton Abbot, 1974).
2. Article 50 of the 1987 Constitution, as interpreted by a majority of the Supreme Court in *Gaffney v Gaffney* [1975] IR 133. See the dissent of Walsh J at 151.
3. [1931] AC 333.
4. [1930] 1 KB 467 at 478.
5. *Corelli v Wall* (1906) 22 TLR 532 at 533 *per* Swinfen Eady J.
6. Contrast the development of the tortious action for invasion of privacy in the United States. Section 652A of the US Restatement Torts (2d) expounds the following general principle.
   '(1) One who invades the right of privacy of another is subject to liability for the resulting harm to the interests of the other. (2) The right to privacy is invaded by
   (a) unreasonable intrusion upon the seclusion of another . . .
   (b) appropriation of the others name or likeness . . .
   (c) unreasonable publicity given to the others private life . . .
   (d) publicity that unreasonably places the other in a false light before the public'.
   The Restatement reflects existing case-law but it is evident that the right of privacy is not confined to these four situations. New forms of invasion of privacy may be established by litigation.
7. E.g. Lord Halsbury in *Monson v Toussauds Ltd* [1894] 1 QB 671 at 687. The pre-1937 English case-law is extensively discussed by Winfield, 'Privacy', (1931) 47 *LQR* 23: see also Neill, 'The Protection of Privacy', (1962) 25 *MLR* 393: Britton, 'The Right of Privacy in England and the United States', (1963) 37 *Tulane LR* 235; the Younger Committee Report contains material on the law of England.
8. E.g. Lord Mancroft's 1961 Bill, introduced into the House of Lords: Alex Lyon's 1967 Bill, introduced into the Commons: Brian Walden's 1969 Bill, introduced into the Commons. These and other measures are discussed by Younger.
9. *Meadox Medicals Inc. v VPI Ltd and Others*, HC, 22 April 1982, unreported.
10. See the discussion in *Seager v Copydex Ltd* [1967] 2 All ER 415 and the judgment in the High Court of Costello J in *House of Spring Gardens Ltd. v Point Blank Ltd* [1983] FSR 213, affirmed by the Supreme Court [1985] FSR 327.
11. [1969] RPC 41.
12. *Ibid.*, at 47.
13. *Robb v Green* [1895] 2 Q.B. 315: *Printers and Finishers v Holloway* [1964] 3 All ER 731: *A.F. Associates v Ralston* [1973] NI 229.
14. Gurry, *Breach of Confidence* (Oxford UP, Oxford, 1984).
15. [1988] 2 All ER 477.
16. E.g. *X v Y and Others* [1988] 2 All ER 648: *W v Egdell and Others* [1989] 1 All ER 1089.
17. *Heywood v Wellers (a firm)* [1976] QB 466.

18. [1964] AC 465: see generally McMahon & Binchy, *Irish Law of Torts*, pp. 397-405 (Butterworths, 1981).
19. McMahon & Binchy *Irish Law of Torts*, pp. 127-148.
20. *Ibid.*, pp. 535-538.
21. *Ibid.*, pp. 463-473.
22. *Wilkinson v Downton* [1897] 2 QB 57: See Tiplady (1981) 44 *MLR* 146.
23. (1861) 30 LJ Ch. 801.
24. [1978] QB 479.
25. See Kerr & Whyte, *Irish Trade Union Law*, p. 239 (Butterworths, London, 1986).
26. See McDonald, *The Irish Law of Defamation* (Round Hall Press, Dublin, 2nd ed., 1989) at pp. 10-18.
27. *Op. cit.*, at pp. 4-6.
28. See above pp. 74 to 79.
29. *Cooke v Carroll* [1945] IR 515.
30. Section 19(1)(b) inserted by section 3 of the Broadcasting Authority (Amendment) Act, 1976.
31. HC, unreported 21 February 1978.
32. *Banque Keyser Ullman SA v Skandia UK Ins. Co.* [1987] 2 All ER 923.
33. Presumably the Gardai, if the information were needed for a specific investigation into crime, or if national security issues were raised, could insist that even natural justice considerations must yield, by analogy with Article 9 of the Council of Europe Convention on data protection.
34. [1974] IR 284.
35. Budd J, Henchy J and Griffin J. Walsh J based his judgment on Article 41.
36. (1965) 381 US 479.
37. See, for example, Kelly, *The Irish Constitution* (1979) at p. 369, citing Budd J in *McGee* itself.
38. [1984] IR 36.
39. Sections 61 and 62 of the Offences Against the Person Act, 1861 and section 11 of the Criminal Law (Amendment) Act, 1885 respectively. It must be conceded that McWilliam J [1984] IR 36 at 45 could have simply been dealing with the balance between alleged rights of privacy and the right to investigate alleged offences; e.g. McWilliam J does not suggest there is no right to privacy if two heterosexual persons live together. Indeed, an argument along these lines was mounted in the recent cohabitation case of *Foley v Moulton and Others* HC unreported, 29 July 1988.
40. [1984] IR 36 at 64, 67 and 80.
41. *Ibid.*, at 71.
42. E.g. possible examples could include the collection of pornographic material or fascist or racist books and pamphlets for private use or consumption: if seized by the police is this a breach of privacy?
43. Judgment delivered 26 October 1988: see O'Malley, 'Norris v Ireland — An opportunity for Law Reform', (1988) 6 *ILT* 279.
44. See the public statement of Mr Noonan, the Minister for Justice of 20 January 1983 at 339 *Dáil Debates*, cols. 1113-4.
45. [1988] ILRM 472.
46. *Ibid.*, at p. 476-477 per Hamilton P.
47. See also *E.D. v F.D.* HC unreported, 23 October 1980. In the United Kingdom it has been held that telephone tapping by the Post Office of a subscriber is not contrary to the law of England where tapping wires are not on the premises of the subscriber. It was specifically held that English law does not recognise a right of privacy in general, or telephone privacy

in particular: *Malone v Metropolitan Police Commissioner* [1979] 2 WLR 700; Elliot (1980) 43 *MLR* 59. The law of confidence however may inhibit disclosure of information illegally obtained: *Francome v Mirror Group Newspapers* [1984] 2 All ER 408.

48. *Meskell v CIE* [1973] IR 121: damages may include aggravated or exemplary damages: see *Kennedy, Arnold & Arnold v Ireland & the Attorney General, op. cit.*
49. Cmnd. 5012.
50. *Ibid.*, para. 37. For criticism on the lack of definition see MacCormick, (1974) 1 *Brit. J of L. and Soc.* 75
51. *Ibid.*, para. 37.
52. *Ibid.*, para. 67.
53. *Ibid.*, para. 68.
54. *Ibid.*, para. 620.
55. *Ibid.*, para. 621.
56. *Ibid.*, para. 623-4.
57. Gerald Dworkin, commenting in (1973) 36 *MLR* 399 at 403 does not take exception to Younger's assertion that the use of computers did not, at that time, constitute a threat to privacy.
58. Cmnd. 6353. See also the accompanying supplementary Report, *Computers: Safeguards for Privacy.* Cmnd. 6353, para. 8.
60. *Report of the Committee on Data Protection*, Cmnd. 7341.
61. *Ibid.*, para. 02.
62. Cmnd. 8539.

CHAPTER TWO

1. The context in which John Browne MP's 1989 Privacy Bill (discussed in Chapter 1), came into being illustrates just how problematic the distinction between freedom of information and privacy can be. While a person is entitled to protect privacy and perhaps business affairs, the public interest in having accurate information on public figures is just as legitimate. See *The Observer*, 7 May 1989 for some further reading on the Browne bill.
2. Cmnd. 7391, para. 204.
3. Cmnd. 7391, p. 10.
4. 375 *Dáil Debates*, cols. 835-6.
5. Ruling of 26 October 1988: see O'Malley (1988) 6 ILT 279.
6. *Norris v The Attorney General* [1984] IR 36.
7. See generally, Castberg, *The European Convention on Human Rights* (Sithoff, 1974).
8. *Slater v Bissett and the ACT Health Authority* (1986) 85 FLR 118, noted in (1988) 62 ALJ 247
9. Article 18.
10. Article 19.
11. Article 3, 1.
12. R (81) 1, 23 January 1981.
13. R (83) 3, 22 February 1981.
14. R (83) 10, 23 September 1981.
15. R (85) 20, 25 October 1985.
16. R (86) 1, 23 January 1986. The present writer has suggested that section 31 of the Social Welfare Act, 1988 is at odds with this recommendation: (1988) 6 ILT 207.
17. 337 *Dáil Debates*, cols. 2846-7.

18. Kilroy, (1987) 81 *ILSI Gazette* 261.
19. 109 *Seanad Debates*, col. 7.
20. 118 *Seanad Debates*, cols. 2172-2193: 119 *Seanad Debates*, cols. 174-213.
21. E.g. see the Peat Marwick publication, *Data Processing Security: An International Perspective* (1982): Mercer, 'Implementing a Computer Security Policy, (1986), *The Accountants Magazine* 50.
22. *Alan v Bushnell T.V. Co. and Broadcast News Ltd* (1968) 1 DLR (3rd) 534.
23. *Esso Petroleum Ltd v Mardon* [1976] 2 All ER 5.
24. Information Technology Statement No. 1 (June 1986).
25. *Ibid.*, p. 5.
26. *Computers and Data Protection: A Guide for the Businessman in Europe* (Deloitte Haskins and Sells, London, 1988). See Semple in 'Business Extra' *Irish Times* 8 December 1987 and the response by Scally, 'Letters', *Irish Times*, 15 December 1987, for an Irish illustration of the debate on data protection and whether it is a benefit or burden to the business community.
27. 375 *Dáil Debates*, cols. 847-8.
28. To be more precise, sections 1, 9, 16 (other than subsection (3)) 17, 18, 20, 26 (other than paragraphs (a), (b) and (d) of subsection (1) and subsection (4)), 32 to 35, and the Second and Third Schedules, came into operation on 9 January 1989. Other provisions, save for section 6(2)(b) and 10(7)(b) came into operation on 19 April 1989. See the Data Protection Act, 1988 (Commencement) Order, 1988 (SI No. 349 of 1988).
29. *Ibid.*

CHAPTER THREE
1. See generally Cross, *Statutory Interpretation*, 2nd ed., London 1986.
2. The leading cases include *Heydon's Case* (1584) 3 Co Rep 7a: *River Wear Commissioners v Adamson* (1877) 2 App. Cas. 743: *Stock v Frank Jones* (Tipton) Ltd. [1978] 1 All ER 948.
3. It is possible that a secondary meaning may be selected, by reference to the canons of construction, in order to avoid unomalies.
4. [1985] 1 All ER 257.
5. E.g. computer, hardware, software, database, key-in. These words do not appear in the Act.
6. It is permissible to look at the long title to the Act, see the Interpretation Act, 1937.
7. Combatting Computer Crime with Criminal Laws (1986) *5 Reeks Information en Recht* 103.
8. 382 *Dáil Debates*, col. 2143.
9. 382 *Dáil Debates*, col 2142-3.
10. Data Protection Act, 1984, section 1(7).
11. Guideline 2, 7.3.
12. 382 *Dáil Debates*, col. 2138.
13. 375 *Dáil Debates*, cols. 850-51, 860, 865, 875.
14. 382 *Dáil Debates*, cols. 2144-5.
15. *Ibid.*
16. See *Words and Phrases Legally Defined*, Vol. II, pp. 102-3.
17. *Hayes v Brown* [1920] 1 KB 333.
18. *Hill v R* [1945] 1 All ER 414.
19. [1974] 3 WLR 221.

20. *McCarthy v Flynn* [1979] IR 127.
21. *Senior v Holdsworth ex parte Independent Television* [1975] 2 WLR 987.
22. [1945] 1 All ER 414 at 417.
23. Because of the definition of data in the Irish Act, the problem of already processed data (which falls outside the UK definition of data) does not require specific attention.
24. See generally Hanbury & Maudsley, *Modern Equity* (1985) pp. 544-553; Wylie, *Irish Land Law* Chapter 9 (Professional Books, Oxford, 1986). Irish Life, in its document, *Pension Plan Information Leaflet No. 3* (March 1989) provide a useful summary of the law *vis-à-vis* data controller and data processor status. I am grateful to Joe Lynch for providing of this document.
25. See Ussher, *Company Law in Ireland* (1986) pp. 18-20. However, the Interpretation Act, 1937 indicates 'person' includes a partnership.
26. Moved by Deputy Colley: 382 *Dáil Debates*, col. 2273-2276.
27. *Ibid.*
28. See section 1(1).
29. 382 *Dáil Debates*, cols. 2159-2170.
30. 382 *Dáil Debates*, col. 2172. Presumably the Minister has in mind the principle of vicarious liability (see Chapter 10).
31. Article 3, Dublin 1988 2.b.
32. See Minister for Justice Mr Collins: 375 *Dáil Debates*, col. 843-4.
33. See generally McCutcheon, *The Larceny Act 1916* (Round Hall Press, Dublin 1988).
34. The dead cannot be defamed: see McDonald, *The Irish Law of Defamation*, 2nd ed., *op. cit.*
35. *Policy Statement on Privacy Legislation, Data Protection and Legal Persons* (1983).
36. Data Protection and Privacy Laws: Should Organisations be Protected? (1988) 37 *ICLQ* 336.
37. 382 *Dáil Debates*, col. 2170-1 (Deputy Jim Mitchell).
38. This is the result of the definition of 'processing'.
39. Workmen's Compensation Act, 1934, section 15: Social Welfare (Consolidation) Act, 1981, section 38.
40. Lord Loreburn in *Moore v Manchester Liners* [1910] AC 498 at 500-1.
41. *Butler v Breen* [1933] IR 47.
42. See however *Sullivan v Kerry County Council* [1954] IR 120.
43. E.g. *St Helens Colliery Co. Ltd v Hewitson* [1924] AC 59: *Carroll v Irish Steel* (1945) 79 ILTR 151.
44. *Mullaney v Kilcawley, Malone & Taylor Ltd* (1944) 82 ILTR 69: *R v Industrial Injuries Commissioner ex. p. A.E. U.* [1966] 2 QB 31.
45. *Foster v Federal Commissioner of Taxation* (1951) 82 CLR 606 at 614-615 per Leatham CJ. The case dealt with penalties for failure to disclose information to tax authorities when the information was already known to them and on this ground is distinguishable.
46. Guideline 2, 9.2.
47. 382 *Dáil Debates*, col. 2152.

CHAPTER FOUR

1. Section 10(1).
2. Section 13(1).
3. Section 13(2).
4. Section 13(3).

5. The UK Act is, significantly, worded differently: 'the information to be contained in personal data shall be obtained, and personal data shall be processed, fairly or lawfully'. This definition includes activities that take place before information or data becomes personal data.
6. Schedule 1, Part II.
7. Guideline 4, paras. 1.1. to 1.7.
8. In the case of the Council of Europe's 1986 Social Security Recommendation the restrictions on data gathering are substantial. Wherever possible, personal data should be obtained by the social security institutions concerned. Data obtained from other sources may be obtained, but in the case of sensitive personal data, only with the informed and express consent of the data subject or in accordance with other safeguards laid down by law.
9. Guideline 4, para. 1.4.
10. Press reports in 1988 indicated that some local authorities were doing this.
11. Minister for Justice Mr Collins: 382 *Dáil Debates*, cols. 2313-9.
12. At Committee Stage in Dáil Éireann alternative suggestions were made: 'in accordance with the law' seemed to be generally acceptable but no change was made at Report Stage: 382 *Dáil Debates*, col. 2318.
13. *The People (A.G.) v O'Brien* [1965] IR 142: *The People v Farrell* [1978] IR 13: *The People v O'Loughlin* [1979] IR 85: *The People v Shaw* [1982] IR 1: *The People v Walsh [1980] IR 294: The People v Lynch* [1982] IR 64: *The People v Trimbole* [1985] IR 550. See generally O'Connor, 'The Admissibility of Unconstitutionally Obtained Evidence in Irish Law' (1982) 17 *Ir. Jurist* 257.
14. See Deputy Kelly 375 *Dáil Debates*, col. 887.
15. Section 2(3).
16. Article 9 2.a.
17. Section 2(6) of the Data Protection Act, 1988.
18. 382 *Dáil Debates* Col. 2325
19. *Smith v Land and House Property Corporation* (1884) 28 ChD 7; *Delany v Keogh* [1905] 2 IR 267: *Brown v Raphael* [1958] Ch. 636.
20. *Esso Petroleum Co. Ltd v Mardon* [1976] QB 801.
21. *Edgington v Fitzmaurice* (1885) ChD 459.
22. [1927] AC 177.
23. See *Bisset & Wilkinson* [1927] AC 177 at 184: contrast *Esso Petroleum Co Ltd v Mardon* [1976] QB 801 with the recent Ontario case of *447927 Ontario Inc. v Pizza Pizza Ltd* (1987) 44 DLR (4th) 366.
24. [1977] IR 305.
25. *Dimmock v Hallett* (1866) 2 Ch. App. 21: *Smith v Lynn* (1954) 85 ILTR 57.
26. A precise definition is found in section 1(1): 'data kept only for the purpose of replacing other data in the event of their being lost, destroyed or damaged.'
27. Sections 19(2)(a) and (b) and 19(6) of the Act.
28. Where sensitive personal data is compiled however, within the terms of section 16(1)(c), the Commissioner is given additional regulatory powers: see section 17(3) and the Chapter on Registration below.
29. On civil liability by virtue of industrial action see generally Kerr & Whyte, *Irish Trade Union Law*, Chapter 8 (Professional Books, Oxford, 1985).
30. Section 17(2)(a).
31. Section 19(2)(b).
32. Section 19(a)(d).
33. Section 19(6).

34. *Locker & Woolf Ltd v Western Australian Insurance Co.* [1936] 1 KB 408.
35. *Horne v Poland* [1922] 2 KB 364.
36. *Aro Road and Land Vehicles Ltd v Insurance Corporation of Ireland Ltd* [1986] IR 403: see also *Schoolman v Hall* [1951] 1 Lloyds Rep. 139: *Woolcott v Sun Alliance* [1978] 1 All ER 1283: Clark, *Property Insurance* (1987) 9 *DULJ* 117.
37. *Lambert v Co-operative Insurance Society Ltd* [1975] 2 Lloyds Rep. 485.
38. *March Cabaret Club & Casino Ltd v London Assurance* [1975] 1 Lloyds Rep. 169 at 177.
39. There may not however be a disclosure under the definition in section 1(1).
40. Accidental in the sense of an 'unlooked-for mishap or untoward event which is not expected or designed' by the victim: *Fenton v J Thorley & Co. Ltd* [1903] AC 443 at 448 *per* Lord Macnaghten: See also *Trim Joint District School Board of Management v Kelly* [1914] AC 667.

CHAPTER FIVE

1. 382 *Dáil Debates*, col. 2329.
2. As initially presented, a fee was to be payable in all cases. The Bill was amended at Committee Stage in the Dáil to make this permissive.
3. SI No. 347 of 1988.
4. Section 4(7).
5. Recommendation No. R (81) 1.
6. Annex, Regulation 6.
7. SI No. 82 of 1989.
8. Data Protection (Access Modification) (Social Work) Regulations 1989 (SI No. 83 of 1989).
9. For a discussion of the social work provisions in UK law see Pearce, 'Data Protection in Social Services', [1985] *JSWL* 125.
10. The section 8 non-disclosure exemption in these circumstances is discussed in the following chapter.
11. SI No. 84 of 1989.
12. 382 *Dáil Debates*, col. 2343.
13. [1979] 2 All ER 1169.
14. *Anderson v Bank of British Columbia* (1876) 2 Ch D 644 at 649.
15. 'lawyer' includes solicitor, barrister legal consultants: *Alfred Crompton Amusement Machines Ltd. v Customs & Excise Commissioners (No. 2)* [1974] AC 405. Solicitor's clerks may also assert the privilege according to *Steel v Stewart* (1843) 13 Sim. 533. An attorney or barrister's clerk is also covered: *Taylor v Foster* (1825) 2 Car. & P. 195. An interpreter translating at an interview between barrister and client is also bound according to the old case of *Du Barre v Livette* (1791) 1 Peake 108.
16. On which see *Reg. v Hay* (1860) 2 F. & F. 2; *Cooke v Carroll* [1945] IR 515: *Forristal v Forristal* (1966) 100 ILTR 182; *R v R* [1981] ILRM 125.
17. In *Re Kevin O'Kelly* (1974) 108 ILTR 97.
18. See generally Casey, *Constitutional Law in Ireland* (Sweet & Maxwell, 1987). On privilege *vis-à-vis* communications between a police officer and superior officer see *A.G. v Simpson* [1959] IR 105.
19. See Kindersley V.C. in *Lawrence v Campbell* (1859) 1 Drew. 485 at 490 cited by Lord Edmund Davies in *Waugh v British Railways Board* [1979] 2 All ER 1169 at 1181.
20. *Herring v Clobery* (1842) 1 Ph. 91.

21. [1930] AC 558.
22. *Baughe v Cradocke* (1832) 1 M. & Rob. 182.
23. [1980] 3 All ER 457, reversed on other grounds [1981] 3 All ER 616 (HL).
24. (1976) 135 CLR 674.
25. [1979] 2 All ER 1169: *Guardian Royal Exchange of New Zealand v Stuart* [1985] 1 NZLR 596: *Guinness Peat Properties v Fitzroy Robinson* [1987] 1 WLR 1027. For an illustration of how difficult this test is in practice see *Neilson v Laugharne* [1981] 1 All ER 829.
26. A sole purpose test, as countenanced in *Graham v Bogle & Mills* [1924] 1 IR 68 is too narrow.
27. [1985] 2 All ER 809; *Balabel v Air India* [1988] 2 All ER 246.
28. Not all communications are privileged: *Caldbeck v Boon* (1872) Ir. R. 7 C.L. 32. See *Balabel v Air India* [1988] 2 All ER 246 for a recent discussion.
29. *Balabel v Air India* [1988] 2 All ER 246.
30. (1803) 1 Sch. & Lef. 209 at 226.
31 (1831) Hayes 174.
32. [1905] 2 I.R. 38, following *Worthington v Dublin, Wicklow & Wexford Ry. Co.* (1888) 22 LR Ir. 310.
33. *Welsh v Roe* (1918) 87 LJKB 520: *Conlon v Conlons Ltd* [1952] 2 All ER 462: *Century Insurance v Falloon* [1971] NI 234.
34. See Taylor LJ in *Balabel v Air India* [1988] 2 All ER 246 at 255 and *Caldbeck v Boon* (1872) Ir R 7. CL 32.
35. *R v Board of Inland Revenue, ex parte Goldberg* [1988] 3 All ER 248, see also *Frank Truman Export Ltd. v Metropolitan Police Commissioner* [1977] 3 All ER 431.
36. [1989] ILRM 257.
37. (1884) 14 QBD 153.
38. Goff J in *Butler v Board of Trade* [1971] Ch. 680.
39. [1988] 3 All ER 775.
40. *Per* Lord Griffiths, *Ibid.*, p. 789 and Lord Goff, *ibid.*, p. 797.
41. Caulfield J in *R. v Barton* [1972] 2 All ER 1192 at 1194.
42. *Schneider v Leigh* [1955] 2 QB 195: *Lee v South West Thames R.H.A.* [1985] 2 All ER 385: *Porter v Scott* [1979] NI 6.
43. *R. v Ataou* [1988] 2 All ER 321. The proposition is based on *R. v Barton* [1972] 2 All ER 1192 and *R. v Craig* [1975] 1 NZLR 597.
44. *Great Atlantic Insurance Co. v Home Insurance Co.* [1981] 2 All ER 485.
45. *General Accident Fire and Life Assurance Corp. Ltd v Tanter* [1984] 1 All ER 35.
46. *Alfred Crompton Amusement Machines Ltd v Customs & Excise Commissioners (No. 2)* [1974] AC 405; *Wilson v Liquid Packaging* [1979] NI 165. See also *Tromso Sparebank v Beirne, Forde, Grimson, Northern Bank Ltd* [1989] ILRM 257.
47. See section 8(h).
48. Data Protection Act, 1988 (Restriction of Section 4) Regulations, 1989 (SI No. 81 of 1989).

CHAPTER SIX

1. See 382 *Dáil Debates*, cols. 2277-2311.
2. 382 *Dáil Debates*, cols. 2277.
3. E.g. see *Robertson v Minister for Pensions* [1949] 1 KB 227 for an example of personal data with security implications.
4. See in particular his observations at 382 *Dáil Debates*, cols. 2289-90 and 2294.

5. See Hogan & Morgan, *Administrative Law* (Sweet & Maxwell, London, 1986), pp. 401-406.
6. [1972] IR 215.
7. See *The State (Comerford) v Governor of Mountjoy Prison* [1981] ILRM 86. For the position in Australia under the Freedom of Information Act 1982 see *Baveris v Commonwealth of Australia* (1987) 75 ALR 327.
8. See 382 *Dáil Debates*, cols. 2311.
9. 382 *Dáil Debates*, cols. 2313.
10. *Ibid.*
11. 382 *Dáil Debates*, cols. 2313.
12. *Rice v Connolly* [1966] 2 QB 414; *Collins v Willcock* [1984] 3 All ER 374.
13. Lord Goddard CJ in *Hinchliffe v Sheldon* [1955] 3 All ER 406, applied in *Steele v Kingsbeer* [1957] NZLR 552.
14. *Betts v Stevens* [1910] 1 KB 1.
15. *Hinchliffe v Sheldon* [1955] 3 All ER 406.
16. See 120 *Seanad Debates*, cols. 2062 *per* Mr Collins.
17. 120 *Seanad Debates*, cols. 2062-3 *per* Mr Collins.
18. 120 *Seanad Debates*, cols. 2062-3 *per* Mr Collins.
19. High Court, unreported, 21 February 1978.
20. See *Aro Road & Land Vehicles Ltd v Insurance Corporation of Ireland Ltd* [1986] IR 403: *Banque Keyser Ullman S.A. v Skandia (UK) Insurance Co.* [1987] 2 All ER 923.
21. See, by way of analogy, Kerr & Whyte, *Irish Trade Union Law* pp. 159-65 (Professional Books, Oxford, 1985) on the rights of a trade union to represent the membership and effect changes to the contract of employment.
22. *Singh v B.S.C.* [1974] IRLR 131.
23. See pages 65-70.

CHAPTER SEVEN
1. See the Minister for Justice, Mr Collins: 375 *Dáil Debates* cols. 840-1.
2. Within the Civil Service Regulation Acts, 1956 and 1958 (see section 19(1) of the Data Protection Act, 1988).
3. SI No. 115 of 1976, giving effect to Council Directive 73/239/EEC.
4. SI No. 57 of 1984, giving effect to Council Directive 79/267/EEC.
5. See Deputy Ahern: 375 *Dáil Debates*, col. 866.
6. See *Mandla v Dowell Lee* [1983] 1 All ER 1062.
7. E.g. persons of the Jewish faith, Sikhs, Romany Gypsies.
8. E.g. Tamils in Sri Lanka.
9. Article 14, the non discrimination article is much more specific.
10. *South Place Ethical Society: Barralet v A.G.* [1980] 3 All ER 918.
11. (1982-3) 154 CLR 120, refusing to follow *South Place Ethical Society: Barralet v A.G.* [1980] 3 All ER 918. See also Latham CJ in *Adelaide Co. of Jehovah's Witnesses Inc. v Commonwealth* (1943) 67 CLR 116 at 123.
12. See the UK Rehabilitation of Offenders Act, 1974 and in particular *Herbage v Pressdram Ltd* [1984] 2 All ER 769.
13. The preparation of the text of a document exemption inherent in the definition of processing in section 1(1).
14. Section 16(2).

15. Section 16(3)(a).
16. SI No. 347 of 1988.
17. Section 16(3)(b).
18. Section 16(3)(c).
19. Section 16(3)(d).
20. See McGrath, 'Tort, Negligence, —The Duty of Care and the World at Large' [1987] 9 *DULJ* 163.
21. SI No. 351 of 1988, regulation 7.
22. Section 17(1)(a).
23. SI No. 351 of 1988.
24. *Ibid.*
25. *Ibid.*, regulation 4.
26. *Ibid.*, regulation 5.
27. Change of address must be notified to the Commissioner if an entry is made: section 19(5).
28. Section 20(2).
29. SI No. 347 of 1988.
30. Section 17(3).
31. Section 17(4).
32. Section 17(5).
33. SI No. 350 of 1988.
34. Section 18(2).
35. Section 18(1).
36. Section 18(3).
37. Section 18(4).
38. SI No. 351 of 1988, regulation 4 and Schedule thereto.
39. SI No. 347 of 1988.
40. SI No. 351 of 1988, regulation 3 and Schedule thereto.
41. SI No. 347 of 1988.
42. SI No. 350 of 1988.
43. A copy of the statement is available from the Commissioner, on request.
44. S.I. No. 347 of 1988.
45. 375 *Dáil Debates*, col. 890.
46. See section 19(5).
47. Section 19(4). The section 20(2) offence of knowingly furnishing false or misleading information is not applicable if correct at the time of application.
48. SI No. 351 of 1988, regulation 4 and Schedule thereto.
49. SI No. 347 of 1988.
50. Section 19(1) and (6).
51. Section 19(4) and (6).

CHAPTER EIGHT
1. Section 9(1). The Commissioner's address is Earl Court, Adelaide Road, Dublin 2.
2. Second Schedule, para. 1.
3. Section 9(2).
4. Second Schedule, para. 1.
5. Second Schedule, para. 2.
6. For a parallel in relation to appeals officers under the Social Welfare Acts, 1981 to 1989 see *McLoughlin v Minister for Social Welfare* [1958] IR 1; *Kiely v Minister for Social Welfare* [1977] IR 267.

7. Second Schedule, para. 5.
8. Second Schedule, para. 3.
9. *Iris Oifigiúil* 29 July 1988.
10. On the rules of constitutional justice to be observed see generally, Hogan and Morgan, *Administrative Law* (Sweet & Maxwell, London, 1986)
11. Second Schedule, para. 2(2).
12. Second Schedule, para. 4(1).
13. Second Schedule, para. 4(2).
14. With the consent of the Minister for Finance and subject to a negative Oireachtas procedure: Second Schedule, para. 7.
15. With the consent of the Minister for Finance: Second Schedule, para. 8(1). Members of staff shall to be civil servants: Second Schedule, para. 8(2). It is not clear whether this means that persons who are not civil servants at the time of appointment are ineligible for appointment. This seems an unlikely construction.
16. Those held under the Civil Service Commissioners Act 1956 and the Civil Service Regulation Acts, 1956 and 1958: Second Schedule, para. 8(4).
17. Second Schedule, para. 7(3).
18. *Ibid.*, para. 9(1) and (2).
19. Where a complaint has been made there is a duty to investigate: Section 10(1)(b).
20. 375 *Dáil Debates*, col. 839.
21. Section 1(4)(1).
22. See 375 *Dáil Debates*, col. 892 *per* Mr Collins.
23. Section 4(3): 375 *Dáil Debates*, col. 891 *per* Mr Collins.
24. See section 5(1)(a).
25. Section 8(f)
26. Section 8(d).
27. Section 8(a).
28. Section 13(1).
29. Section 14(1).
30. Section 16(2).
31. Section 24(1).
32. Section 30(1).
33. S.I. No. 350 of 1988.
34. S.I. No. 351 of 1988.
35. In Irish, an Coimisinéir Cosanta Sonraí.
36. There is no requirement that the complaint be in writing.
37. [1895] P. 87 at 90-1.
38. *Lawrance v Norreys* (1890) 15 AC 210; *Willis v Earl Howe* [1893] 2 Ch.D 545
39. *Ibid.*
40. *Hamilton v Anderson* (1858) 6 WR 737.
41. See *Kenny v Cosgrave* [1926] IR 517; *Mulgrew v O'Brien* [1953] NI 10.
42. *Barrett v Day* (1890) 43 Ch. D. 435 (a patents case): *Chatterton v Secretary of State for India* [1895] 2 QB 189.
43. Section 10(2). The enforcement notice can be withdrawn at any time: section 10(8).
44. See section 7 of Civil Liability.
45. Section 2(3).
46. Section 2(4)(a).
47. Section 10(5) provides that no offence is committed by not complying with the stipulated requirement if an appeal is lodged.
48. Section 10(6).

49. Save for the further appeals provision in section 26(3): see section 10(6).
50. Section 10(7).
51. Section 10(5).
52. The Act also applies to information transferred from Ireland to another place for conversion into personal data: see section 12(a).
53. Section 11(6).
54. Subsection (3) need not to summarised, i.e. the High Court appeal provisions.
55. See section 15.
56. See Chapter 1.
57. *Scorer v Seymour Johns* [1966] 3 All ER 347.
58. Section 12(2)(a).
59. Section 12(2)(b).
60. See pages 128-130.
61. 'Material'. See Chapter 4 for a discussion on what this means in insurance contracts.
62. Section 14.
63. Section 15 and Chapter IV of the Convention, especially Article 13.
64. Section 16 and Schedule 4 of the 1984 Act.
65. *Ibid.*: there is provision for waiving this in urgency or exceptional cases see para. 2 of Fourth Schedule.
66. See section 1(1).
67. Section 24(4).
68. (1982) 17 Ir. Jur. 257.
69. For Constitutional reasons section 27(1)(c) directs that a document purporting to be a certificate is deemed to be such a certificate only until the contrary is proved. The document cannot be final and conclusive.
70. Section 3.
71. The code need not deal with the issues of physical or mental health or social work access rights covered by section 4(8).
72. Sections 2, 3, 4 and 6.
73. 120 *Seanad Debates*, cols. 2016-7.

CHAPTER NINE
1. Section 31(1).
2. Section 31(2).
3. Section 10(9).
4. Section 11(13).
5. Section 12(5).
6. Section 19(5).
7. Section 21(2).
8. (1875) LR 2 Cox. CR 154.
9. (1884) 13 QBD. 207.
10. *Sherras v de Rutzen* [1895] 1 QB 918, applied in Ireland in *Toppin v Marcus* [1908] 2 IR 423 and *McAdam v Dublin United Tramways* (1929) unreported, cited in Findlay & McAuley, *A Casebook of Irish Criminal Law*, 2nd ed. (Dublin, 1985) p. 67.
11. *Hobbs v Winchester Corporation* [1910] 2 KB 471.
12. *Gammon (Hong Kong) Ltd. v A.G. of Hong Kong* [1984] 2 All ER 503.
13. *R. v Lim Chin Aik* [1963] AC 160; *Sweet v Parsley* [1970] AC 132.
14. [1984] 2 All ER 503.

15. *Ibid.* at 508.
16. [1951] TLR 284 at 288.
17. *People v Murray* [1977] IR 368.
18. [1981] 2 All ER 280.
19. *Ibid. per Ackner* J at 286.
20. The section 24(6) offences however are not within the section 26 appeals provision.
20a. See *Leck v Epsom Rural District Council* [1922] 1 KB 383 which supports the view that expense or the economic hardship of meeting the requirements of a legal requirement may provide a reasonable excuse.
21. 'Excusable Mistake of Law' [1974] *Crim. LR* 652 at 661. See *R. v Reid* [1973] 1 WLR 1983.
22. E.g. see section 19 of the Consumer Information Act, 1978.
23. [1987] 2 All ER 608.
24. Cmnd. 7341.
25. *Ibid.*, Chapter 33.
26. *Roche v Peilow* [1985] IR 232.
27. Cmnd. 8359.
28. Section 21 of the Data Protection Act, 1984.
29. Section 22 of the Data Protection Act, 1984.
30. It must be made before the criminal penalty is imposed or varied as the case may be: section 17(3)(a).
31. See section 22 of the Employment Equality Act, 1977.
32. In *Lawton v BOC Transhield Ltd, supra,* this point was not taken.
33. For a recent High Court of Australia case in which the distinction between aggravated and exemplary damages was taken see *Lamb v Cotogno* (1987) 61 ALJR 541. See also White, 'Exemplary Damages in Irish Law' (1987) 5 *ILT* 60.
34. (1987), pp. 150-153. For damages for fraudulent misrepresentation see *Smith Kline & French Laboratories Ltd. v Long* [1987] 3 All ER 887.

CHAPTER 10
1. A very dangerous attitude to adopt, regardless of how data or information is stored. Civil liability may result in tort law generally.
2. And unconstitutional in this context: see Chapter 1.
3. The UK Institute of Personnel Managers have produced guidelines which indicate to members of that body what procedures should be followed by members. These guidelines have not been expressly adopted in Ireland but they provide excellent advice to anyone involved in personnel administration on the pitfalls of the data protection principles, which are common to the UK and Ireland.
4. It may not always be possible to rely on the section 4(4) exemption.
5. Section 2(4).
6. See p. 5 of the publication, *Data Protection Act 1988 Applications for Registration — Guidance Notes,* produced by the Commissioner.
7. See Chapter 1.
8. [1978] ICR 401.
9. *Ibid.* at 403 *per* Kilner-Brown J.
10. *F.C. Gardner v Beresford* [1978] IRLR 63: *Murco Petroleum Ltd v Forge* [1987] ICR 282.
11. [1987] ICR 282.

12. *B.A.C. v Austin* [1978] IRLR 332.
13. While most cases concern the duty of an employee there is, after *Stephens v Avery* [1988] 2 All ER 447 no reason to doubt that personal details given in confidence to an employer are also covered.
14. [1987] 2 All ER 608. See above p. 133.
15. Section 19.
16. E.g. *R v Howe* [1987] AC 417; *R v Conway* [1988] 3 All ER 1025.
17. Section 22(2) exempts from the offence persons who are employees or agents of the data controller or data processor.
18. E.g. defamation, breach of statutory duty.
19. See the discussion by Atiyah in *Accidents, Compensation and the Law* (1980) at p. 253-9.
20. *Turberville v Stamp* (1697) 1 Ld. Raymond 264.
21. On express authorisation see *Bayley v Manchester, Sheffield & Lincolnshire Ry.* (1873) L.R. 8 C.P. 148.
22. *Rose v Plenty* [1976] 1 All ER 97.
23. [1955] AC 130. If however an act is done for the benefit of the employers business it is generally regarded as being committed in the course of employment! See Denning MR in *Rose v Plenty (supra)*.
24. [1912] AC 716.
25. *McNamara v Browne* [1918] IR 215.
26. E.g. *Coogan v Dublin Motor Co.* (1914) 49 ILTR 24: *Nixon v Cairns* [1941] NI 21.
27. *Rose v Plenty* [1976] 1 All ER 97.
28. [1988] 3 All ER 867.
29. *Ibid.*, p. 869.
30. *Morris v C.W. Martin* [1966] 1 QB 716.
31. [1987] IRLR 286.
32. E.g. *McNamara v Browne* [1918] IR 215.
33. McMahon & Binchy, *Irish Law of Torts* (Profession Books, Oxford, 1982), p. 102, citing *Moynihan v Moynihan* [1975] IR 192.
34. [1985] IR 362.
35. *Lloyd v Grace Smith & Co.* [1912] AC 716; *Morris v C.W. Martin & Sons Ltd* [1966] 1 QB 716.
36. *General Engineering Services Ltd v Kingston & St Andrew Corporation* [1988] 1 All ER 867.
37. *Heasmans (a firm) v Clarity Cleaning Co.* [1987] IRLR 286.
38. E.g. section 22.

Index